# Vancouver Island
## Fishing Guide

## D.C. Reid

Frank Amato
PUBLICATIONS, INC.

## About the Author

D.C Reid caught his first fish at age 5—by sticking his hand in a creek and pulling out a trout. Switching to conventional gear after that first experience, Reid has fifty years of fishing experience, landing more than 500 salmon in a good year.

Reid has been a sportfishing journalist for 15 years. His articles have appeared in more than 50 fishing magazines across North America, and on more than a half dozen websites. His column, "On Fishing", appears weekly in the Victoria Times Colonist, and is syndicated across Canada. This is Reid's fourth fishing title, his other books are: How to Catch Salmon, Fishing for Dreams, and his most recent book, published in 2007, Maximum Salmon. Reid is currently working on two fishing books, and, as President of the League of Canadian Poets, has had five literary books published as well. Reid's websites are: www.dcreid.ca and www.catchsalmonbc.com.

Published in 2008 by Frank Amato Publications, Inc.
P.O. Box 82112, Portland, Oregon 97282
(503) 653-8108
ISBN 13: 978-1-57188-429-9
UPC: 0-81127-00263-4
All Photographs: D.C. Reid
Cover & Book Design: Craig Wann
Printed in SINGAPORE
1 3 5 7 9 10 8 6 4 2

# Table of Contents

## Saltwater

## Freshwater

# Introduction

Vancouver Island has been a destination for salmon fishing for more than a century. Campbell River's Tyee Pool has drawn the rich and famous since its inception in the 1920s. The Cowichan River has been drawing people from Europe for even longer. The island's steelhead are legendary and many of the great men of fishing legend, for example, Brigadier General Noel Money and Roderick Haig-Brown, fished here, and, the latter, wrote his stories.

It's surprising, given the bountiful nature of the 12 month of the year calendar for both fresh- and salt-water fishing, that a good all-encompassing book has not been written before. But now it has. Amato Publications got in touch with me and asked me to put together the best spots to fish and the book you hold in your hand is the result. These are, in my estimation from fishing here for more than 30 years, the must do fisheries for anyone interested in Vancouver Island. The purpose of this book is to give those who live here and those who come here, including families on holiday with their children, a good all around and up to the 21$^{st}$ century rundown on all the fishing on the island.

Within these covers is nitty gritty fishing information on an island that is 300 miles (500 km) long and 150 miles (240 km) wide. The island is set along a coast line where millions of salmon nurse and return to - and swim by - every year. Added to this are more than 100 watersheds on land and thousands of lakes. Both the Department of Fisheries and Oceans Canada (DFO), and the Freshwater Fisheries Society of British Columbia stock trout, salmon and other species. Quite literally, you could fish Vancouver Island for your entire life and not be able to do all there is to do. This book will help you do as much as you can.

This book is organized in two sections. First, all the saltwater fisheries around the island are listed. Along with these are charts of locations and text that describes what you need to do to catch fish. The gear and tackle that are catching the big ones today - and for years to come - are listed for your use. Useful websites and contacts for accommodation, information, restaurants, special events and points of interest are summarized to inform you. I have also suggested various resorts and guides from time to time, ones who have served me well in the past.

The second section of this book reviews the freshwater fisheries. You are directed to the major water courses and to a selection of lakes among ones that are stocked with a million fish each year. Again, specific rods, gear and tackle are set down along with tactics so that you will have confidence approaching the water for the first time. Do refer back to the saltwater write-ups for its general information, for example, accommodation, as this is the same whether you are fishing salt- or fresh-water from a specific town or locale.

Good Fishing.
D.C. Reid
Catchsalmonbc.com

Shawn Stiffler caught these 25-pound chinook while fishing offshore.

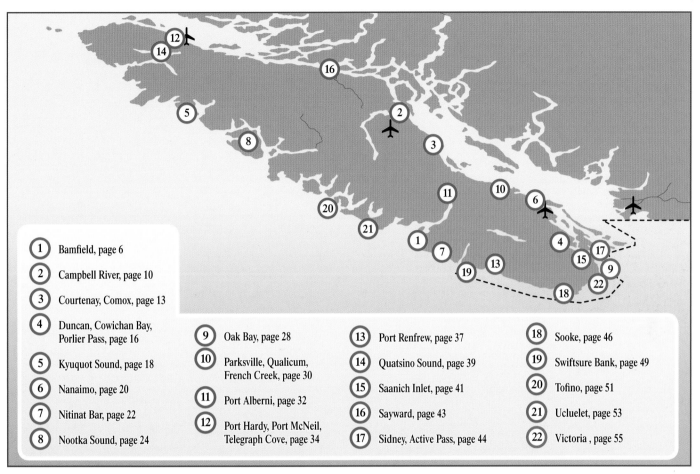

| | |
|---|---|
| ① | Bamfield, page 6 |
| ② | Campbell River, page 10 |
| ③ | Courtenay, Comox, page 13 |
| ④ | Duncan, Cowichan Bay, Porlier Pass, page 16 |
| ⑤ | Kyuquot Sound, page 18 |
| ⑥ | Nanaimo, page 20 |
| ⑦ | Nitinat Bar, page 22 |
| ⑧ | Nootka Sound, page 24 |

| | |
|---|---|
| ⑨ | Oak Bay, page 28 |
| ⑩ | Parksville, Qualicum, French Creek, page 30 |
| ⑪ | Port Alberni, page 32 |
| ⑫ | Port Hardy, Port McNeil, Telegraph Cove, page 34 |
| ⑬ | Port Renfrew, page 37 |
| ⑭ | Quatsino Sound, page 39 |
| ⑮ | Saanich Inlet, page 41 |
| ⑯ | Sayward, page 43 |
| ⑰ | Sidney, Active Pass, page 44 |
| ⑱ | Sooke, page 46 |
| ⑲ | Swiftsure Bank, page 49 |
| ⑳ | Tofino, page 51 |
| ㉑ | Ucluelet, page 53 |
| ㉒ | Victoria , page 55 |

Vancouver Island has something for every fisher person, whether it be the urbane streets and nightlife of the capital of the province, Victoria, after a day on the water or the trip of a lifetime to the completely wild west coast that is as powerful and magical as the Queen Charlotte Islands farther north. There is a lot of complete wilderness on the west and north coast of the island and it is a special introduction to fishing to do so among such beautiful surroundings.

The big hatcheries of the Conuma, Gold, Robertson Creek, Nitinat and others add to the big runs for British Columbia and those destined all the way south to California. All five species of salmon pass these shores every year. Literally millions of salmon are out there to be caught. Along with these are halibut, ling cod and 35 species of white-fleshed rockfish lurking in the depths.

The open Pacific Ocean is beautiful but also a tough and demanding arena for fishing. You should always take a guide or go with a thoroughly experienced captain. Venture forth on your own only after you have a lot of west coast fishing under your belt. All boats heading out need to be fully tricked out with vital electronic gear, including, depthsounder, GPS chartplotter, radar, and if you can afford it, a satellite phone for areas beyond cell phone range, not to mention the humble compass and back up electronics, too. Paper charts to backup the GPS should be considered mandatory. Check your VHF weather channel before going out and leave it on during your day to be prepared for new developments. Fog is an every day reality in August and September.

Inside waters have their exciting moments, too, but are usually less demanding. Still, a good array of electronic equipment will help you out anywhere you boat. And remember, don't leave shore without full tanks of gas. I once got lost in the fog and ended up in Washington State. I needed every ounce of fuel to get home. And when I hit the dock, my feet marched me directly to the marine supply store where I bought a GPS.

And remember to bring that cooler, too. Make sure it's a big one. You'll need it.

Other information that you can access from your home computer includes the following:

For saltwater boat launches, check out the following website: http://marineguides.com/~watersport/launch_ramp.html.

There is also a list of ramps on this site: http://marineguides.com/~watersport/launch_ramp.html

The best source of information is usually the local Chambers of Commerce, many of which offer printable maps of local roads. A good central source of Chamber information is Tourism Victoria's site: http://tourismmall.victoria.bc.ca/chambers.htm

And for all your information requirements about the province, check out the Tourism BC. Website: HelloBC.com; Phone: 1-800-HelloBC.

For a road map of Vancouver Island, take a look at: www.britishcolumbia.com/Maps/?id=31

The schedule of the various ferry crossings may be access at: www.bcferries.com.

You can find out the latitude and longitude of any location at: http://www.env.gov.bc.ca/bcgn-bin/bcg10?name=4062.

For current fisheries information, including limits and closed areas, always check with DFO. Pick up their Tidal Waters Sport Fishing Guide that includes the BC Freshwater Salmon Supplement. This booklet includes all the local office phone numbers that should be checked with before your fishing begins. View saltwater regulations at: www.pac.dfo-mpo.gc.ca.

The Sport Fish Institute has good up-to-date fishing and resort info: www.sportfishing.bc.ca/.

Two local magazines have fishing reports, too: Island Angler and Island Fisherman.

You will require a federal short-term saltwater licence - $7.49 - $34.17 - for an adult, non resident or year licence for $108.07, with a chinook tag of $6.42. While those under 16 do not need licences, they must pay the chinook tag. Website: www.pac.dfo-mpo.gc.ca/recfish. Refer to the freshwater section of this book for river and lake fishing licences.

# Bamfield

Along with Nootka Sound, Bamfield is one of the most historically interesting places on the entire island. With its calm harbour in the middle, it is also one of the prettiest—the kids in their yellow boots and orange lifejackets get taken across the inlet in the "school boat."

Bamfield was the terminus of the Trans Pacific Cable Corporation transmitting messages to Winston Churchill in World War II, the site of innumerable ship wrecks, the end of the West Coast Life Saving Trail, and sits beside the Broken Island group in the world-recognized Pacific Rim National Park. The Cable Corporations concrete "bunker" is now a major marine research centre owned by five universities.

While few people fish here in winter, there is good access to winter spring fishing in Barkley Sound among the sheltering islands. In summer it serves as a port of access to Swiftsure Bank, the Broken Islands and to some of the Big or Laperouse Bank that gives Ucluelet, 18 miles northwest across the sound, its outstanding fishing.

## Local Winter Hotspots

When others are digging out from snow banks, March is high time for winter chinook fishing in Rainy Bay. Herring gather in large numbers for a February-March spawn on Barkley Sound's northern shore, particularly Vernon Bay, drawing resident feeder chinook into deep-water holding areas. Fish to 30 lbs. are recorded annually, making this a fishery for larger than average feeders.

Winter fishing concentrates at Swale Rock and in Vernon Bay, as the chinook follow the spawning herring. The presence of large bait necessitates large lures, trolled deep. Herring also spawn in the kelp at the harbour mouth, so if it's rough out there, you can fish five minutes from the dock.

## Winter Lures

Spawning herring can be 12 inches or more. Thus large whole herring or anchovies in green or clear teaserheads will catch the eye of a winter chinook. Fish 180- to 200-feet deep. You can fish with a flasher on a 6-foot leader or do without, which is preferred by the winter feeder chinook any way. With bait this large and with the ultra-clear waters of winter, the fish will see your offering much more readily than in the summer.

In hootchies use a glow Gatorback in green and white or an Angel Wing with a 5-foot leader to a flasher. Winter spoons include the silver/green and the glow/green commonly called a Coyote spoon. Winter plugs include the 264 and 242. You can also mummify your bait in coarse salt in the freezer for a few days to toughen it up. Then modify your teaserheads by moving the exit hole for the leader to the middle of the front edge. This makes the bait roll like a bullet shot from a gun, rather than the spiral favoured in summer fishing that is the result of the 'offset' hole on the teasers' front edge.

## Local Summer Hotspots

In May the weather calms enough to allow access to Swiftsure Bank and the Bamfield fleet motors out to troll for both 20- to 30-pound chinook as well as the onshore migrating halibut.

Summer fishing is influenced by proximity to the Alberni Inlet. Large runs of sockeye (as high as 1.8 million fish) destined for the Stamp/Somass River system and chinook headed for the Robertson Creek hatchery swim by Bamfield on their way to Alberni Inlet rivers. Fishing occurs close to many rocky, island hotspots and success depends entirely on finding bait. And of course all the Puget Sound and Strait of Georgia and Nitinat chinook fin by the opening to Barkley Sound all summer long.

While most islands support some summer chinook structure, some islands receive more fishing pressure. Tight to Cape Beale is the most consistent shallow water structure for the high flying chinook of summer. Drag your balls across the 36 foot ledge on the north west corner and when they drop off the edge, big chinook (20- to 50-pounds) are waiting. This entire fishery is one that typifies the expression: stick and stay and make it pay. That is, you grind the kelp beds until the waiting chinook turn on to the bite.

Robertson Creek chinook begin moving in at the end of July. August is the

*Heading out from Bamfield, Tyee Lodge, past King Folger Island on the way to South Bank, part of Laperouse Bank. The Continental Shelf stretches from the south some 25 miles out to the north end of Vancouver Island, where it is only a few miles wide.*

hot month for chinook to 40 pounds, which generally move from Cape Beale to Diplock and the Rainy Bay areas. Pill Point and Chup Point have excellent structure and this is the spot to fish at the end of the ebb, as the summer chinook move in from all over the sound, but will not move on until the flood tide begins.

On the outer islands, find the structure under very rocky shores where needlefish crash in the surf. Try King Edward, Folger, and Bordelaise Islands, and off Cape Beale at Whittlestone. But if the points get crowded with anglers, move on and find your own. All the rocky points from Cape Beale to and including Bamfield Harbour mouth on its east side will be home to the moving fish. These include, Keehin Rock, The Blow Hole, Brady's Beach and Scott Bay. These are less often fished but it is common to catch fish when the crowd is elsewhere.

Guides are pretty cagey, speaking in code on their VHFs: "I'm thinking of going to where we talked about last night," they'll say, or move quickly to talk on their cell phones. Make sure you know who the guides are; if they pick up and move it's probably a good time to follow.

The Stamp and Sproat River sockeye arrive in Barkley sound in late May and hold until early July when most have entered the Somass System. June is the peak month at Papermill dam for shore anglers. Summer sockeye school in mid-channel waters and move through to the entrance to the Alberni Inlet. Fishing depth is 45- to 75-feet. Add extra flashers to the downrigger line, i.e., stack rods and flashers.

Coho size peaks in mid-September at 15 to 19 pounds. Look for good lingcod and rockfish off Seabird Rock. In August and September, chum and coho crowd into the Sarita River and Carnation Creek Hatchery.

## Summer Lures

Bamfield's secret weapon is: a sardine brined so tough as to give meaning to the expression "fish leather." Pour pickling salt until it covers a tray of bait and leave in the freezer for a few days until every last molecule of water is extracted. The tough tough bait can be inserted into a clear Rhys Davis Anchovy teaserhead without a toothpick being required to hold it there—but do add one anyway. Also, modify the teaser by drilling a hole, with a hook point, in the middle of its front edge and put the leader through this hole; it will make the bait spin like a bullet in a narrow diameter spiral. The common pattern elsewhere of a 4- to 5-inch spiral does not catch as many big chinook as the bullet roll. Note that this rig works well in the winter, too.

For plastic baits, try the Army Truck, Red Army and Tiger Prawn squirts where you note needlefish. White, white pearl, green and white, and Army Truck hootchies work for May feeders on a very long leader of 44 inches to a dodger. For sockeye, try pink plankton squirts, or orange hootchies on 18- to 25-inch leaders slow trolled with a red, or Army Truck Hotspot flasher. Also

*Rod Leland, one of my old friends, with a lapful of halibut.*

Radiant's small spoons in red and pink do the deed, too.

Tomic plugs in 4- to 6-inch models take some fish, too. The numbers to choose are: 156, 158, 301, 500, 602 and 700. Use larger plugs when mackerel abound.

For those who like the cleanliness of spoon fishing, pick up the half glow half green Coyote or Devil's Tail spoon, as well as the Cop Car pattern. And remember that Bamfield was the area to develop the use of the 7-inch white Apex with a yellow stripe, also a silver Apex, trolled quickly without a flasher. This lure is good all along the outside of Vancouver Island.

Barkley Sound used to be the site of a commercial fishery for coho and, before the practice spread to Cowichan Bay, 7-inch bucktails were trolled fast, including the Grey Ghost, white, green and white, and purple and white with abalone spinners. Troll the fly 25 feet back in the prop wash in Imperial Eagle Channel.

Coho are sometimes fished for with drift fishing lures among the islands, but seldomly do anglers do so for chinook. When they do they use 60 gram MacDeeps and Stingsildas in white, white pearl with purple, green or black edging. Also pink pearl Zzingers.

For Swiftsure halibut pipe bombs, adorn the 1- 1 ½ lb. bomb with green, pink and clear striped hootchie skirts.

**Launching Ramps:** Port Desire. See instructions in this small town of one—just one—stop sign.

Tackle shops: The Kingfisher Inn in the harbour is the gas dock and while not a complete tackle shop has a fair bit of useful terminal tackle.

Access: The bumpy route is 150 miles (240 km) from Victoria through the Nitinat valley. At the Nitinat Junction, you turn right and follow the poorly marked road. The more comfortable route is to go north from Victoria on Highway 19 and turn off to Port Alberni on Highway 4. Signs on the highway at the information booth going into Port Aberni give you directions to the gravel road to Bamfield—this is in better shape. Count on at least 3.5 hours.

A prettier option is taking the MV Lady Rose from Port Alberni and the scenic ride down the Alberni Inlet, 35 miles (56 km) to Barkely Sound and 10 miles (16 km) more to Bamfield Harbour. If you prefer to fly from Renton Washington or Vancouver, the plane ties up at the Tyee Resort floats. Check their website for info.

You can come by plane: Sound Flight: Access through Tyee Resort website or: www.soundflight.net.

Accommodations: The Tyee Resort is a gem. A very charming, west coast cedar chalet and outer buildings on the cliff at the harbour mouth. Tyee Resort, PO Box 32, Bamfield, BC, V0R 1B0; 1-888-493-8933; Website: www.tyeeresort.com; Email: info@tyeeresort.com.

Fishing Guides: Coastline Salmon Charters, Doug Ferguson, 2530 Cosgrove Crescent, Nanaimo, V0R 1B0, Phone: 1-250-728-3217, Email: coastlinecharters@hotmail.com.

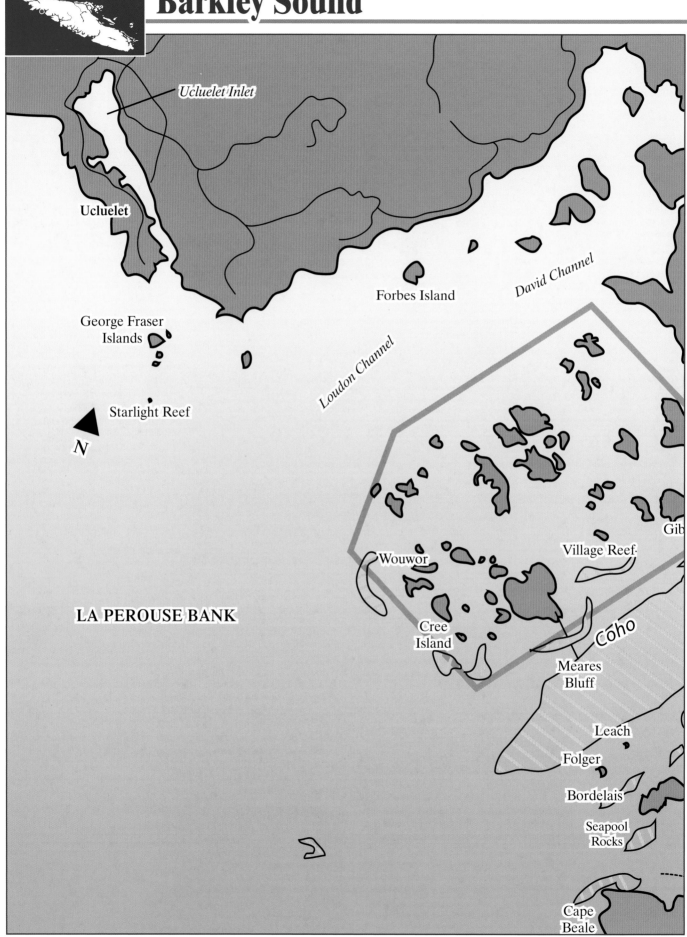

Ucluelet Inlet

Ucluelet

Forbes Island

David Channel

George Fraser
Islands

Loudon Channel

Starlight Reef

N

Wouwor

Village Reef

Gib

**LA PEROUSE BANK**

Cree
Island

Coho

Meares
Bluff

Leach

Folger

Bordelais

Seapool
Rocks

Cape
Beale

N

Henderson Lake

Vernon Bay

Pill Point

Swale Rock

Gibraltar

Imperial Eagle Channel

Diplock Is.

Rainy Bay

To Port Alberni

Chup Point

Adamson Rocks

Coho

Sandford Is.

Trevor Channel

Diana Is.

Poett's Nook

Bamfield

Scott's Bay

Port Desire

Whittle Stone

# Campbell River

Campbell River was *the* spot to fish salmon, right into the 1960s. Out in your lapstrake, Briggs and Stratton putt putt, you would be cheek by jowl with the big boats of celebrities like Bob Hope, John Wayne and Bing Crosby. To this day, the self proclaimed, Salmon Capital of the World, still produces fish year-round. The reason for this is that the choke point between the town and Quadra Island across the way funnels all the five species of salmon destined for rivers to the south on their fall migration. In winter, chinook entering or exiting Georgia Strait must do so on Campbell River's doorstep.

In the summer time, get your gillie to row you around the Tyee Pool with the required gear for your chance to enter the auspicious Tyee Club. Just catch a 30-pound chinook and you're in.

Take care in Seymour Narrows north of town. Even though Ripple Rock, a treacherous impediment to shipping travel, was blasted to smithereens in 1958, boats are still taken down today in whirlpools that form on 15.3 mph (25 km) speed tides.

The well known conservationist and writer, Roderick Haig-Brown, lived in Campbell River for decades and his house is now a historical site open to all who care to make the pilgrimage to the great man's abode.

## Local Winter Hotspots

Winter fishing is influenced by the presence of bait in the Shelter Point, Willow Point and Cape Mudge Lighthouse areas. A mile back from Mudge, the Hump also receives chinook hugging bottom structure.

Resident chinook and blueback coho inhabit local areas year-round. Fishing for deeper, 12 - to 16-lb. winter chinook typically begins in November with 1 to 2-lb. blueback coho showing in March of some years.

In most areas you are fishing almost right on the bottom, particularly at Cape Mudge, right on the bottom along the 200- to 230- contour, keeping your downrigger lines close to straight down. Cape Mudge fishes best on the ebb, due to its back eddies. Willow and Shelter fish well on flat water, either ebb or flood. Keeping your gear down is the real key to success in such fast water currents.

Off the Hump, troll 90- to 150-feet, on either the ebb or flood. Remember that the Lighthouse Rip is right beside you—and it blasts right on through—at Cape Mudge; it fishes best on a flood. And with bait at Willow and Shelter points, and further north, at Separation Head, Deepwater (flood tide) and Brown's (last half of flood) bays.

## Winter Lures

Consider this a hootchie and plug fishery. Troll fast with the Tomic 565 Rattler, pink pearl, 700 and 500 in 3- to 5-inch lengths. In hootchies, the Jack Frost (a yellow green combination), Army Truck, pearly white, purple and white, fluorescent green and yellow, Peanut Butter, and needlefish glow-in-the-dark for winter fishing at 80- to 120-foot depths in 180- to 240-feet of water off the Lighthouse, Willow Point and Shelter Bay. Cop Car spoons also take their share, 4 feet behind a glow-in-the-dark flasher

For those that like to troll bait, use the glow green or clear teaser head, with stick on eyes. Surprisingly, some guides still use cutplugs for these deep fish.

In years when bluebacks appear at the end of winter, in April and May, try bucktails off April Point in pink, orange or grey on white polar bear hair. When the tide rip forms, put out the flies.

*A nice shot of Painter's Lodge in Campbell River.*

## Local Summer Hotspots

Campbell River is one of the few areas on the coast where there are so many hotspots and such a variety of annual fisheries, it is difficult to summarize its angling opportunities; however, the salmon fisheries of Discovery Pier, Tyee Pool, Cape Mudge (and around to Francisco Point) and up Seymour Narrows should all be sampled.

The local fishing pier, built for shore anglers and kids, provides a solid chance to catch all five species of salmon without going out in a boat. It is wheel chair accessible, has a food concession, rod holders built into the pier railings and has a big net lowered to retrieve fish that anglers catch below the high dock.

Tyee Pool is a tightly demarcated spot right in front of the Campbell River estuary for local chinook waiting to go up the river. It starts at Earthquake Drop and continues 500 yards to the Tyee Spit boat ramp and is 200 yards wide. The rules state that motors cannot be used so your gillie rows you around in the July 15 to September 15 official season. You may use only a plug or spoon, 20-pound test line and 6- to 9-foot rod as set out in the rules, originally laid down in 1924. Catch a chinook over 30 pounds and you can gain membership in the "exclusive" Tyee Club. Best fishing occurs at the top of the flood or the latter part of the ebb, i.e., slower water gives the right action to the lure. Row boats are often seen plying the waters as the sun sets and the water calms.

The main summer season between late June to early September focuses on chinook returning to all Georgia Strait waters, including Columbians that may reach 50 pounds and Harrison river white chinook. First light and last light are the best bite times. Troll in the same direction as the current. This covers territory faster and pushes the lure directly in the face of the salmon. Try this neat trick to dispel dogfish: set your Black Box at .70 volts.

Whiskey Point, Copper Cliffs and North Bluff are good cutplug spots, for chinook using an 8-oz. banana weight. At Plumper Bay, and Chatham Point, the springs are 60 to 120 feet down.

During July to September, sockeye, pink and coho salmon in their millions migrate through the channel between the town and Quadra Island. Concentrate on the Green can buoy and Red can buoy in a delightfully simple fishery: 1 to 2-oz. weight, a cutplug and 15- to 20 two-foot pulls. At the same time, springs begin to show in Francisco Bay. If other anglers are catching sockeye and you are not, change directions as they have a decided preference for biting on only one direction of the tide. Stack as many rods with flashers as you can get on each downrigger. Sockeye respond overwhelmingly to flash

*Randy McCammon, head guide at Painter's Resort LLodge, with an ocean-caught chum from the sizzling October fishery up Seymour Narrows.*

and follow along until they bite the lure. The lowest rods should be at 80 feet.

In late September and October before the big rains come, chum for southern rivers stage above Seymour Narrows in Brown's and Deep Water bays. This is fabulous fishing that you must try at least once in your fishing life. Make a date and keep it. Without doubt a 12- to 15-lb. chum can pull as hard as a 35-lb. chinook, screaming off more than 100-yard run and appear here there and everywhere. Painter's Lodge has a sensational seasonal October rate for nice rooms. Pick one of their experienced guides for the trip through the Narrows, on a blue sky, high pressure, fast flood tidal flow day for the best fishing. If you are motor mooching, chum can drive you crazy taking up to 30 seconds mouthing bait and having extremely hard mouths to penetrate. Fortunately they are more persistent than other species.

## Summer Lures

Motor mooch a cutplug for summer chinook and fall chum. When towing herring use a glow green or clear teaserhead with stick-on eyes. For a strong tide, use a blunter cut to achieve a slower roll. In slower water, use a sharper angle to establish a faster roll.

Local hootchies of note include the Purple Haze, purple and white, Army Truck, pearly white, mother of pearl and fluorescent green and yellow. Try pink and blue, Bubblegum, the Googly Eyed Wild Thing (a local concoction) or pink with white spots for chum. For sockeye, utilize pink plankton squirts on a 36" leader to a red Hot Spot flasher. Pink salmon mill the river mouth looking for pink 1-inch streamer flies. Then they migrate up to pools where they await your lure or fly.

Tomic plugs of choice include two of the outside patterns, 602 and 500. Add the Army Truck for summer chinook. A 3-inch, 225 plug (which is pink) stimulates both pink and sockeye salmon.

The venerable red Krippled K works for surface fish. The Gibbs #8 is a traditional spoon, as would a half brass/half silver (or blue) for the Tyee Pool. Dig out the old Lucky Louie Plugs, or mount a 4/0 or 5/0 single hook on a drift-fishing lure and drift through.

Traditional Cowichan Bay bucktails can be trolled fast in the fall. Try flies such as the Pink Shrimp, Grey Ghost, Green Ghost, as well as orange or purple flies for coho. Look for polar bear hair as it is more sinuous in the water than standard buck's tail fibres. These can be up to 7 inches.

There is also a well-subscribed beach fishery for coho, pink and chum in front of Rotary Park, at the big rock (don't worry, you won't miss it), "Driftwood" Bay and Salmon Point. Typically fished with a fly rod, you want 1-inch streamers in pink, green, white, with some silver tinsel for flash coupled with a floating line and at least 10 feet of 6- to 8-lb. test leader. Add the ever-present California Neil and Pearl Mickey. You will find useful variations up and down the beach. A 6-weight rod with a full floating line will work best. For distance, use a Spey rod, double-handed rod, with a full floating line and a plus-10-foot leader. The extra distance will put you on fish that other guys can't reach. It'll drive them crazy and make you happy as a clam.

Shore anglers with spinning rods use pink Rooster Tail spinners, pink or red spoons, a silver Krok and at the pier, green jigging lures, Zzingers and white Buzz Bombs

**Launching Ramps:** Tyee Spit, off Spit Road, near the river mouth.
Freshwater Marina, parking, boat launch, turn east off Highway 19 on Baikie Road after you cross the Campbell River Bridge.
Government Marina and Discovery Pier, south end of harbour on Highway 19.
Discovery Harbour Marina and Argonaut Wharf, just north of the Government Wharf
Salmon Point Resort, marina, launch, pub, ten minutes south of town.
Pacific Playgrounds resort at Oyster River south of town, marina and launch, a few minutes farther south from Salmon Point.

**Tackle Shops:** River Sportsman has a full range of items for the out doors, salt- and fresh-water and a particularly good fly selection; 2115 Island Highway, V9W 2G6; Website: www.riversportsman.com; Email: info@riversportsman.com; Toll free: 1-800-663-7217.

Tyee, 880 Island Highway on Pier St, a good, professional tackle shop, 50 years in business. Website: www.tyeemarine.com; Toll Free: 1-877-287-TYEE.

**Access:** By air, water and road. Campbell River is a 3.5-hour, 280-km drive north from Victoria on Highway 1 that becomes Highway 19, aka the Inland Highway.

**Information:** Campbell River Chamber of Commerce, PO Box 400, 900 Alder St, V9W 5B6; Phone: 1-250-287-4636; Website: www.campbellriverchamber.ca; Email: chamber@campbellriverchamber.ca.

Fishing information updated weekly at: www.vquest.com/crtourism/.

**Accommodations:** Campbell River has a full range of all types of accommodations, in and out of town. Painter's is a good bet for a full-feature resort and also the spa across by shuttle to April Point. See: obmg.com.
The Coast Discovery Inn, 975 Shoppers Row, V9W 2C4; Toll Free: 1-800-716-6199.
The Haida Harbourside Inn, 1342 Shoppers Row, V9W 2E1; Phone: 1-888-673-9247; Email: haidainn@island.net. I and the Hell's Angels stayed there once. They were surprisingly quiet.

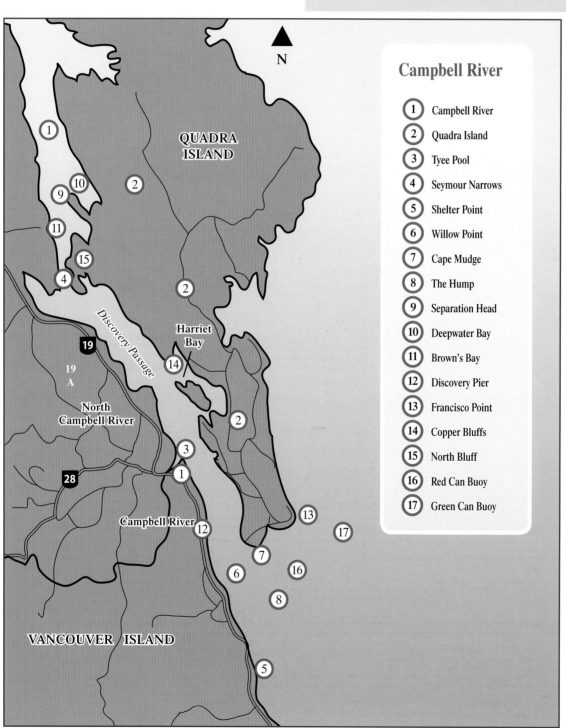

**Campbell River**

1. Campbell River
2. Quadra Island
3. Tyee Pool
4. Seymour Narrows
5. Shelter Point
6. Willow Point
7. Cape Mudge
8. The Hump
9. Separation Head
10. Deepwater Bay
11. Brown's Bay
12. Discovery Pier
13. Francisco Point
14. Copper Bluffs
15. North Bluff
16. Red Can Buoy
17. Green Can Buoy

A long with Qualicum a bit more to the south, the twin towns of Courtenay and Comox comprise the nicest urban areas on Vancouver Island. And, situated on Cape Lazo, they are close to a number of fish hatcheries: the Campbell River and the Qualicum River hatcheries put out chinook and coho, along with other species; the local Puntledge River also has a hatchery.

While southeasters and northwesters can pummel the Cape, boaters find calmer waters in the lee of Hornby and Denman Islands, which are, happily, home to one of the highest concentrations of herring in January and February during their annual spawn.

Oyster River is the northern edge of the area, where there is good cutthroat fishing as well as volunteer hatchery supplied pink and coho salmon on the beach near Pacific Playgrounds RV Park.

Prawns may be had off Denman and Hornby islands. Set your crab traps off Comox spit.

*A nice saltwater trolling setup: A Sage rod and an Islander single-action reel.*

## Local Winter Lures

Seal Bay lures include white, green and white, Tiger Prawn, and Army Truck hootchies towed 35 inches behind a glow green or blue flasher. Use squirts when needlefish predominate, hootchies when herring predominate.

In Apexes, the black/white is the lure of choice, followed by pearl in 4-inch models—without a flasher. Try light-coloured Tomic plugs in 4- to 5-inch models. The standard green/glow 4-inch spoon commonly called a Coyote should be fished on a long 4- to 5-foot leader behind a flasher; Titan and Wonder spoons, too on plus-4-foot leaders.

Bait-fishermen use cutplug herring, anchovy and herring strip in Purple Haze teasers on 4- to 6-foot leaders. Hootchies from hook to swivel should be 40 inches.

## Local Summer Hotspots

Bluebacks appear in mid-May in some years. The first migratory chinook move in in June as 20 pounders. Qualicum River chinook swim by in early August to mid-September and can exceed 30 pounds.

The early chinook cruise the 100- to 200-foot deep levels in Seal Bay, just south of the Powell River ferry terminal and the north side of the Cape Lazo buoy.

The largest chinook taken from the King Coho beach was 51.1 lbs., by Winston Murphy in 1987 on a pink Zzinger tossed from shore. Other shore casting spots include Comox Harbour, Royston waterfront, Little River estuary and the Oyster River mouth.

July and August are the months for fly-fishing the beaches for pinks from the Oyster River in the north, to the Comox Harbour and south to Nile Creek, in the Qualicum area. September and October beach fishing features coho and chum salmon. It is the local blast and is as easy as sauntering across the beach. You must try the beach fisheries.

Big runs of chum enter the Puntledge Rivers, so give a try with the fly on the sheltered beaches inside the harbour—look for the line of casters. Though they are available much longer, the traditional day to fish the river for chum is November 11, Remembrance Day. There are so many fish sometimes that there are too many!

## Summer Lures

For summer coho use a dodger and 1 1/2-inch Apex or hootchie in pink, red or orange, then switch to white with greens or blues and the Army Truck. Late

# Saltwater Fishing

## Local Winter Hotspots

The hatcheries in Campbell, Puntledge and Qualicum rivers combine to give good winter feeder fishing. The large supply of herring also contributes to these springs being available 12 months of the year. Fish where bottom contours drop from 200 feet to 300 feet.

Seal Bay, and The Hump just off it, are the winter hotspots for feeders in the 6- to 12-lb. range. This tack runs all the way north to Kitty Coleman Beach Park and south, past the Little River ferry terminal, past Kye Bay and Cape Lazo. The chinook are in 300 feet of water here. On the Miracle Beach to Bates Beach run most fish are taken in 130 to 235 feet of water.

Fish Lambert Channel for winter feeders and the southern ends of Denman and Hornby islands. This is usually a calm area with little tidal flow. In the clear winter water, you can dispense with the flasher and have an unhindered fight.

In the south end of this fishing area, try the Lighthouse on Chrome Island, Norman Point, Norris Rock, Downes Point and east to Flora Islet. On the north end of Hornby Island try Manning Point and Collishaw points.

In Deep Bay, fish off the point on a run that starts just north of the Bowser mark in the southern end of this fishing area.

In late spring, halibut are taken as there are lots of sandy, muddy bottoms with gravel in the Comox area.

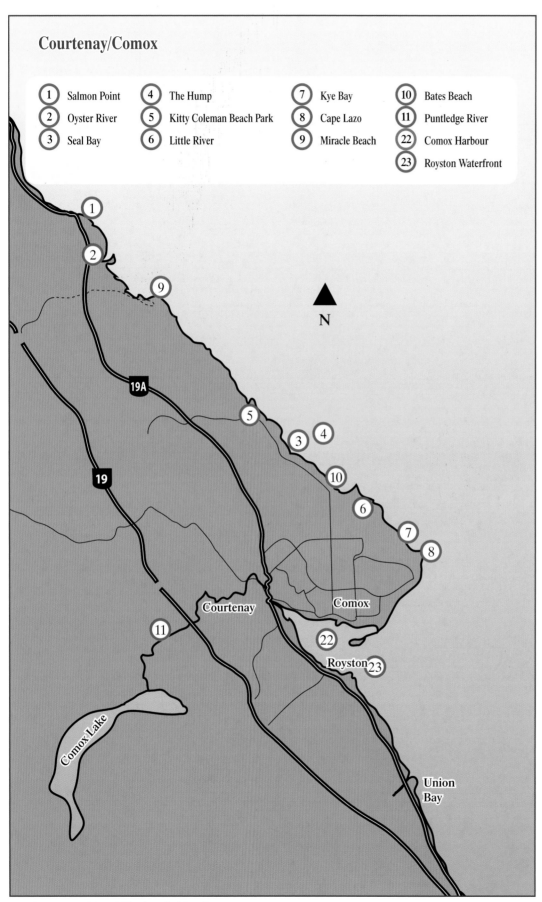

## Courtenay/Comox

1. Salmon Point
2. Oyster River
3. Seal Bay
4. The Hump
5. Kitty Coleman Beach Park
6. Little River
7. Kye Bay
8. Cape Lazo
9. Miracle Beach
10. Bates Beach
11. Puntledge River
22. Comox Harbour
23. Royston Waterfront

19A

19

Courtenay

Comox

Royston

Comox Lake

Union Bay

N

in the season, try lime-green, grey, yellow and pink, black and white. Use a 32-inch leader. Black or green Apexes work, too, along with the Coyote spoon, fishing from the surface to 200 feet. Troll anchovy fast. Try the Oyster River to Little River run trolling for coho with blue, green, clear and glow hootchies with green or blue flashers at 30- to 100-feet deep.

Fish the June chinook with white, green and white, green ghost and Army truck hootchies. Use the 602 Road-runner spoon all summer. Other good spoons include the Cop Car and Army Truck patterns. Buzz Bombs and Zzingers are the drift jigging lures of choice. Consider motor mooching the Hump and just off Little River and Comox sand bar for chinook.

September beach fishing marks the end of the pinks and beginning of coho. Use No. 3 and 4 Vibrax Blue Foxes in silver or gold for coho, but make sure to wash these later in fresh water to prevent rust. Other casting spoons include Krocodiles, Kit-A-Mats and Kohos in brass, chrome, blue, and green.

Beach patterns for pinks in July and August are sparse and small, with a hint of pink. For coho try the California Neil and Clouser minnows in chartreuse/white and pink/white, the local Neil Cameron's Copper Clouser being a good example. Remember those clear intermediate tips and slow-sink clear lines. Tie shrimp patterns in pink. Flies for coho around Flora Islet include euphasid patterns then sandlance patterns such as the Firecracker. If you want to bucktail, try flies in green, blue and chartreuse.

Qualicum River chinook appear from early August to mid-September as 20- to 30- lb fish. They take large spoons, 4-to 6-inch plugs in pink, white, green, pearl, blue or grey. Start at 30 feet at the crack of dawn and move deeper following the 50- to 120-foot contours.

In October troll for chum at 50 feet, using a green and white, or Army Truck hootchie on a 36-inch leader.

Launching Ramps: This area is serviced by at least a dozen ramps from Hornby Island north to Miracle Beach. These include the central Comox Harbour, and Kitty Coleman Beach north of town. Miracle Beach, Bates Beach Resort, Point Holmes, Roystron and Union Bay, Fanny Bay and Hornby Island. Ask at the tackle shop or chamber for the ramp nearest you.

Tackle Shops: Gone Fishin', #3-2720 Cliffe Avenue, Courtenay, V9N 2L6; Phone: 1-250-334-2007; Website: gonefishinshop.com; Email: info@gonefishinshop.com.

Peters Sport Shop, 505 Duncan Ave., Courtenay; Phone: 1-250-334-2942.

Fishing Guides: Island Sport Fishing, Steve Patterson, 6575 Rennie Road, V9J 1V1; Toll free: 1-877-338-9413; Website: islandsportfishing.com; Email: steve@islandsportfishing.com.

Access: Drive north from Victoria 2 hours 30 minutes on Highway 1 that becomes Highway 19 and take the turn off for the twin towns of Courtenay/Comox.

If you are coming from Powell River on the mainland shore (but reached by ferry from Vancouver) you can take the ferry to the Little River terminal just north of Comox.

Information: Comox Valley Chamber of Commerce, 2040 Cliffe Ave, Courtenay, B.C., V9N 2L3; Toll Free: 1-888-357-4471; Website: http://www.comoxvalleychamber.com/; Email: admin@comoxvalleychamber.com. The Chamber runs the Visitor Information Centre from this site, too.

Accommodations: There are dozens of resorts in this area, many right on the sea. Check the Chamber and the Info Centre. King Coho Resort, 250-339-2039, info@kingcohoresort.bc.ca, kingcohoresort.bc.ca.

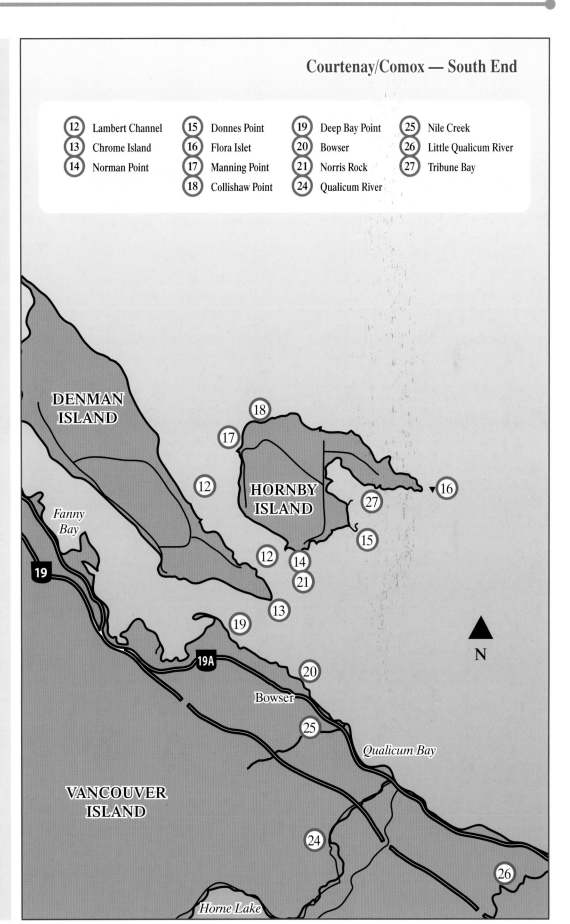

## Courtenay/Comox — South End

| | | | | | | | |
|---|---|---|---|---|---|---|---|
| 12 | Lambert Channel | 15 | Donnes Point | 19 | Deep Bay Point | 25 | Nile Creek |
| 13 | Chrome Island | 16 | Flora Islet | 20 | Bowser | 26 | Little Qualicum River |
| 14 | Norman Point | 17 | Manning Point | 21 | Norris Rock | 27 | Tribune Bay |
| | | 18 | Collishaw Point | 24 | Qualicum River | | |

# Duncan, Cowichan (Including Porlier Pass)

**D**uncan is the first major town north on Highway 1 from Victoria, an easy one hour drive over the scenic Malahat Drive. It is also the town most commonly associated with the historic Cowichan River that flows through it.

South east of Duncan, Cowichan Bay is where you launch for saltwater fishing.

## Saltwater Fishing
## Local Winter hotspots

Most of the winter fishing takes place between Vancouver Island and Saltspring Island. Sansum Narrows has good strong tides that push bait and chinook salmon into well-defined back eddies. These make drift jigging popular all year-round. The hotspots include Separation Point, Bold Bluff Point, Octopus Point across from it and the narrows north of Maple Bay, a very pretty and charming retreat of a town.

If you want to motor north, fish off the town of Vesuvius and all around the south end of Tent Island. Currents are less speedy than through the Narrows.

Porlier Pass to the north is also a drift jigging spot, with the best water associated with the downstream side of the current. First you fish one end, and then, when the tide changes, you motor to the other side of the pass where the rip forms anew. Take care, many reefs dot the area.

April spots include Tent Island and Porlier Pass for early Columbians. Troll 100- to 150- feet along the steep walls and pay great attention to your depth-sounder in Porlier Pass.

## Porlier Pass

This pass to Georgia Strait is to the south of Nanaimo, between Valdes Island and Galiano Island. The Gap is good for springs January to September. The pass is particularly reef studded—Dionsio Pt and other reefs actually break the surface—and with currents as fast as 9 knots, it is difficult water, best taken with a guide. Fish on the east side when the tide is in flood and off the west entrance on the ebb.

*What's a book without a shot of a boat and a rainbow, provided it's in color.*

Fish with 8- to 10-oz of weight, cutplugs and 3/0 single hooks in the back eddies created by the main tidal flow. Look for rocks and reefs that attract bait schools. On dark days, use green/glow, green/white spoons or the venerable silver Tom Mack on four-foot leaders. Local hootchies on 34-inch leaders include glow varieties: Cop Car, Army Truck, Blood and Bones, green gator splatterback, the Radiant Purple Haze and Irish Mist.

## Winter Lures

Fish across the change of tides, not when the current is blowing full speed through Sansum Narrows.

Use herring in glow teasers 4 feet behind glow flashers. Fish four-inch spoons in green/glow, silver/green, Tiger Prawn and Mongoose.

Try black/silver and pink/silver Apexes.

Local favoured hootchies include the Army Truck, Cop Car and jelly fish patterns.

Buzz Bombs and Rip tide Strikers work for drift jiggers.

## Local Summer Hotspots

The summer hotspots are the same as the winter ones. They include Separation Point, Burial Island and the Power Lines.

In autumn fish between the fish marker and Sherard Point There is a big hole in the Vancouver Island side. Fishing 90- to 125-feet deep in the 150 foot hole can produce springs to 20 pounds and in the odd year a pink or two, a surprising catch as pinks should be miles away going around the south end of Saturna Island as they beetle toward the Fraser River.

Cowichan Bay was a location of great fishing history, with the traditional Cowichan Bay Bucktails with abalone spinners (4 and 5) developed to take coho that grew to 30 pounds.

Today, the fish are fewer, but when there are fishing openings, fish the mid-channel waters where you see jumping coho. Chum can be distinguished as they fall on their flanks and jump 6- to 8-times in a row in a semi-circular pattern. They seldom bite but you can chase them around in the early morning and later in the evening.

## Summer Lures

Drift jiggers use jigging lures year round for salmon, including Buzz Bombs and Rip Tide Strikers in green and yellow and red and white and the King of Diamonds. Moochers use herring and 6 oz banana weight to reach 125 feet.

**Launching Ramps** (among others): Hecate Park public ramp. Cowichan Bay Road, Cowichan Bay, BC. Turn left on Koksilah Road, left onto Cowichan Bay Road, a good launch.

Pier 66 Marina, 1745 Cowichan Bay Rd., Cowichan Bay BC, VOR INO; Phone: 1-250-748-8444; Website: pier66marina.com; Email: pier66@shaw.ca.

**Tackle Shops:** Bucky's Sports Shop, 171 Craig St. Duncan, B.C. V9L 1V8; Toll Free: 1-800-667-7270; Website: buckys-sports.com/fishing; Email: rkennett@buckys-sports.com.

**Access:** Duncan is an hour north of Victoria on Highway 1. Turn right on Wilmot before Duncan to access Cowichan Bay. The several marinas on the waterfront can be accessed via water from Nanaimo to the north and Sidney to the south.

**Infomation:** Contact the Chamber of Commerce, 381 Trans Canada Highway, Duncan, B.C., V9L 3R5; Phone: 1-250-748-1111; Website:www.duncancc.bc.ca/ContactUs.htm; Email: manager@duncancc.bc.ca.

**Accommodations:** See cowichanbay.com for a good listing of local accommodations, restaurants and marine facilities.

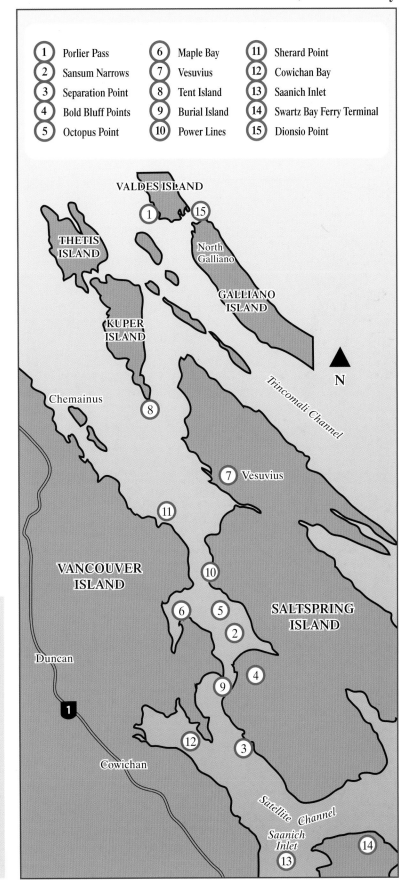

| | | | |
|---|---|---|---|
| 1 Porlier Pass | 6 Maple Bay | 11 Sherard Point | |
| 2 Sansum Narrows | 7 Vesuvius | 12 Cowichan Bay | |
| 3 Separation Point | 8 Tent Island | 13 Saanich Inlet | |
| 4 Bold Bluff Points | 9 Burial Island | 14 Swartz Bay Ferry Terminal | |
| 5 Octopus Point | 10 Power Lines | 15 Dionsio Point | |

*Peter the guide all smiles and his not-so-amused lingcod. It smiled and gave Peter the old face wash—after it was released.*

## Saltwater Fishing

### Local Winter Hotspots

Leave the winter hotspots to the locals—past Fair Harbour there is no road, no power, no hotel. But if you just can't do that, Fair Harbour has a good winter fishery right off the dock for feeder chinook to 15 pounds. If you are a real glutton for punishment, you may survive infamous Spaghetti Hill, boat in tow. Troll around points of land in the inside channels and where good structure changes direction along steep rock walls. Run your gear 75 to 140 feet (24 to 45 metres) down.

### Local Winter Lures

The venerable, green/white hootchie behind a glow flasher is gear enough. But if bait is your thing, medium herring in a glow teaser will connect you with a winter feeder. Flashers are optional with bait—there are lots of naïve fish here and they stay this way until June when they move offshore, just before the summer season begins.

### Local Summer Hotspots

Kyuquot Sound has had no fishing pressure in the past and thus must be considered a prime pristine area for fishing, both for bottom-dwellers and pass-through chinook, coho, chum, sockeye and pink salmon. Chinook season is June 1 to September 15; coho peak August 15 to September 15.

Like the sportfishing destinations to the south, Kyuquot gets the same pass-through stocks from as far away as California early in the season and sequential run bell curves that bring the local Vancouver Island river stocks home later in the season; for example, Nootka Sound's Conuma Hatchery fish in later August. They are on the same underwater freeway but here bottom features concentrate the chinook into a narrow band a mile or two (1.6 to 3.2 km) wide. And the big chinook, 25 to 45 pounds, pass right on shore among the maze of open-ocean rocks and kelp lines. This is prime-time stuff without another boat in sight.

Also of advantage, the Continental Shelf is narrower than farther south. This means that, on days when halibut are the target, the farthest out the boats travel is 14 miles (22.4 km), half the distance of deep-sea trips farther south.

The small town of Kyuquot on Walter's Island is 10 minutes from the local hotspot Spring Island. This is one of the typical on-the-rocks fishery on a near-shore area with the troll pattern precisely defined hard to the rocks with swells crashing a boat length from the boat. This is dangerous fishing without the proper guide, but is the spine-tingling motor-mooching ballet that is beautiful to watch skilled guides move and glide, move and glide one behind the other.

Take a guide until you are thoroughly familiar with this remote area. If you subsequently take a boat, the etiquette in power mooching is to get in behind another boat. When he puts his motor in gear, then you put your motor in gear. When he takes his boat out of gear, then you then take your boat out of gear. Every boat does this and it is beauty to watch, making your lines move from 90 degrees at the end of the glide to, say, 45 degrees on the go. When a boat has a fish on, the other boats try to form a hole in the line and let the fish be fought on the outside.

Your boat should be welded aluminum; fiberglass is not tough enough. Do not explore on your own. On the west side of Spring Island in Brown Channel, when the ebb meets the north-westerlies of afternoon, the waves make boats and then their aerials disappear. You can fish here all day and not see another boat. So go safe or don't go.

*Releasing a fine, fly-caught coho at Catface Bar, Clayoquot Sound (Tofino).*

**K**yuquot Sound is one of the few locations on Vancouver Island that was not submerged half a mile under the ocean by a mile's thickness of ice in the last ice age, 10,000 years ago. This results in a far greater abundance of rock projections in the sea. Thus you are strongly advised, in this very remote area, to take a guide service until you are fully familiar with the thousands of uncharted rocks. And then take careful marks with your GPS before boating this area yourself.

Rocks do have one good use, though: they confer a much greater abundance of bottom fish such as ling cod, rock fish, red snapper and halibut. They also provide the kind of surf-plowed rock walls that mature chinook move along in search of food and home and that impress you with their efficient motiveless power.

The Sound seems to have more sea otters than herring. Ten were brought from the Aleutian Islands to escape a nuclear test circa 1970 and now thousands lie on their backs, rocks on tummies, breaking open sea urchin shells just like on National Geographic.

Another of the landfalls for south-bound chinook is Rugged Point 20 minutes to the south. When the bite comes on in July and August, all the boats get fish, as the period lasts more than an hour. When the bite is on it is almost too easy to catch big chinook—some problem.

Typically there are on-shore boundaries for chinook protection later in the season. At this time, boats move out onto the banks five to 15 miles (8 to 24 km) off shore. They produce the best fishing but this is, again, serious ocean, hence it is fished only when safer fishing is out of bounds. Fish the edges of contours, the high and low spots, 130 to 300 feet down. There are days with "silly" coho fishing when you lower the downrigger balls at rocket speed and can't reach the chinook beneath the 10- to 20-pound coho.

Later in August when the waters are calmer, some boats run up to the pinnacles and holes just south of Brooks Peninsula Park for halibut on average a healthy 60 lbs.

If you are a fly-guy, bring along an 8-weight fly rod for coho and try to contain your glee when they race to the plop of a fly. Coho are focused-on only late in the summer when chinook fishing slows and coho are at their maximum size nearing 20 pounds. With no rain to push them into the rivers, they remain in saltwater chomping everything that comes their way.

## Summer Lures

The number one bait for power mooching is large cut-plug herring. Second is anchovy in a clear teaser. Hootchies are put down when mackerel abound, whacking every bait and making you annoyed. When skip-fly fishing for coho at higher speed, put down some Tomic plugs, the 602, for example, at 20 feet and see if some chinook don't speed up to catch them.

For off-shore chinook fishing use anchovy or herring in a clear teaser on a 4- to 8-foot leader. The fish are so unpressured that the simple white hootchie is the artificial of choice. The green/glow spoon commonly referred to as Coyote spoons (though half a dozen manufacturers also produce the identical spoon and usually a full complement of 25 other colours) is king. Again, any colour will work out here in the boondocks. Take out some Road-runners, the large and beautiful spoons from Tomic, 602, 429, the Cop Car and my favourite, the pink/blue white spoon that changes colour as you rotate it. Troll them without a flasher.

As for flies, make up some Clouser Minnows in chartreuse/white, pink/white, silver and any combination of colours for bucktails. Add some Krystal Flash or Flashabou for sparkle.

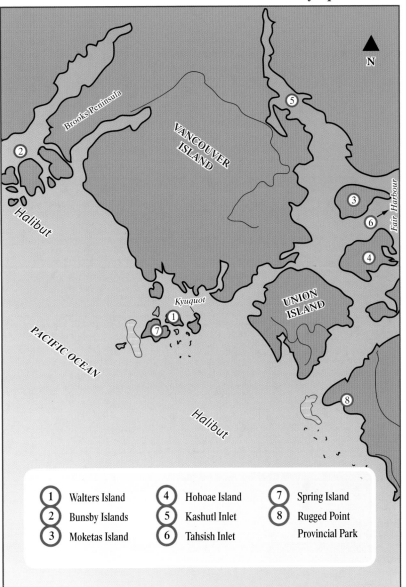

| | | | | | |
|---|---|---|---|---|---|
| 1 | Walters Island | 4 | Hohoae Island | 7 | Spring Island |
| 2 | Bunsby Islands | 5 | Kashutl Inlet | 8 | Rugged Point |
| 3 | Moketas Island | 6 | Tahsish Inlet | | Provincial Park |

**Launching Ramp:** Fair Harbour has a gas dock and a rough gravel boat launch.

**Tackle Shops:** Bring all your own tackle.

**Access:** Access is by boat or by air. Visit Westjet.com for flights to Comox and pickup by Walter's Cove. See Nootka Air in the Nootka Sound chapter or Harbour Air: Phone: 1-800-665-0212; Website: www.harbourair.com for flights from Vancouver landing on the water at your resort.

Boat access is aboard the *MV Uchuck* from Gold River. It has a Thursday sailing to Kyuquot on Walter's Island.

Road access north from Victoria to Campbell River is 280 km or 3.5 hours and from there to Fair Harbour is a long drive, 230 km north and west, or another 4 hours. Take Highway 19 north from Campbell River to the Zeballos turnoff 20 km past Woss. Then it is 39 km to Zeballos on gravel, after the big hill (you will know), take the left fork to Zeballos, or right to Fair Harbour. It is 9 km to Western Forest Products and Little Espinosa bridge, 16 more to Kaouk River Bridge. Bear left after the bridge, 10 km to Fair Harbour (a total 22 miles/35km from Zeballos which is 26 miles/42km west of Highway 19). From Fair Harbour it is a 35-minute scenic boat ride to Kyuquot.

Package trips that include air passage to the lodge of your choice are an easier way to go—though fog can delay your landing or take-off until later in the day.

**Information:** Try www.gov.bc.ca/sm/ and type in Kyoquot to find info. This is a remote spot, even today. Kyuquot has a few amenities: B&B, motel restaurant, general store, medical centre, boat charters and water taxi.

Zeballos Board of Trade, Phone: 1-250-761-4090

**Accommodations:** Walters Cove Lodge: West Coast Resorts, #2 7100 River Road, Richmond, BC, V6X 1X5; Phone toll free: 1-800-810-8933; Email: info@westcoastresorts.com.

Dave Murphy's presence is reason enough to fish here. A well-respected name in island fishing, he offers water-based and land-based accommodations for a total of 30 guests. Toll Free: 1-877-218-6600; Website: murphysportfishing.com; Email: murphy@island.net.

Swan Song Campsite beside the government dock in Fair Harbour has fuel, campgrounds, store, tackle, boat ramp.

Dixie Cove Provincial Park campground is about 10 km from Fair Harbour by water (25 km (16 m) west of Zeballos by water). An undeveloped site, but has good, safe moorage.

Rugged Point Provincial Marine Park, campground is about 22 km from Fair Harbour by water (35 km by water west of Zeballos). Pit toilets and that's it.

In the beginning was the bath tub and Nanaimo was proud to be known as the Bath Tub Capital where races in the said item ran from the waterfront all the way across to Vancouver on the east side of Georgia Strait. Surprisingly, some of the perilous craft actually made it. But that was yesterday and now Nanaimo likes to call itself the Hub City.

Without doubt Nanaimo has one of the prettier, sheltered harbours on Vancouver Island, with a waterfront strip having the Bastion fortress on one end, the new performing arts centre and condo high rises and then the Departure Bay ferry terminal on the northern end.

The harbour is protected from the full force of winter south easters by Newcastle and Gabriola islands. The latter is long and justly famed for its extensive, beautiful and weird sandstone foundations at water's edge. This high island drops right into the sea more than 300 feet on the harbour side. Thus, with the Strait of Georgia on the other side, Nanaimo has one of the deepest fisheries for winter chinook on Vancouver Island, with trollers using their electric downriggers—you don't want to hand crank a manual this far—as much as 250 feet down.

# Saltwater Fishing

## Local Winter Hotspots

With the general long-term demise of Georgia Strait chinook stocks, Nanaimo's fishery, along with many other inside fisheries, had been declining for a long time. More and more, anglers had moved to the more blustery Georgia Strait side of Gabriola Island with its strong south-easterly winds. With the improvement of Campbell River's winter fishery and DFO's attempt to bring east-side stocks back, the fishery is slowly reviving.

Do note that because winter feeder chinook are fish of absolutely specific behaviour, if you know the patterns that existed in the past when stocks were more plentiful, when stocks increase, the fish can be expected to do exactly the same things, at the same depth in the same spots as their ancestors did. This is the reason for knowing the fishing grounds in such areas.

Winter chinook season is December to early April with 8- to 15-lb fish filtering in along with a few large 20-pound fish, and growing larger over the season. Dawn and dusk are peak periods along with tide changes and you should actively troll in search of the fish. When you connect, concentrate your effort in that area.

Early in the winter concentrate effort near the oil dock and the ferry terminal. Allowing for ferries slipping in and out, this sheltered area is also shallower, with 80 to 120 feet the downrigger depth. You may drift fish in this area, too.

In January and February, fish just off the Cannery along the northern shore of Gabriola Island in 250 to 300 feet of water, downriggers at 180- to 240 feet. Fish toward Entrance Island, a local hotspot in summer as well as winter. A deep "slot" lies between Orlebar Point and Entrance, so fish the outside as well as inside of the island. But do steer clear of the reef on Orlebar. Here and off the south end of Snake Island a lot of diving traffic takes place. The Canadian Naval Destroyer *H.M.C.S Saskatchewan* rests near Snake, and you must stay away 300 feet (100 metres) when diver signs are posted.

In March, shore anglers try the rocky promontories north of Neck Point. Access is from the adjacent park.

Arguably the best or second most productive spot in the area—year-round—is Five Fingers. Try 150 to 200 feet deep in the winter. The same depths hold for Snake and Entrance islands. Hudson Rocks near Five Fingers deserve a pass as do the Clarke Rocks just beyond. Icarus Point marks the northern end of the Nanaimo fishing area and the beginning of the Lantzville, Nanoose Bay fishery area.

When you fish the outside islands, keep your eyes trained on the southern and northern horizons. If you see a black line, indicating wind on the water, it's time to pick up stakes and move more within the gap afforded by Gabriola Island. And watch the ferries coming and going, too, as a number of the hotspots lie directly in the path of these large vessels that have little or no ability to thread their way among sport boats. Not to mention that you are supposed to get out of their way.

## Winter Lures

Early in winter, use 3-inch plugs to match local bait supplies of needlefish and immature herring. Plug choices include the 191, 232 (good on coho in the fall, too), 500 and 727. Your bait should present a narrower silhouette, too, particularly closer to the harbour, where needlefish prevail most of the time. One local initiative is Tiny Strip "narrowed" down, or the un-slimmed, small anchovy and small herring. The green and clear Anchovy Specials are standby teaser heads, though the newer green glow, Purple Haze and pearl (like a 602 plug) deserve attention, too.

Some diehards use cutplug herring even though this is a very deep fishery and bait may be blunted simply by being let down 250 feet. Trail cutplugs 6 feet behind a chrome Hot Spot or O'ki flasher. As the season progresses, increase lure or bait size to match baitfish and switch to flashers with green or red trim. As the saying goes: "Go with whatever bait you can roll the best."

Glow in the dark hootchies find their best use in deep fisheries. Try the Cop Car, Army Truck and the Purple Haze, 34 inches behind a glow flasher. Use longer leaders, to 42 inches, later in the season.

The Coyote spoon, or Radiant's, Green Ghost, glow/green and the Campbell River favourite, the Cop Car work here, too. Troll 4- to 6-feet behind a flasher. The older angler may have more faith in the half green/half silver Krippled K spoon or the silver Tom Mack.

In April, winter fish change depth based on weather. Cloudy days and early in the morning, the fish are in the 80- to 110-feet levels. Sunny days or later in the afternoon, the fish descend to 150- to 210- feet. Try the Brickyard, Entrance Island, Five Fingers, Orlebar Point and the old Cannery.

Later plugs also include the larger sizes of 4- to 6-inches. Try out the 191, 158, 203 and 602. The 158 and 602 are the best plugs on the west coast of Vancouver Island as well. For those who fish Luhr Jensen J-plugs, try chrome, white, pearl, with green, blue or grey trim.

Shore anglers use the long standing drift jigging lures, the Buzz Bomb, Pirkens, Pirks, Mac Deeps and so on.

## Local Summer Hotspots

Fish out around the islands concentrating on Entrance Islands and Five Fingers, along with Snake Islands and Neck Point. Depth should be 120- to 150-feet. Then there is also the Cannery and Silva Bay.

Shore anglers amble out to Rocky Point, Pipers Lagoon Park, and Neck Point, some of the same spots they use for winter fishing.

## Summer Lures

In spoons pick up the Monkey Puke, Army Truck and Cop Car from Radiant or Luhr Jensen. Also herring strip in the tyee size and short cutplugs trolled fast, i.e., fire crackers for coho, and anchovy in glow teasers for chinook. Green Apex lures from Hot Spot are also effective.

Summer hootchies include the Cop Car and green/white on 36- to 42-inch leaders.

Drift fishers move to the venerable Buzz Bomb, the fishy Stingsilda, Zzingers and the rest.

In odd numbered years, for example, 2009, pinks destined for the Fraser pass through and pink in hootchies and squirts will put you on them, along with pink Roostertails from the beaches to the north.

Where the Nanaimo area butts up against the Parksville fishing area, the same lures come into play: Blood and Bones, Moby Dick, and Frogman patterns in hootchies. Try spoons in glow/green, Cop Car, Watermelon and Mongoose. Use plaid flashers in water shallower than 75 feet and the Betsy, red or green Hot Spot or Purple Haze when fishing deeper. Try Icarus and Neck Points fishing 90- to 150-feet deep.

---

**Launching Ramps:** Launching ramps are found right beside the Departure Bay terminal at Brechin Point, operated by the City and the smaller Charlaine ramp near Pipers Lagoon. Many marinas and waterfront businesses lie along the shore facing Newcastle Island.

**Tackle Shops:** Johnson Hardware Ltd, 39 Victoria Crescent, V9R 5B9; Email: gunsfish@nanaimo.ark.com; Phone: 1-250-753-2531.

Bill's Reel and Downrigger Shop, 3260 Departure Bay Road, V9T 1B4

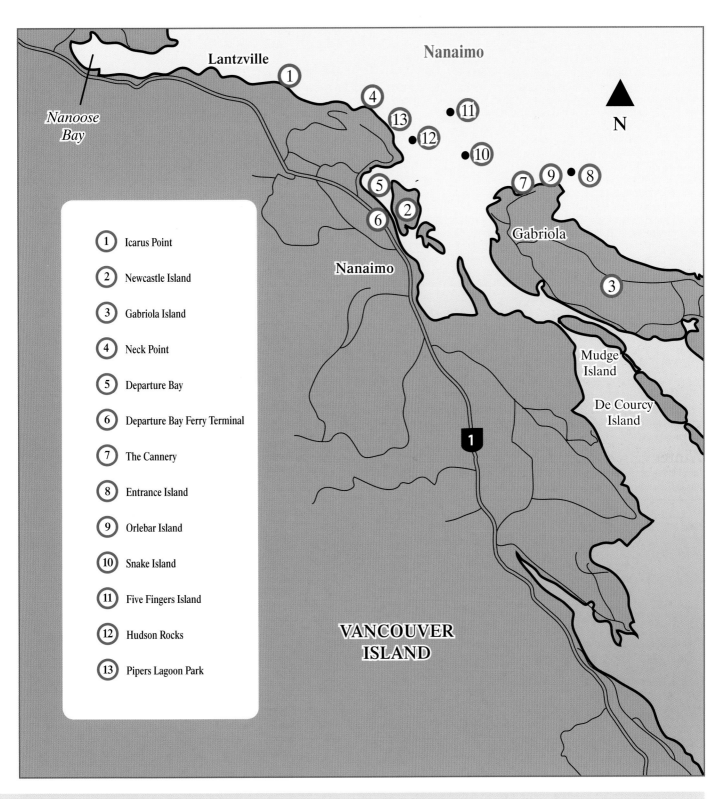

**Legend:**

1. Icarus Point
2. Newcastle Island
3. Gabriola Island
4. Neck Point
5. Departure Bay
6. Departure Bay Ferry Terminal
7. The Cannery
8. Entrance Island
9. Orlebar Island
10. Snake Island
11. Five Fingers Island
12. Hudson Rocks
13. Pipers Lagoon Park

**Access:** By car from Victoria, north on the Trans-Canada highway, 66 miles (110 km), an hour and a half easy drive. Coming from Vancouver by BC Ferry, you have two choices, either the older, Departure Bay terminal in the centre of town or Duke Point to the south. Flying in from Vancouver is a third option.

**Information: Greater Nanaimo Chamber of Commerce**, 2133 Bowen Road, V9S 1H8; Phone: 1-250-756-1191; Website: nanaimochamber.bc.ca; Email: info@nanaimochamber.bc.ca.

Tourism Nanaimo, Website: tourismnanaimo.com

**Accommodations:** Nanaimo has a full range of accommodation from the harbour front to B&Bs. Check out the City of Nanaimo Website: cityofnanaimo.com/hotels-motels/index.html.

# Nitinat Bar and Lake Fishery

orty miles (64 km) across from Washington's Olympic Peninsula, Nitinat Bar is one of the most infamous spots on Vancouver Island's southern coast. The bar, actually two sets of rocks, jams the neck of the saltwater lake of the same name, and has taken down many ships when the ocean waves meet the tidal outflow. People are lost here almost every year, so be aware and take no chances.

While you must take care, the Bar can produce fantastic results in August when the Nitinat chinook, 20- to 45-pound bullets, plug the ledge on the ocean side. Provided all boats work together to "mine" the ledge in front of the narrow channel, all can come away with big chinook.

The Nitinat has a major hatchery returning, in average years, 20,000 chinook, 30,000 coho and 700,000 chum. The last number has been as high as 1.8 million chum, hence the reason for the solid fishing.

Nitinat Lake is one of the top 10 North America destinations for wind surfers. This is because a natural convection wind of 30 miles an hour (50 kmph) forms virtually every day and the hundreds of brightly coloured wings zing the surface from noon until 7 p.m. when the wind dies. Typically this wind does not bother anglers, who are out in the Narrows near the ocean, or traveling that way early in the morning when there is no wind and going back, with the wind, later in the day. Do note that if you decide to venture from Ditidaht after 11 a.m. in the morning that you will be banging into three to four foot waves for the entire 18 mile (28.8 km) journey. So leave earlier.

## Local Winter Hotspots

Nitinat Bar is about 15 miles (24 km) from Owen Point near Port Renfrew and about 15 miles (24 km) from Cape Beale near Bamfield.

No one fishes here in winter as it is too rough and the running distance is too far. Note that the prevailing wind is South East in winter and South West in summer

## Winter Lures

The obvious lures, were one to fish, would be anchovy in a glow teaser head, purple Haze hootchie and Glow/Green spoon.

## Local Summer Hotspots

### Nitinat Bar

The Bar is fished in August for chinook and in September for coho. The Ditidaht First Nation runs a zodiac around the two sets of rock. Check your chart carefully, and follow their route, if you must cross to or from the lake—at high slack. The left passage is close under high rock and the almost invisible channel on the Whyac side is hardly passed by boats larger than a canoe. Crossing the Bar is not recommended. The water swirls so much that you can't see the bottom in 12 feet of water.

The peak bite period is the last two hours of the rising tide. When this occurs at about 8:00 am, you have prime fishing conditions. You want to catch your fish and motor to port before the daily southwesterly blows.

The best fishing is to be found in the gap between the rock walls on the Whyac shore and the opposing cliff. The chinook crowd close to the Bar in water as shallow as 12' in the natural ocean "pool" that develops. Every boat passes through parallel to the shore. The recent big fish is 53 pounds. I have caught a 60 pounder in the river and the hatchery has recorded a 68 lb. male.

With the surf plowing across the outer bar on a low tide, the "pool" where salmon reside waiting to proceed into Nitinat Lake on a high tide is very shallow. For this reason, fishing is less successful, that is, the fish are not concentrated in as defined a spot and thus are encountered less frequently by trolling fishermen.

In the instance of a low tide, make sure to troll as far east as the point of Clo-oose and as far west as Tsusiat Falls, where the river of the same name falls directly off the cliff onto the shingle beach and is spectacularly beautiful. Between the two kelp beds is a good spot to try while waiting for the tide to build. This shore holds the Nitinat chinook earlier in August and should be fished before moving to the bar in late August and September. If September remains dry the chinook hold on the bar and fishing can continue to be great until rain shoots them through the narrows.

For a couple of weeks when the high slack begins to ebb, the big hogs holding in the lake drop back to the bar and make for an outstanding bite. Fishermen can't get the lines back in the water fast enough.

In September the obliging chum take cutplugs in the deeper waters off the Bar as do the carnivorous coho.

Fish the 180 foot spires offshore as they are good halibut holders.

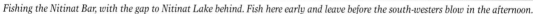

*Fishing the Nitinat Bar, with the gap to Nitinat Lake behind. Fish here early and leave before the south-westers blow in the afternoon.*

## Nitinat Lake

The other summer hotspot is the inside of the narrows during the Labour Day weekend. The chinook typically build in August and a week either side of Labour Day they slip over the bar with the flood.

Lake-side anglers run up into the narrows and drift back with the incoming tide—at a good clip—fishing with Buzz Bombs and any other drift fishing lure. Two thirds the way into the narrows there is a good rock ledge where the incoming chinook drop down to the bottom 35 feet below and rest in a vertical eddy. This is the hotspot for drift fishers. The fish are so thick at times they may be fin "biters" rather than mouth biters. As the lake is tidal, the federal saltwater regulations apply and foul-hooked fish may be retained, provided you did not deliberately foul hook it, in which case the fish must be let go.

Although used by few anglers, cutplug herring rigged in the traditional manner on two single hooks and let down 15 feet, will also over a good day of fishing produce, many mouth-hooked chinook in this area, when the boat moves around on a slow troll.

Because the neck is narrow, filled with rocks and boats, and has a swift tidal bore, many anglers choose to fish other structure. Both of the two unnamed points east north east of the narrows provide structure for the chinook that, as mature summer fish, follow the shoreline all the way to the river. On the Labour Day Weekend you will find a pretty group of 50 or so boats trolling these two points with traditional saltwater trolling gear. This is flood tide fishing, all the way to the closed areas near the Nitinat River.

## Summer Lures

Utilize clear, blue, chartreuse or pink teaserheads with stick-on eyes for herring, a minimum 42-inch leader behind a Hot Spot or Oki flasher and with a one-second flop-roll. If you are unsuccessful, lengthen leaders to 6-feet and try again. For simplicity, most anglers use one large treble and embed one barb in a straight line from the wing on the teaserhead up behind the dorsal fin. Clip toothpicks (used to secure bait in the teaser) flush with good quality pliers-style clippers.

On the ocean side of the bar, the ground swell calls for longer leaders for cutpluggers: 7- to 9-feet, but don't be tempted to go longer as it gets increasingly hard to net fish. Use 4- to 6-oz. banana weights. Cutplug leaders usually feature two single 3/0 to 6/0 silver, Kirbed hooks 4 inches apart, the leader of which hooks into the high or meat side of the plug and the trailer is buried in the lateral line behind the dorsal fin. A fast, tight, cutplug roll is best. Chinook are greedy at the Nitinat and it is common to find cutplugs in their stomachs.

While bait should be the lure of choice, carry some hardware, too. Pick up some spoons in glow white/glow green and Army Truck. Carry green and Army Truck squirts to fish behind a flasher.

For cutplug anglers, fluorescent weights, particularly in day-glo orange, out fish other keeled weights 3 to 1. Fish these in close to the Bar.

If you wish to troll, move out from the Bar and let the lines on either side down to 25- to 35-feet with an anchovy 6 feet behind a flasher. Run a middle line with a 4-ounce keeled weight and without a flasher. Sometimes the fish are as shallow as 6 feet under the surface, so it is best to offer two different depths between the boat and the shelf below.

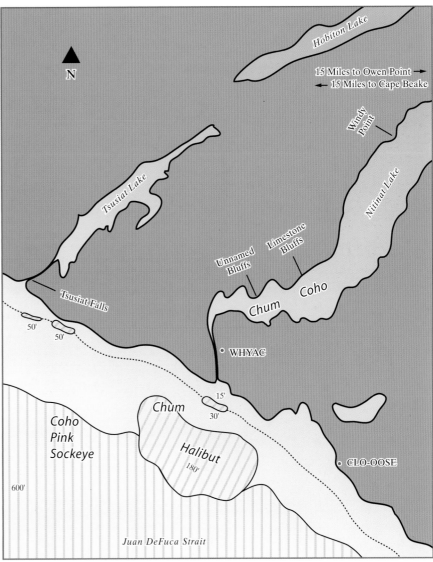

**Launching Ramps:** There is no local launching ramp on the open ocean side. You must run up Juan de Fuca Strait 15 miles (24 km) from Port Renfrew or down the same distance from Cape Beale, 5 miles (8 km) west of Bamfield.

There are two ramps on Nitinat Lake, one near the Indian village of Ditidaht—add 18 miles (24 km) to get to the narrows—and one at the campground down the lake on the Rosander Main, about 8 miles (12.8 km) from the narrows.

**Tackle Shops:** There is no tackle shop. You must bring all your gear with you.

**Access:** Port Renfrew: a 60 mile (100 km), 90 minute drive from Victoria. Stay the night in town and launch early.

Nitinat Lake: the campsite is a 3.5 hour drive north from Victoria, on Highway 1 to Duncan, west on Highway 18 to Youbou and then varying quality gravel roads to the Nitinat Junction where you turn left and follow Rosander Main. It has some tight, high switch backs.

Bamfield: a 3.5 hour vehicle trip from Victoria on the same roads as to Nitinat Lake. On this trip you turn right at the Nitinat junction and proceed. Bamfield is also accessed through a better quality

gravel road 1 hour south from Port Alberni, which is itself 2.5 hours on Highway 1 and then Highway 4 to the Bamfield sign posts near the information kiosk. Same time, better road.

**Accommodation:** The Ditidaht First Nation has a small, nine room motel. There is also a provincial campground near the town and the campground out the Rosander Main

**Information:** There is no local Chamber of Commerce. Ditidaht has a gas station that usually has fuel. There is no vehicle service. You must be self-sufficient.

*Thatcher Beatty and a typical Nootka Sound spring, taken at Ferrer Point on a late-September afternoon where all 18 boats had big springs on for three hours.*

**B**.C.'s most important historical site, Friendly Cove, at one entrance to Nootka Sound, is where Captain Cook landed in 1778. Both Cook, from England, and Narvaez, from Spain, claimed the area for their respective countries. The two countries were on the brink of war and had Spain won, the entire Pacific shore from Alaska to Tierra del Fuego would have been Spanish speaking today.

Instead of remaining at war readiness, the two captain's enjoyed one another's company so greatly they agreed to wait for their two nations to duke it out, while they spent the winter in the tiny harbour of Yuquot, which translates as "blows right over" (and does it ever) having hunting and fishing parties and toasting one another with their ample supplies of wine and spirits.

Nootka Sound still retains its remote nature more than 200 years later. And this means loads of fish. It also is such a large area, 40 miles (64 km) across the mouth, with 9 major fjord inlets with high cliffs of 4000 foot rock faces and many 30 miles (48 km) long, you could set out to fish the salt and freshwater fishing and

not come back for a year. The Inlets are: Muchalet Inlet (Gold River), Tlupana Inlet (Moutcha Bay), Tahsis Inlet (Tahsis), Esperanza Inlet, Zeballos Inlet (Zeballos), Espinosa Inlet, Little Espinosa Inlet, Kendrick Inlet and Nuchatlitz Inlet.

The area is home to the Conuma River hatchery, and the tens of thousands of chinook it returns is the big reason why Nootka Sound enjoys such wonderful fishing, including being a nursery ground for maturing feeder chinook on the Continental Shelf out front. As in all west coast Vancouver Island fisheries, the Shelf receives sequential runs from "Springers" in February, then chinook from California rivers, then Oregon, then Washington on the outside, and so on through the summer, including the surfline Robertson Creek and Nitinat hatchery chinook and finishing up with Conuma, all being in the 20- to 45-pound range.

It says loads about today's fishing that the commercial troll fleet fished off Friendly Cove until 1998 when it was curtailed to give sport anglers first crack at the coho and chinook. Now the fish are here in great numbers but the fleet is gone and that spells great fishing for sport anglers. As recently as 2007, a commercial "test" troll fishery was authorized—further evidence that this is a great place to fish.

As with all other fisheries, you must check the annual regulations for fisheries closures, areas and times aimed at protecting, in this case, the other non-enhanced chinook runs in Nootka Sound.

## Local Winter Hotspots

Two and three year old, 6- to 14-pound, winter feeder chinook from as far away as California move into and mature in Nootka Sound from November right through to June when the first local summer sockeye arrive. Fish them, inside the Sound at 18- to 36-metres, with small spoons, hootchies and anchovy. If you can reach them—a weather issue—try the kelp lines along Nootka Island's outside edge as it is the best spot for springtime feeders in March to May.

Of course, the traveling feeders on the Shelf are here 12 months of the year and if you could get off shore they are available 12 months of the year.

In rough water, fish for halibut on the flats just off Burdwood Point and off Escalante Point, and Perez Rocks in water as shallow as 105 feets in February and March when the spawning halibut come on shore. This is lazy fishing: you put down a cutplug on the downrigger, ball just off bottom and drift along, ocean swell improving bait action.

After spawning, the bulk of the halibut move offshore one to two and one half miles (2- to 3-km) for a short period and then return in May as 20- to 50-pound fish, just as they do in most waters off Vancouver Island. Look for them anywhere from the Nootka Light to Ferrer Point, in June, 150- to 175-feet, on sand and gravel bottoms Along with rockfish and the present feeder chinook come early coho as bluebacks in the 2- to 5-pound range that you fish when you see them on the surface.

On the northern entrance to the sound, the water between Ferrer Point (pronounced locally as fair-ee-er) and Catala Island is also relatively shallow and protected and good for early bottom fishing. Also move to between the whistle buoy in Gillam Channel to 1 mile (1 km) off Ferrer Point, bouncing your spreader bar baited with squid. Drop your prawn traps in the 300- to 350-feet range on your way out.

Ask the wily locals for winter hotspots. They'll point out there is a good winter fishing right off the dock for springs to 15 pounds. The same can be said of Zeballos, the best fishing being off the points of land pretty well every where all the way out to Steamer Point, 75- to 140-feet down.

## Winter Lures

For halibut, bait is key, a cutplug, squid or large herring, along with an octopus tentacle. Due to its toughness octopus isn't as easily inhaled off the large 6/0 to 9/0 Kirbed or circle hooks as easily as other baits, so your rig is fishing longer with this addition.

For feeders, medium herring in clear or glow teasers, with or without a flasher and the traditional green/white hootchie, the coast-wide favourite, Purple Haze, Army Truck, Tiger Prawn, with a glow flasher. Always use glow in the winter, as the fish are usually deeper than light penetrates.

For those who like plugs, give a try to the 602, 158, 700 and 530. Local Apexes include Cop Car, black or pink pearl.

## Local Summer Hotspots

As with any open Pacific spot, it's offshore in the morning and on-shore in the afternoon. From May on, if you don't hit swells going past Steamer Point at 6 a.m., it's usually flat on the outside. Ferrer Point is 50 minutes away from Zeballos. Move south following the 110 foot contour as much as one mile (1.6 km). Use a Gibbs green/brass flasher early in season with a clear teaser, small anchovy, to 60 feet. If the wind rises, move inshore to Rosa Island, trolling at 40 feet.

Mature chinook arrive in waves, moving down the outside shelf and shores from July 15 on. Local fish begin arriving a week or two later, followed by surfline chinook destined for Vancouver Island rivers for the first three weeks of August and then, of course, the Conuma River fish increasing in numbers. Burman, Tahsis, Gold, and Lernier river chinook now move into the Sound and are protected by local closures in some years.

Local sockeye infiltrate the fishing holes late in July, favouring, strangely, for their herbivore natures, an anchovy with a corkscrew roll. Hordes of coho begin arriving by the second week in July.

On the Friendly Cove end of Nootka Sound, calmer, inside places for afternoon fishing include the entrance to Hanna Channel, between Bligh (yes, named for the Mutiny on the Bounty, Bligh) and Vancouver Island, Camel Rock, Hoiss Point and Boston Point named for the ship's crew massacred by chief Maquinna in the early 1800s. Try San Carlos and the Wall on Tlupana Inlet.

Just outside the lighthouse at Yuquot Point is popular. Troll the little sandy bay close to the rocks near the point, but expect tangles in this small spot. On the outside of Nootka Island, try Maquinna Point, rocky islets nearby, the bay near Beano Creek and inner and outer Bajo Reef. Troll for chinook, 25- to 40-feet in 50- to 70- feet of water and remember that most success comes within 200 feet of shore and often tight to rocky cliffs.

There are fully-loaded halibut banks 8 and 10 miles (13 and 16 km) off shore from Friendly Cove.

The best bite in any terminal fishery—chinook on the rocks in the surfline or inside the sound headed to the many rivers—is the crack of dawn with sporadic action at tide changes and then a 10 p.m. bite to end the day. Outside hotspots also include tight to Maquinna Point. When fishing the rock piles on the open shores, you will be fishing 15.5 to 46 feet on the downrigger.

There is also shallower fishing too, with the 30- to 40-foot ledges holding the chunky wanderers in highest concentrations July 15 to August 30, and then extending halfway through September. When the bite comes on, everyone catches fish. Ferrer Point can offer up tyee—chinook over 30 pounds—to every boat in the fleet. But when the Point gets crowded move away from the fleet and fish the rock piles toward Pin Rock which has lots of good structure for fishing 20- to 50-feet on the downrigger.

When motoring from Tahsis or Zeballos down Esperanza Inlet in September you are usually looking at calm water and fewer boats. Along with Ferrer Point try Low Rock, Black Rock, Outer Black Rock, Pin Rock, Rosa Island, Catala Island, and unnamed rock piles along the surf line. When the wind rises, fish inside for coho and chum, from Esperanza Inlet to Steamer Point. Try Nootka Island shoreline between Rosa Island and Centre Island for afternoon trolling in calmer water, 10- to 46-feet on downriggers or cutpluging.

And then there is Moutcha Bay in September for fly guys and their kick boats. I was introduced here, bumping down the logging road into the river valley down the spline of road still bedrock in places. From the hill extended a view of the long mountainous Moutcha Bay before the Conuma River estuary. Out on the calm water was what looked like waves here and there, but without intending to go anywhere. Then I realized the "waves" were actually large fish coming down with very large splats. For gear anglers, troll the wall a mile "row" across the often glassy bay in August and early September.

Row out in your kick boat, 8-weight fly rod on board and various sparse terminal patterns. Think chartreuse, orange, small silver flies with small bead eyes. The chinook stir the water under the surface and you watch intermittent

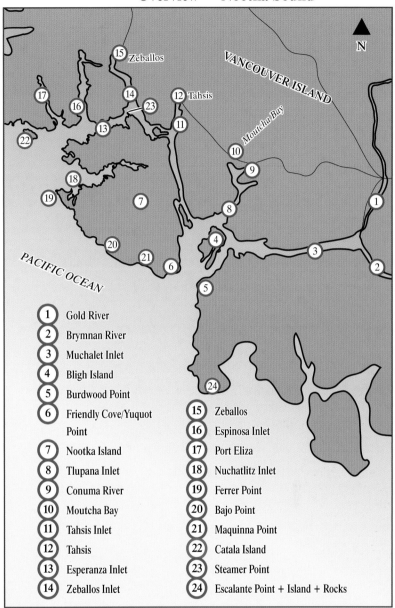

| | |
|---|---|
| 1 | Gold River |
| 2 | Brymnan River |
| 3 | Muchalet Inlet |
| 4 | Bligh Island |
| 5 | Burdwood Point |
| 6 | Friendly Cove/Yuquot Point |
| 7 | Nootka Island |
| 8 | Tlupana Inlet |
| 9 | Conuma River |
| 10 | Moutcha Bay |
| 11 | Tahsis Inlet |
| 12 | Tahsis |
| 13 | Esperanza Inlet |
| 14 | Zeballos Inlet |
| 15 | Zeballos |
| 16 | Espinosa Inlet |
| 17 | Port Eliza |
| 18 | Nuchatlitz Inlet |
| 19 | Ferrer Point |
| 20 | Bajo Point |
| 21 | Maquinna Point |
| 22 | Catala Island |
| 23 | Steamer Point |
| 24 | Escalante Point + Island + Rocks |

upwellings coming and going with fish adrenaline all around you once you are in the school of rapidly moving fish. It's almost scary. They hardly seem to know you are there and, though they are a little terminal in late September, you will land half a dozen chinook per day. And if you want to take a look at chinook in the river, row yourself to the estuary and take a short walk up to schools of 5000 chinook—just waiting for you to toss in your lure or fly.

Coho show in Moutcha Bay in late September and October, which is true about all the major rivers, including the Tahsis, Gold and Burman. If you don't have kids to be back to school, stick around, this is like fish in a barrel. It should be called Mucha Bay, not Moutcha.

Do pay close attention to Nootka Sound fishing boundaries (meaning area closures in specific summer timeframes). In early July when chinook drain into the sound, DFO closes much of the inside water from July 15 to October 15. But they do so in a way that allows anglers to fish, say, one side of a channel, while the other side is closed, so there is both fishing opportunity and fish protection. Typically there is open water from the outside all the way into the Conuma River, close to 25 miles (40 km). One way of beating the summer crowds in this area is to fish the middle of Tlupana Inlet or troll Perpendicular Bluff with mature chinook leaping around your boat and then head into the wall in Moutcha Bay.

## Summer Lures
### Gear-Fishing Lures

Anchovy or large herring with a clear, chartreuse, glow green or glow white, yellow, blue or chrome teaser, 4- to 6-foot, 25 lb. leader to your choice of green or blue Hotspot or Gibbs Farr Better Flashers—along with medium and fast action, the latter can be set for slow action, which is preferred by big chinook. Switch to cutplugs when the fish bunch up—motor mooch, a spine tingling method of fishing. Some hotrods use a shorter 33-inch leader theorizing that keeping the bait and flash close together keeps the fish focused on the bait and not losing sight of it when it zips in to bag some chow. Use gold-plated flashers for later chinook that are turning to their golden hue. Do note that the water is so clear and the chinook so turned on that you can troll without a flasher if you prefer.

In late June and in July local sockeye arrive, and favour small sparse hootchies in pink, red or orange, 27 inches behind a flasher with orange trim. October chum will take this sockeye gear, too.

When dogfish abound, move to artificial lures, including the Tomic 300, 602, 212, 530 and 500 plugs, the brass/silver Wonder spoon, or the classic commercial spoon: Tom Mack in silver/gold. Locals use needlefish squirts, green spoons and chrome teasers in May to July, also the white and Army Truck hootchies on Pacific shores. For inside fishing, add the drab J79 hootchie.

Use 5- to 7-inch spoons for chinook and smaller 3.5 to 4.5 inch spoons for coho. Good names include Roadrunner, Clendon Stewart, Coyote, Titan, Gypsy and Radiant in black/white (Cop Car), green/glow and watermelon in 500 or 602. I don't think that scent matters much to these fairly willing fish, but if you are a true believer, try Smelly Jelly, Mike's, X 10 or, for bottom fish, the simple aniseed oil. Troll spoons faster, at 3.5 to 4.5 knots.

In August, tens of thousands of prime condition Conuma hatchery chinook come into Tlupana Inlet and its calmer water. Briskly troll anchovy or hootchies for the first two weeks of August in the top 60 feet. But when the fish bunch up into larger schools in the last two weeks of August, they move down to 90 feet, and you should offer them a larger bait or spoon trolled dead slow. The opening from the Nootka Light across to Burdwood Point produces bright, actively feeding fish. Most are 30- to 40-lbs. (13.6- to 18.2-kg), but some 60 pounders (27.3 kg) are taken, too, in the later dates.

For coho move to smaller spoons, anchovy and hootchies in the top 30 feet, in August and September during their feeding frenzy along kelp lines at the entrance to the Sound when these shores are calmer.

For cutpluging use 10.5- to 12.5-foot mooching rods, with four to eight oz., keel shaped sinkers, and a six-foot leader to a two single, 3/0 to 6/0 Kirbed Octopus style hook arrangement.

September is the best month when fishing Esperanza Inlet from Zeballos or Tahsis. It's less breezy, has less rain and the crowds have gone home. Now come the largest local chinook. Use anchovies and herring, switch from green/silver flashers to bronze and gold (Oki's Old Betsy), slow trolling large spoons, Tomic Plugs, 20- to 46-feet (deeper at mid-day) at Ferrer Point, Nuchatlitz Inlet, Catala Island and inside Esperanza Inlet, especially Steamer Point with silver/dark green hootchies. Buzz Bombs and Zzingers for drift fishers.

Chum arrive in the entire sound at the end of September and go for slow-trolled small hootchies or pink or red spoons, early or late in the day on a rising tide, well into late October until rain cues them to move into the rivers.

The calmer seas allow you to run offshore for halibut 5- to 6-miles (9- to10-km) from Tatchu and Ferrer Points. Mark a depth contour change around 110- to 185-feet on an otherwise fairly level sand and gravel bottom. Pull out the spreader bar, the 2 lb. (.91 kg) ball, salmon belly, add octopus for its toughness, and bounce the rig along bottom.

Troll for large 12- to 20-pound (5.5- to 9.1-kg) coho faster and shallower in offshore waters. If it is rough, come into Cliff Cove, Black Rock and outside Rosa Island. Fog arrives quickly so sound electronics are required.

Lucky Jigs, Riptide Strikers, Spinnows and Mudrakers in 18- to 24-oz (.51- to .68-kg) sizes have their place in halibut fishing. Try orange and black, yellow and red, green and white and other bright colours and thunk them off bottom as you drift between Burdwood and Friendly Cove. You can also try Maquinna and Escalante Points at 150 feet. Berkley Power Grubs make good re-usable plastic scented baits.

## Summer Fly-Fishing Flies

The coho fly fishing off shore is of the frenzied type never encountered on shore and thus it's another corn cob pipe fishery. Make your self up a box of Clouser Minnows, Lefty's Deceivers, streamers and so on. Polar bear hair is better than bucktail but it little matters to coho fattening up on anything that moves. Try red/white/blue (Coronation), purple and white, Green/white (Green Ghost), chartreuse, white, silver, pink, dark green/white, also add Krystal Flash and Flashabou. Anything to attract attention, these can be from 7 inch varieties for fast bucktailing on windy days, down to 2.5 inch streamers for casting. Even black on white works well. You make it, they eat it. Add a trailing single hook on a loop of 25 lb (11.4 kg) test.

And don't think that being able to cast 80 feet is required. For the not so talented, strip off 20 feet of (Type 3, full sinking) line and let the fly hang straight down in the water. You may outfish your more competent casting crew, as the coho smash anything that moves or doesn't move.

For black bass along the kelp beds on Bajo Reef throw out a good sinking fly and once you get them up and following the boat, fling out a bass popper and the action becomes so hysterical you'll have to stop or a few ribs will break from the comedy of 12 fish trying to bite the fly at the same time. I have one beat up chartreuse Clouser Minnow that took 15 fish in 15 casts.

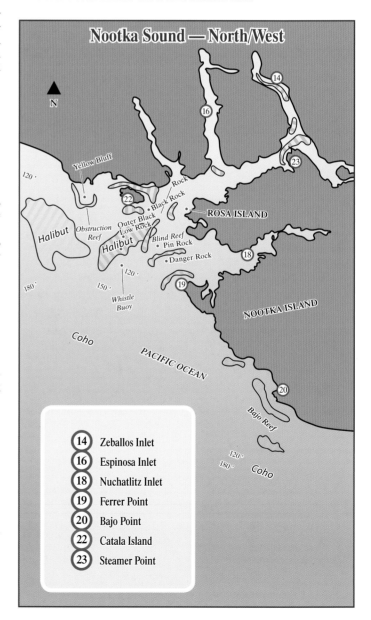

### Nootka Sound — North/West

| | |
|---|---|
| 14 | Zeballos Inlet |
| 16 | Espinosa Inlet |
| 18 | Nuchatlitz Inlet |
| 19 | Ferrer Point |
| 20 | Bajo Point |
| 22 | Catala Island |
| 23 | Steamer Point |

**Launching Ramps:** Boaters take note that thermal winds arise before noon and blow strongly on shore, funneled by high inlet walls from noon to 6 pm.

Gold River's ramp is actually 10 miles (16 km) down the Gold River gorge from town on Muchalet Inlet by the eerily quiet mill site. A two foot tide is the minimum and, as this is a one boat at a time place, you can expect to arrive early or wait. There is limited parking along the highway and you can walk as much as a mile. The run to outside waters is 35 minutes.

Check with Muchalet Marina next door, 1-250-283-2029, as larger boats typically launch here.

Cougar Creek halfway between Gold River and Tahsis has an 18 unit campground with a small gravel boat launch.

Moutcha Bay, 12 miles (20 )km short of Tahsis, has a good-angled gravel boat launch. It also has mid-grade fuel and a small store.

Tahsis has a good ramp at the Municipal Dock and Public Boat launch. The facility has washrooms, tables, telephones. See also Westview Marina for a full service marina, including restaurant, laundry, fuel and limited accommodation; Website: westviewmarina.com; Email: info@westviewmarina.com.

Zeballos has a good all-tide boat ramp. Weston Fuels operates its fuel dock seven days a week.

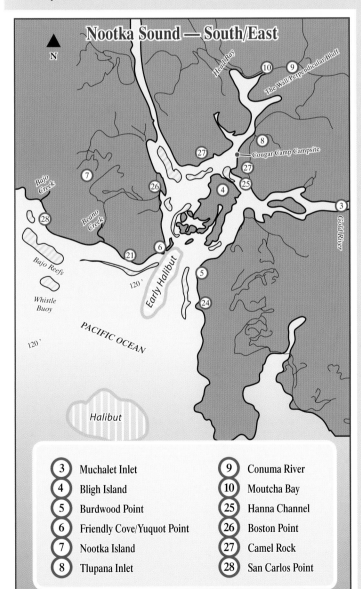

### Nootka Sound — South/East

| | | | |
|---|---|---|---|
| 3 | Muchalet Inlet | 9 | Conuma River |
| 4 | Bligh Island | 10 | Moutcha Bay |
| 5 | Burdwood Point | 25 | Hanna Channel |
| 6 | Friendly Cove/Yuquot Point | 26 | Boston Point |
| 7 | Nootka Island | 27 | Camel Rock |
| 8 | Tlupana Inlet | 28 | San Carlos Point |

**Tackle Shops:** Take all you gear and stock up at local shops on terminal tackle.

Critter Cove Marina, accessed from the water, on your starboard in Nootka Sound en route to Friendly Cove.

Ralph Osha's tackle shop in Gold River. Turn left at the stop sign, cross the Muchalet River and it's on your left.

Westview Marina in Tahsis has bait.

Zeballos General Store has limited tackle.

**Access:** You can drive into Gold River, Moutcha Bay, Tahsis, Cougar Creek and Zeballos. From Victoria it is a long 6.5 hour, 260 mile (421 km) drive. North to Campbell River. Turn left onto Highway 28, 54.3m (89 km) to Gold River. Turn left at the stop sign (the only one in town) and proceed 10 miles (16 km) following the Gold River gorge until the launch site is reached near the old mill site on Muchalet Inlet.

You may drive further, to Moutcha Bay, and Tahsis to launch. From the Gold River stop sign, carry on straight through for another hour. You will be taking the gravel road to Moutcha Bay 27.5 m (45 km), and Tahsis another 39 m (64 km). This is a bumpy twisty, road with a few doozies of hills to go down (though easier than coming up on the return).

Air Nootka float planes offer a 10 minute, 20 mile (30 km) run down the inlet from Gold River to fishing lodges and other spots: Website: airnootka.com; Email: info@airnootka.com. Phone: 1-250-283-2255.

The MV U-Chuck moors in Gold River and offers boat access to Nootka Sound and Kyuquot Sound. Phone: 1-250-283-2325; Website: mvuchuck.com; Email: info@mvuchuck.com. Reservations required.

Many lodges offer air travel from Campbell River or Vancouver airports as part of their package prices. If they do, take them up on it – the drive is long and bumpy.

Zeballos is the most northerly town on the Sound and is accessed by road but by a different route. Carry on north from Campbell River on Highway 19, turn left between Woss and Port McNeill, onto the 26 mile (42 km) gravel road. Campsites are available four miles (7km) north, at Cevallos campsite in town, Rhodes Creek campsite four miles (7 km) south of town on the road to Fair Harbour.

Fuel may be located at land-based service stations in Gold River, or Tahsis (also has a fuel dock at Westview Marina) or at Critter Cove and Hoiss Point on the water. This is a huge area so being adequately fueled is vital.

**Information:** Village of Gold River, Phone: 1-250-283-2202; Website: village.goldriver.bc.ca; Email: villageofgoldriver@cablerocket.com.
Village of Tahsis, Box 519, Tahsis BC V0P 1X0; Phone: 1-250-934-6344; Website: www.tahsis.ca; Email: admin@villageoftahsis.com.
Tahsis Chamber of Commerce: www.tahsischamber.com.
Zeballos Tourist Visitor Info, Website: www.zeballos.com; Phone: 1-250-761-4070.

**Accommodation:** Perhaps two dozen floating and land-based lodges and campgrounds lie within the sound. Pacific Safari, is new and comfortable. Toll Free: 1-877-488-0045; Website: pacificsafaris.com; Email: info@pacificsafaris.com.

Some of the others include: Nootka Island Lodge (nice people); Hoiss Point; CeePeeCee, Chinootka Lodge; Critter Cove; Nootka Island Fish camp and so on.

Moutcha Bay Resort and RV Site, Jim Davis: Phone: 1-250-923-2908; Email: info@moutchabay.com; Website: www.moutchabay.com.

Zeballos Inlet facilities include Mason's Lodge, Iris Lodge, Zeballos Hotel and Zeballos Inlet Lodge. Consider also: Dan O'Connor, Zeballos Expeditions, PO Box 111, V0P 2A0, Zeballos; Ph: 1-250-761-4137; Email: kayak@netcom.ca; Website: www.zeballoskayaks.com.

**Guides:** D.C. Reid, Toll Free 1-877-610-1011; Website: catchsalmonbc.com; Email: dcreid@catchsalmonbc.com.

Steve Patterson: Phone: 1-250-338-9413; Email: steve@islandsportfishing.com; Website: www.islandsportfishing.com.

Rollie Rose, Sooke Salmon Charters Ltd., Phone: 1-250-380-7018; Cell: 250-13-3055, Email: rrose@pacificcoast.net; Website: fishingbc1.com.

# Oak Bay

*So who says you can't catch flatfish on the fly?*

## Saltwater Fishing
## Local Winter Hotspots

The best spots to fish for salmon in this area are known as the Flats and The Gap. The flats is a broad area of relatively flat mud/sand bottom between Trial Island and Discovery Island where fishing occurs close to the bottom from the 100 foot level out to 150 feet. The south end of Trial Island is also a good spot on the Victoria side on an ebb tide and on the east Oak Bay side during a flood at about 135 feet on the downrigger. There is a large rock on the Victoria side 500 yards from Trial that rises sharply to 85 feet, so take care. There is also Brodie rock on the east side of Trial that can be, well, a trial.

The Gap is between Discovery and Chatham Islands. There is a pronounced reef on the south side, so watch your gear. The best water is on the Chatham Island end and you follow the 97-foot contour on the bottom, watching the depth sounder for reefs.

## Winter Lures

The choice of lures is dependent on the fact that local feed is needlefish, that is, smaller than herring. Thus the smaller version of lures is the best. For example, the 4" Coyote spoon 4 feet behind a flasher. In bait, small anchovy or Tiny Strip are fished in glow teaserheads 4 feet behind a glow in the dark green flasher.

Squirts of note include the Purple Haze, Jelly fish, both fished behind a Purple Haze Flasher, J-49, Irish Mist and the common green and white squirt.

Discovery Island, Darcy Islands, Border Bank and Hein Banks are local spots that give up large numbers of halibut each year. This is one of the areas where you need to pay particularly close attention for DFO rockfish conservation areas, as there are many.

## Local Summer Hotspots

Oak Bay is fished the same way as in the winter, on the bottom, in the Gap or on the Flats, mostly on the latter. You fish the bottom for chinook salmon with the same lures as in the winter.

I f you're looking for a "more English than the English" spot on the map, Oak Bay is the place. Teashops in "The Village," as Oak Bay Avenue is known, supply what this affluent city butting up to Victoria is all about.

On Willows Beach is the home of the famous and infamous architect, Francis Mawson Ratternbury. Now part of the Glen Lyon Norfolk House private school, take a look inside for the marble and the fire grates that he absorbed when he was the architect of the Parliament Buildings in the centre of Victoria's Inner Harbour.

Standing on the back lawn you can look across the bay to the Oak Bay Marine Group head office that has resort properties in the US, Canada and in the Caribbean.

Beach Drive is a popular marine drive to motor around this scenic and well-to-do municipality.

The other species tend to migrate up Juan de Fuca Strait south of the Flats and you motor a couple of miles south of Trial Island and then commence fishing heading south until you connect with pink, sockeye or coho salmon. In the past, these were usually taken in the top 40 feet, but now, plumb the depths to 95 feet.

In odd years, coho come right into Oak Bay between the Royal Victoria Golf Course almost all the way to the Oak Bay Marina breakwater. If you see action in the evening, fish here, other wise head south into Juan de Fuca Strait.

A small slot in McNeill Bay, aka Shoal Bay, of 60 feet deep is also a good spot for summer fishing for advancing spawning chinook, at 25- to 30-feet deep. Spawning chinook stop and bide their time on an ebb tide and then move on the flood. This slot holds the big fish—to 50 pounds (22.7 kg)—on the ebb. The Chinese Cemetery in Gonzales Bay has a small slot in front of it to 35 feet. Fish it 12 feet deep and 25 feet back and be prepared to lift your lines if you can't turn around before the rocks in the bay.

Oak Bay is also a port of departure for Constance Bank, discussed in the Victoria area report.

## Summer Lures

Fish for chinook with the same lures as would be used in the winter, again, deep on the Flats or in the Gap.

For sockeye, pink and coho, use any pink squirt or hootchie, ripping out a few fronds for sockeye as, less is more. These are set on leaders from shortish ones for sockeye of 28 inches to as long as 36 for coho. And speed up to 1000 rpm, and continue heading south until you contact fish. Note that speeding up makes you contact more fish in the same period of time. It also has the effect of 'shortening' your leaders as it transmits more snap to the squirt.

Try Slam Dunk spinners in any red or pink variation, also towed behind a red flasher. Plaid flashers are good here, too.

Shore fishers can try their luck on the point of the golf course, the Marina breakwater, or Ten Mile Point, with the venerable white Buzz Bomb. Fly fishers know that coho tend to stage off Douglas Park to the north of Gordon Head and head up to the beach in September and October.

**Launching Ramps:** Cattle Point, deep in Oak Bay, has two free public ramps. The more northerly of the two is more sheltered.

Oak Bay Marina has a ramp, but it is used by their guests. You will have access if you intend on mooring at the marina. The next ramps are those listed for Victoria.

**Tackle Shops:** Island Outfitters on Douglas Street, is Victoria's best tackle shop for your gear requirements.

Robinson's downtown has the best selection of fly-fishing gear.

**Access:** Oak Bay Marina is a ten-minute drive from the border with the City of Victoria, down Oak Bay Avenue to Beach Drive.

Water access is by boat from ramps and marinas near the Ogden Point Break water in Victoria.

**Info:** Check the Tourism Victoria site: www.tourismvictoria.com.

The Great Victoria Chamber of Commerce, 100 -852 Fort St., Victoria, V8W 1H8; Phone: 1-250-383-7191; Email: chamber@gvcc.org. It serves the five municipalities that comprise the greater Victoria area.

**Accommodation:** Victoria has a full range of all accommodation types. The Travellers Inn is inexpensive and Spartan or visit the tourist info place on the corner of Government St. at the end of the Causeway. The Ocean Pointe Resort and the Empress impress those with greater wallet size. Oak Bay is a residential area and there are few accommodation rentals.

**Guides:** Sanscott Charters. Book at Oak Bay Marina, Toll free: 1-800-663-7090.

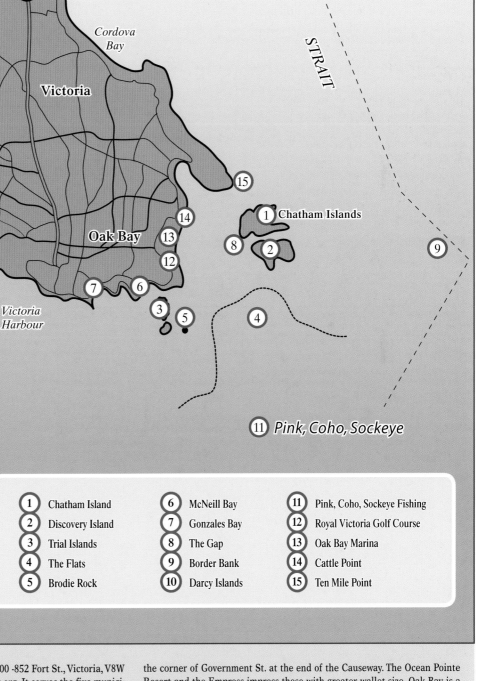

| 1 | Chatham Island | 6 | McNeill Bay | 11 | Pink, Coho, Sockeye Fishing |
| 2 | Discovery Island | 7 | Gonzales Bay | 12 | Royal Victoria Golf Course |
| 3 | Trial Islands | 8 | The Gap | 13 | Oak Bay Marina |
| 4 | The Flats | 9 | Border Bank | 14 | Cattle Point |
| 5 | Brodie Rock | 10 | Darcy Islands | 15 | Ten Mile Point |

Parksville and Qualicum are known for their very broad and wonderful beaches. When the tide is low, walk out with your children on Rathtrevor Beach a half mile and you will come upon lots of sanddollar skeletons for them to pick up and trundle home.

The hotels in Parksville on the waterfront south of town are very fine indeed. Qualicum has the most affluent retired residents on the Island, with a lot of golf courses close by.

## Local Winter Hotspots

Winter fishing is better than more southerly inside areas because of the large herring spawn in the Hornby and Denman Island areas. See also Courtenay/Comox for adjacent hotspot information. At Flora Islet near Hornby Island there are three drop offs in structure that attract chinook: 90-, 125- and 180-feet.

On the south end of Lasqueti Island, troll toward Young Point and along the 300 foot ledge toward Bull Passage.

Fish the broad beach fronts parallel to the shore starting at 180 feet and moving deeper until fish are contacted on depthsounders. Fish the bottom. This includes French Creek, particularly in April and May for late feeders, 160- to 180-feet down and then farther out, 200- to 225-feet.

Fish the southern end of this area at Icarus Point downriggers set at 130- to 200-feet, and then in May, bring your lines up to 100- to 140-feet. (Refer to the Nanaimo area write-up and chart).

## Winter Lures

One half mile off French Creek, troll Purple Haze, green/white, white with green stripe, blue/silver, Cop Car hootchies behind a Purple Haze flasher. In spoons, try the Army Truck, green/glow or glow Cop Car 5 feet behind the flasher at 180 feet. Use large sizes to match the size of the spawning herring, and then move smaller as late winter gives way to spring. Try for the late feeders with the above spoons and the Party Girl.

Do note that on the Lasqueti Island side you use smaller gear than on Van Isle Side.

Off the beach fronts, try a Monkey Puke spoon, or Army Truck or Oil Slick hootchie with a glow/green flasher. Anchovy in a teaser head is the winter bait.

Plug fishermen lean to pink, pearl or white colours, the 6" 191 Tomic being a local favourite.

Try glow in the dark hootchies with a glow or Purple Haze flasher at Icarus Point.

## Local Summer Hotspots

Off the south tip of Flora Island, try mooching cutplug herring at low slack tide in May. Fish down the dropoffs.

Around Lasqueti Island fish False Bay where the ferry comes in, also Jenkins Island (fish chinook on the ebb), Sea Egg Rocks, Young Point (the 180 foot ledge) and Seal Rocks. Do traditional Cowichan Bay bucktailing for coho at

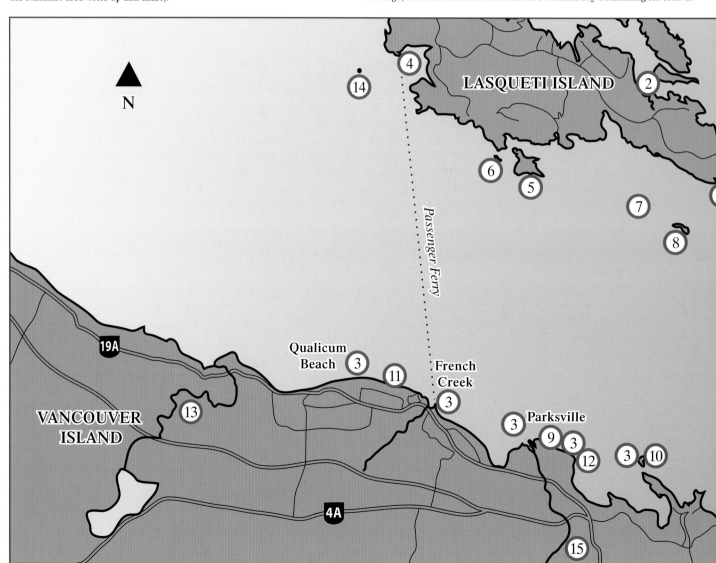

Sangster Island (fish chinook on the ebb).

Fish The Trough off French Creek. Start at Boathouse Door and drift on the ebb if you mooch to French Creek Harbour. Fish the bottom. Moochers and jiggers fish the White Door south of Qualicum Beach.

Troll the shorelines for coho from Columbia Beach to Judges Row, as well as the outside of Mistaken Island and The Hump at False Bay and Brant Point to the Little Qualicum River. For flat water anglers, Sisters Islets offer this in a moochers spot on its south end.

The majority of the local chinook stage in the Bowser and Deep Bay (refer to Courtenay and Comox write-up) shoreline from August to early October, some as far out as the south end of Denman Island and Hornby's Tribune Bay and Flora Islet, and, of course the beach fronts of the Q rivers themselves.

Use plugs in front of local rivers, the Big Qualicum, Little Qualicum and Englishman, in August; 5 and 6 inch Tomics in white or pink. Troll the bottom.

It should be noted that for fly fishermen (and the occasional gear guy who can take the heat for not being a fly guy) the saltwater beaches all along this area —focusing on local streams—offer pink, then coho then chum salmon from July right on through late October. This includes Nile Creek, the Qs, and any trickle of water on which a local volunteer group runs a small satellite hatchery at. Take your binoculars and cruise Highway 19A looking for a build up of cars, signifying good fishing out front, oh, and jumping fish, too.

The southern end of this region leans into Lantzville and then Nanaimo, with Neck Point, Winchelsea Island, Rocky Point, Fiver Finger Island and Entrance Island off Nanaimo's doorstep.

## Parksville, Qualicum, French Creek

1. Young Point
2. Bull Passage
3. Beach Fronts
4. False Bay
5. Jenkins Island
6. Sea Egg Rocks
7. Seal Rocks
8. Sangster Islands
9. White Door
10. Mistaken Island
11. Columbia Beach
12. Brant Point
13. Little Qualicum River
14. Sisters Island
15. Englishman River
16. Winchelsea Islands

## Summer Lures

May and June are good months to mooch cutplug herring in the flat water ebbs. Try 40 pulls (80 feet) and work down from there.

Troll for chinook with herring, large herring or strip in Army Truck, Chartreuse, ultraviolet teasers on a 5- to 6-foot leader before a flasher. Plaid flashers, Green/Glow flashers, green/glow hootchies or 4" spoons in Live Image and Green Glow and large herring in Army Truck, Chartreuse, UV teasers, 6-foot leader, trolling offshore waters early in the season 30- to 50-feet above a 100- to 170-foot bottom. Try three inch green or grey Apexes on 40-inch leaders before a green/glow flasher. For coho, troll Super Herring Strip in a green strip teaser and green Hot Spot flasher.

French Creek favourites include green/white, black/white, black/glow, Purple Haze and gold hootchies and silver, silver/brass, green/glow, Army Truck and Cop Car spoons (Coyote and Roadrunner styles) and green/white plugs six feet behind a flasher. In flashers, use the Army Truck or Purple Haze, and later, the Old Betsy. Troll in a zig zag pattern. Try traditional bucktails for coho in the offshore waters where you see fish jumping.

French Creek has a good sandy bottom and thus there are lots of flounder. Fish for them with pieces of clams you collect off the various marina docks.

Jiggers fish Qualicum Beach and the White Door south of there with Buzz Bombs and Zzingers in chartreuse, orange, pearl, pink, holographic, green, black and blue. Take your pick.

Try pink and pearl Tomic plugs.

On beaches, fishing for coho with flies, try, Clouser Minnows or Mickey Finns in blues and greens, streamers, as well as the Pearl Mickey and the California Neil.

For staging, local chinook try the Gibbs Gypsy in Silver Hex and Witch doctor patterns along with Gibbs Wonder Spoons in chrome/nickel or nickel/brass.

When saltwater trolling for pinks, use pink or blue flies/hootchies at 100 feet. Blue, gold, plaid or red plaid flashers. Troll slowly. For sockeye add the trusty old red Kripped K, as well as Bubble Gum and silver/green hootchies.

For the September/October holding chinook, try the venerable, brass/chrome Gibbs Wonder Spoon behind a Plaid flasher, or a 600 Tomic plug. Fish the water of 30- to35-feet with the slabs running horizontal for ages. Try the evening high tides off the Q rivers. Surprisingly, like Port Alberni, these big springs also like pink squirts, and on leaders from 30 inches right down to the almost unbelievable: 18 inches.

Southern water lures include the Moby Dick, Blood and Bones, and splatter back Frogman hootchies, as well as glow/green, Watermelon, Cop Car and Mongoose spoons. In flashers there are three good choices: Plaid and Old Betsy for higher in the water, and the all around Purple Haze.

**Launching Ramps:** French Creek Harbour is central to all locations and has a good ramp. Website: http://www.frenchcreekstore.com.
Schooner Cove Marina: Phone: 1-250-468-5364; Website: http://www.fairwinds.ca/marina-home.html.
Deep Bay Marina 20 mins north of QB has a good ramp and restaurant.
**Tackle Shops:** Nile Creek Fly Shop, Unit 2, 6590 West Island Highway, Bowser (a half mile beyond the power lines); Phone: 1-250-757-2095; Email: flyfisher@telus.net; Web: www.ogilvieoutfitting.com.
French Creek Charter Boat Association
**Access:** Qualicum Beach and Parksville, 10 miles (15 km) south of Qualicum are both about 2 hours drive north of Victoria on Highway 1 that turns into Highway 19. Nainaimo, about a half hour south of the area has two ferry terminals, receiving boats from Horseshoe Bay in Vancouver and Tswassen nearer to the border with the U.S.A.
**Information:** Parksville and District Chamber of Commerce, Box 99, Parksville BC, V9P 2G3; Phone: 1-250.248.3613; Email: info@chamber.parksville.bc.ca; Website: www.chamber.parksville.bc.ca
Qualicum Beach chamber of Commerce: 2711 West Island Highway, Qualicum Beach, B.C., V9K 2C4; Phone: 1-250- 752-9532; Email: info@qualicum.bc.ca.
**Accommodation:** Search for accommodation on both the Parksville and Qualicum Beach Chamber sites. The ones on Rathtrevor Beach are snazzy, beach front and face the morning sunrise, very pretty.

# Port Alberni

Reflecting the Spanish influence on the B.C. coastline, Port Alberni and its 30 mile (50 km) inlet, were named by a Spanish military garrison for its captain in 1791 when the nation's imperial ambitions were high. Half a century later, the Port became one of Britain's best sources of spars for the big ships and, with the American Civil War imminent, Captain Edward Stamp, who lent his name to the best local fishing river, was sent to commence export of the expensive items.

The fishing grounds of Port Alberni include almost year-round saltwater fishing in the long fjord, particularly in June and July for sockeye and later for big chinook, and fall coho. The town's Labour Day salmon derby lures in hundreds of boats, its prizes being worth the trip. Some years the derby scales record more than 30,000 pounds of fish and prizes top $100,000.

Port Alberni also has access to Barkley Sound (it is 15 miles—24 km—from the inlet mouth to Cape Beale) that both Bamfield and Ucluelet also have as local waters. Some hardy boaters use the Port as access to the La Perouse Bank— a two hour ride, often into wind and wave—off the mouth of Barkley Sound but most people launch in Ucluelet.

The Robertson Creek Hatchery is high on the Stamp River and is justly famous for pumping back 50,000 chinook in the summer. And, while other rivers are sometimes closed in the fall, the Stamp continues to return 60- to 100-thousand coho each August and September. The inlet receives an average of 500,000 sockeye each summer.

The Alberni Inlet, like the Nitinat Lake, usually gets a 30 mile per hour (50 kmph) convection wind by two in the afternoon that blows into the teeth of boaters trying to go out the Inlet. So, go early or get bashed.

## Local Winter Hotspots

The precipitous mountains lining the side of the inlet drop just as steeply under the water to as much as 1000 feet. This influences the chinook to swim more mid-channel than they might with strong underwater features. Fish the ledge at the harbour mouth that runs from 50 feet to 300 feet. Fish 100- to 150-feet in mid-channel areas or following bottom contours. Wherever you get points of underwater structure,

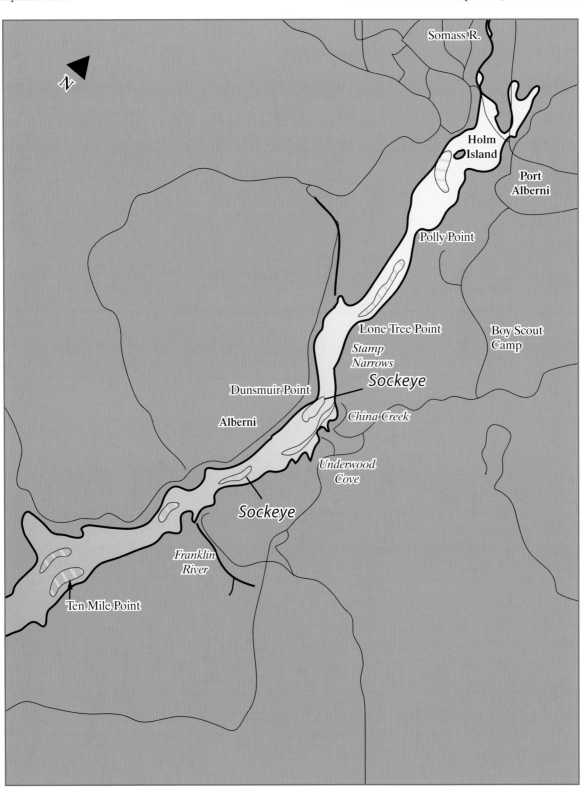

or sharp indentations in other wise straight structure is where you will find the chinook in this low tidal current area. Alternatively, put down a prawn trap near China Creek in the 300 foot mid-channel level and troll this deep flat, and closer in near Franklin River.

Vernon, Rainy Bays and Toquart bays, along with Diplock Island, Pill Point and the Bamfield wall on the north end of Barkley Sound are accessed by boat in 1 hour 15 minutes from Port Alberni. Refer to the Bamfield chapter for details. Fishing peaks from January to March.

## Winter Lures

For winter springs of 8- to 12-pounds (3.6- to 5.5-kg), use anchovy or herring strip trolled in glow in the dark teaser heads, 4- to 6-feet behind a glow in the dark or ultraviolet flasher that thumps out colour in the deep dark water. Surprisingly, white hootchies are fished six feet behind a flasher, a tackle combination that does not impart any of the flasher's action to the lure.

For winter feeders, use 4 inch Tomic plugs. Note the plug numbers in this list, you will see many of them repeated for the outside open Pacific facing fishing spots: 158, 602, 500, 900 and 232. The 232 is also a good fall plug for coho.

The white Apex spoon is also a good bet for winter chinook in Barkley Sound. Fish Coyote or Gypsy half glow/half green spoons with or without flashers as much as 200 feet deep

## Local Summer Hotspots

An inlet with good returns of sockeye, coho, chinook and chum for many rivers including the Somass, Nahmint and Henderson. Most inlet streams have small populations of steelhead in the winter and summer.

Steep mountain slopes descend underwater several hundred feet and most summer runs move through in the top 100' of the water column. As in winter, fishing concentrates in mid-channel waters with little reference to underwater structure.

On the first full moon in June, 100,000 sockeye come in to the Somass River. Troll in deep mid-channel water from Dunsmuir Point to China Creek Campground, also Sproat Narrows to Polly Point near town, Lone Tree Point, Cous Creek, The Slide and The Narrows. Don't bother fishing with the fishers; fish where you mark sockeye at 80- to 110-feet. The biters will be above the school so fish 45- to 85-feet deep. And don't fish jumpers; they don't bite either. As summer deepens the schools do to, and waves of sockeye come all summer long into September.

The other greatly anticipated run is the 30- to 40-pound (13.6- to 18.2-kg) Robertson Creek chinook run that begins in Barkley Sound in mid-June progressing into the inlet toward town through August and into early September. The full moon brings fish onto the harbour ledge, running from the mouth of the Somass River. Do note, however, that closures do apply in Alberni Inlet, and check the current regulations.

Summer chinook fishing concentrates on the ledge—when open—running 50- to 300-feet deep from Port Alberni Harbour. Fish the ebb of a major high tide and expect chinook to sit below the ledge. Downrigger depths are 80- to 100-feet and due to the darker water, a pink hootchie (more ultraviolet than other colours) is the lure of choice. Bait and plugs also take many of the leviathan derby-winning chinook.

Then come good solid numbers of coho from 8- to 16-pounds (3.6- to 7.3-kg), July through September and that may hold in freshwater as late as December in the Taylor River.

## Summer Lures

Think bait for summer fishing—anchovy in a teaser head for chinook and strip in a large strip head for coho. But the best lure for chinook is surprising: a bright pink hootchie, 34- to 36-inches behind a plastic flasher.

Coho take the straight up white and green and white hootchies/squirts, 20- to 30-feet deep in Barkley Sound. When the larger, later, so-called northern coho arrive, try green splatterbacks, white hootchies and green and mother of pearl Apexes. Early Coho spoons include the traditional Tom Mac in blue and silver, silver and silver, and silver and bronze.

Summer chinook bite the same plugs as winter feeder chinook, but prefer larger, 5- to 7-inch models.

## Sockeye-Specific Lures

In early June fish the Ten Mile Point area for pre-runners to the main run. Start with Golden Bait MP15 Mini Plankton and move to MP2s and MP16s as light comes on the water.

When the main schools arrive, Alberni Inlet sockeye prefer a 27-inch leader behind a red Hotspot flasher. Try plankton squirts in pink, blue, purple and clear, green and blue and the J79. Tie the waist of a squirt, making it thinner and remember that less is more: pull out fronds here and there. Squirts that prove effective get better with age, so do not throw away those that begin losing fronds.

In spoons try the standard Krippled K in mother of pearl, Radiant's Pink Shrimp and set the Black Box at .7 volts. Put out at least three flashers on each downrigger line: sockeye like a light show. Or run a spoon on its own, between two other stacked flashers—reduces chances of tangles.

If you like drift fishing with Buzz Bombs and Stingsildas, once you locate a school on the depthsounder, drop your lure to 10 feet above and fish. Remember it is slow up with the rod tip, but quick down.

In the May to June period when sockeye hang just out side the inlet in Barkley Sound, fish mid-channel with pink plankton squirts or orange hootchies. Use 18- to 20- inch leaders and troll slowly at 45- to 75-feet.

Launching Ramps: Check the Port Authority website: www.portalberniportauthority.ca, for local ramps.

Clutesi Haven Marina, turn right at the T-junction on Johnson Street and Clutesi is soon on your left with a good four-lane launch ramp, moorage for boats to 28 feet, fuel and ample trailer parking. Phone: 1-250-724-6837.

China Creek Marina and Campground, five miles (8 km) south on the Bamfield road access, features moorage for 250 vessels, 265 campground sites, four-lane launch ramp, washrooms, shower, laundry facilities, small general store, a café and fuel dock. Phone: 1-250-723-9812.

Tackle shops: Gone Fishn' at the bottom of Johnson Street; Website: www.gonefishinshop.com, has current local fishing reports; Phone: 1-250-723-1172. Clutesi Haven Marina.

Access: A 2.5 hour drive from Victoria over Highway 1, which turns into Highway 19 and then turn west on Highway 4. Alternatively, take the Horseshoe Bay (or Tswwassen) ferry to Departure Bay/Duke Point in Nanaimo for a 1.5 hour drive over Highway 19 and Highway 4.

Information: Chamber of Commerce: Phone: 1-250-724-6535; Website: http://www.avcoc.com/.

DFO: Phone: 1-250-720-4440.

Accommodation: Murphy Sport Fishing, 5560 Cherry Creek Road, Port Alberni, BC., V9Y 7Z2; Toll free: 1-877-218-6600; Website: murphysportfishing.com; Email: Murphy@island.net.

To find other accommodation see: www.portalbernihotels.worldweb.com.

Guides: West Coast River charters, Nick & Darlene Hnennyj; Toll free: 1-866-839-8411; Website: westcoastrivercharters.ca; Email: nick@westcoastrivercharters.ca.

Harvest Salmon Charters, 4526 Beale St., Port Alberni, B.C. V9Y 5P6, Ph: 1-250-723-6551, or, Cell: 1-250-720-6269. Ross Beckett and his father Brian. Murphy Sport Fishing.

# Port Hardy, Port McNeill, Telegraph Cove

On Queen Charlotte Strait at the north east end of Vancouver Island, Port Hardy has to be considered as good year-round fishing as the more remote west-side of Vancouver Island. In fact, it's fairly remote itself, the highway coming only in 1979 when ticked off locals sent every member of the Legislative Assembly in Victoria a card with a carrot attached. They then hounded the Honourable Members until the road was built, ending now in, yes, you guessed it: Carrot Park.

Port Hardy also has a second great wealth: of salmon; all the five species destined for any river in the entire Georgia Strait—the Fraser, for example—pass right by its doorstep in the summer months. It bills itself as King Coho Country, as the coho stage for weeks, starting mid-June in the cool water, before proceeding as more sexually mature fish. Look for scads of bluebacks in April.

The local harbour is a must see as you will be amazed at the high-tech zillions of dollars worth of the northern fishing fleet. Port Hardy is the southern terminus for the scenic Inside Passage ferry trip to Prince Rupert and lies 333 miles (544 km) and 7 hours north of Victoria on Highway 1 and then 19. This area includes Robson Bight where killer whales rub themselves on the bottom gravel to the delight of onlookers

## Saltwater Fishing Local Winter Hotspots

Frequently, strong north winds from Queen Charlotte Strait and southeasters from Labouchere Passage blast Port Hardy in winter. Accordingly, most fishers take the short drive to the more sheltered Quatsino Sound for its dependable 8- to 15-lb. (3.6- to 6.8-kg) chinook action peaking December to February, and extending until April. See Quatsino Sound chapter.

When you can get out of Port Hardy, feeder chinook inhabit local waters January to April. Fish from Port Hardy down to Port McNeill, Alert Bay and Beaver Cove, with chinook to 20 pounds (9.1 kg) available.

Do note that it is far faster to drive to Port McNeill and Telegraph Cove from Port Hardy, and launch there to fish Malcolm Island, Hanson Island and Black Fish Sound.

Robson Bight off Telegraph Cove is the largest viewing site for killer whales on Van Island, as they rub themselves on the gravel at the bottom of the bight. This is a true wonder of the natural world.

## Winter Lures

Fish small herring and anchovies in glow teasers at 50- to 70-feet. In hootchies choose black and white and any with a bluish tinge.

## Local Summer Hotspots

Port Hardy is the first Vancouver Island area to get access to summer runs of all five species of salmon. Migratory chinook start showing in Port Hardy the last week of May and build until August as 20- to 25-lb. (9.1- to 11.4-kg) mature fish bound for the local Quatse or the Nimpkish River a little farther south. Local fishing experts recommend fishing the low slack into a flood tide, particularly at the crack of dawn.

*Looking like he's strumming on the old banjo, Courtney hamming it up with a coho.*

Locals are proud to point out that when the fishing is good you don't have to go out of the bay. That includes blueback fishing (immature coho migrating out to sea in their third and final year) in April—huge schools, as they assemble from dozens of southern rivers.

If you do venture forth, you have at least 25 hotspots to choose from—many more than most other areas. You may fish many of them in the same day with Duval Point being the most highly rated of the bunch: Daphne Point, the Masterman Islands, the Deserters, the Gordon Islands, Christie Pass and the Jeanettes, Fisherman Rock, top end of Hope Island, Nigei Island, Goletas Channel and Shelter Passage near the Deserters. Open water in the surrounding areas can provide excellent action for coho, sockeye and pink. Take your A535 as it is not uncommon to hook 40 coho in a trip.

The Masterman Islands lie at the eastern entrance to Hardy Bay. Thence there are many points to fish, including Dillon Point to Peel Island, Round, Deer and Cattle islands in Beaver Harbour. Duval point to Frankham Point is a good long fish. Add also, Duncan Island, the Gordon Islands, Boxer and Hussar points on Nigei Island as well as Scarlet Point on Balaklava Island. Farther islands include Walker, the Deserters and the Millar group.

From June 15 to August 30, Fraser River sockeye pass through. This is a major fishery—80% of the 4- to 20-million fish divert down Johnstone Strait in a cool water year. In an El Nino year—warmer water—the percentage may climb to 100%.

In contrast to more southerly areas on Vancouver Island, pink salmon runs occur every year; however, the odd-numbered year runs are heaviest. These July - August humpies average 4 to 7 lbs (1.8- to 3.2-kg). Most are caught offshore, however, the Quatse River run some of these fish right into Hardy Bay. May you experience a day when you simply stop fishing because you are too worn out to catch any more. Local coho for the Quatse and Cluxewe (near Port McNeill) rivers stage off Duval, Masterman Islands and Daphne Point.

Coho fishing begins in June and the 3- to 5- pounders give way to sequential runs of 10- to 12- pound (1.4- to 5.5-kg) fish, with 20 pounders taken in late August. And then the Northern (even bigger) coho arrive in September and hold until the seasonal monsoons set in in earnest. In late August, 10-pound (4.5-kg) chum eat their way south to provide the fabulous Campbell River October fishery—and the waters of Port McNeill and Telegraph Cove.

## Port McNeill, Telegraph Cove

Black Fish Sound is southeast of Port Hardy and a special salmon fishery of its own. Either do the longer run from Port Hardy or the shorter run from Port McNeill or Telegraph Cove. Fish from Donegal Head at the southeastern end of Malcom Island. Continue down past the Plumper Islands and Hanson Island through Blackney Passage to the mouth of Baronet Passage and from Cracroft Point to the Sophia Islands at the southwestern end of West Cracroft Island. The true hotspot is the end of Black Fish Sound and the point off Hanson Island.

Also on Malcolm Island is Lizard Point, Dickenson Point and just beyond, Pulteney Point. Fish the kelp bed on the north shore of Malcolm Island.

Telegraph Cove is south east of Port McNeill and is reached from Highway

19 by turning right on Beaver Cove Road. You can fish the same spots as from Port McNeill, as there is good structure in the form of islands in front of Telegraph Cove.

The south end of Cormorant Island holds chinook in summer as do the Pearse Islands to their south and in Cormorant Channel. Check out the south tip of Weynton Island on the flood, where the rips form. The same can be said of Blackney passage at the south end of Hanson Island. Even further south, the hotspots on West Cracroft Island include, Cracroft Point, and the Sophia Islands. Try the northeast shore of Malcolm Island between Donegal Head and Lizard Point, these spots produce halibut during salmon trolling.

Swanson Island to the east of Malcolm has a good ledge on its western flank. Try also Baronet Pass that channels the fish going to Knight Inlet. The inside waters in this area are fairly calm and flat.

## Summer Lures

The fish are so plentiful that the successful rigs are quite simple: for bait, try cutplugs (5/0 tandem singles) and banana weights of 4- to 6-ounces, or on the downrigger at 15- to 150-feet, depending on location. Also an anchovy in a white glow teaser in the morning. At Duval Point try anchovy in a Purple Haze teaser and Purple Haze flasher. Strip and whole herring will also work.

Hootchies of note for the biggies include the venerable green and white and whole white, and, surprise, surprise, the coast wide favourite, the Army Truck. For pinks, sockeye and chum try the local Googly Eyed Wild Thing, a bead and rubber strip concoction in red, trolled behind a red or green Hotspot flasher. Or rip out most of the fronds from a red or hot orange hootchie and try that. Dayglo orange or yellow cuttlefish also take sockeye, or as an alternative, green hootchies and green Hotspot or No. 1 or 2 Abe and Al flasher. Add back-up pink hootchies and Coyote spoons, and fish 20- to 110-feet. Coho warm up to pink hootchies early in the season and then hootchies in light greens and blues, including the blue and white and Mint Tulip.

For chinook try Wonderspoons in the standard, half chrome/half brass, #5 Clendon Stewarts or Tom Macks at 45- to 125-feet. Coho will be at 30- to 60-feet. The red Krippled K, orange and pink Apexes can be good for pink and sockeye salmon.

Many Tomic Plugs work in this large area. Try 4- to 5-inch models, numbered: 900, 500, 700, 632 and 602.

If bucktailing is for you, try the Coronation or white for chinook at 30- to 120-feet. Try purple and white with an abalone spinner for coho on the surface.

Drift jiggers try the 2.2 ounce Yellowtail Zzinger, 3" Polar Bear Buzz Bomb, Deadly Dick, MacDeep or Stingsilda in either black or green.

Fly guys target river estuaries for pinks and coho with pink/white, chartreuse/white Clouser Minnows, deceiver patterns and sparse 1.5 inch streamers. The Quatse River is only a few minutes by car from the Port Hardy harbour.

In the Telegraph Cove area, try an anchovy in a teaser behind a Hot Spot flasher, trolled fast for coho.

## Halibut

Port Hardy is a best bet for large halibut from 80 pounds (36.4 kg) up. In fact a record 225 lb. (102.3-kg) fish was taken across the way from the harbour floats in 1998. June is when the biggies move in and open water spots of 200- to 400-feet regularly produce during the summer season. Popular spots include Bolivar Passage, Ripple Passage, Richards Channel and the open water areas of Taylor Bank and Morgan Shoal. With such deep water, fishing slack water—low slack into a flood—and the slower tides is essential to get the lure to the bottom and keep it there.

The best bet is whole herring and octopus on a 2 lb. (.9 kg) spreader bar. Large 8/0 or 9/0 hooks prevent bottom snags, as do circle hooks.

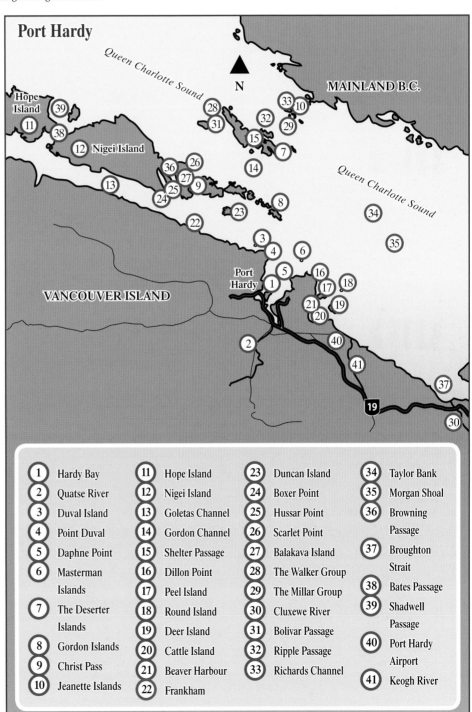

| | | | | | | | |
|---|---|---|---|---|---|---|---|
| 1 | Hardy Bay | 11 | Hope Island | 23 | Duncan Island | 34 | Taylor Bank |
| 2 | Quatse River | 12 | Nigei Island | 24 | Boxer Point | 35 | Morgan Shoal |
| 3 | Duval Island | 13 | Goletas Channel | 25 | Hussar Point | 36 | Browning Passage |
| 4 | Point Duval | 14 | Gordon Channel | 26 | Scarlet Point | 37 | Broughton Strait |
| 5 | Daphne Point | 15 | Shelter Passage | 27 | Balakava Island | 38 | Bates Passage |
| 6 | Masterman Islands | 16 | Dillon Point | 28 | The Walker Group | 39 | Shadwell Passage |
| 7 | The Deserter Islands | 17 | Peel Island | 29 | The Millar Group | 40 | Port Hardy Airport |
| 8 | Gordon Islands | 18 | Round Island | 30 | Cluxewe River | 41 | Keogh River |
| 9 | Christ Pass | 19 | Deer Island | 31 | Bolivar Passage | | |
| 10 | Jeanette Islands | 20 | Cattle Island | 32 | Ripple Passage | | |
| | | 21 | Beaver Harbour | 33 | Richards Channel | | |
| | | 22 | Frankham | | | | |

Utilize 1- to 2-lb. lures such as the Lucky Jig, Spinnow, Dymara, Mudraker or Halibut Hammer jigs that have glow-in-the-dark halibut-sized hootchies in black and orange, black, purple and red, green, yellow and red together, also fluorescent colours. Add scent to the foam insert or an octopus tentacle to one hook.

Halibut can be found at the 30 to 50 fathom line off Cormorant Island as well as Malcolm and Pearse Islands (see Port McNeill map). Fish with the current down a slope rather than up. The latter tends to hang up your gear on the bottom. Do remember that Port Hardy enjoys a special reputation for large red snapper up to 25 lbs (11.4 kg). Fish 250- to 500-feet over pinnacles or steep drop offs. But you don't have to go too far as Duval has halibut and snapper and some pretty big ling cod, too. For halibut and ling, try herring or octopus off Browning Pass to 250 feet.

In March and April try large whole herring at Stubbs Island, Broughton Strait, the Deserter Group, Christie, Browning and Bate Passes in only 60- to 150-feet. In the fall, find halibut in Ripple Passage, 240- to 400-feet at the slack. Try also Taylor Bank, Shadwell Passage, with home made pipe bombs with large skirts. Look for sand or gravel bottom. This is the time to try in front of the river mouths, too, as halibut lie there vacuuming up the dead salmon that pass out from them.

In June try Shadwell Passage, in front of the airport and Keogh River, in Nowell Channel. In summer move on to Christie Pass, Duval Point, Gordon Islands, Masterman Islands, Lizard Point and Blackfish Sound (see Port McNeill map). Run out into open water onto Taylor Bank in 200- to 300-foot areas.

Remember to use a braided line when fishing deep. It doesn't stretch an inch, which leads to more secure hook sets. It has a thinner diameter which means it gets your gear down in comparison with monofilament line.

**Launching Ramps:** The municipality has a free boat launch facility at its dock at Bear Cove on the road to the BC Ferries terminal. The Fishermen's Wharf, has a cement launch ramp. Phone the Harbour Authority at 1-250-949-6332 for information.

**Tackle Shops:** Quarterdeck Marina Resort, 6555 Hardy Bay Road, Box 670 Port Hardy, B.C., V0N 2P0, Phone: 1-250-949-6551. Email: info@quarterdeckresort.net; Website: quarterdeckresort.net. Has a boat launch.

Telegraph Cove Resorts Ltd., Box 1, Telegraph Cove, British Columbia, V0N 3J0; Toll Free: 1-800-200-HOOK (4665); Info: tcrltd@island.net; Website: www.telegraphcoveresort.com.

**Access:** By vehicle, 300 miles (502 km), and six hour drive North from Victoria on Highway 1, 19A and 19 North.
Water access by BC Ferries from Prince Rupert.
Air access at the airport, 3675 Byng Road, Port Hardy, B.C.; 1-259-949-6424.

**Information:** Port Hardy & District Chamber of Commerce, PO Box 249 Port Hardy, B.C. V0N 2P0; Phone: 1-250-949-7622; Email: phcc@cablerocket.com.
Port McNeill District Chamber of Commerce, P.O. Box 129 - 351 Shelley Crescent, V0N 2R0; Phone: 1-250-956-3131; Email: pmccc@island.net;

**Accommodation:** See Chamber of Commerce Listings

**Guides:** Catala Charters, 6170 Hardy Bay Road Box 526 Port Hardy British Columbia, V0N 2P0; Toll Free: 1-800-515-5511; Email: info@catalacharters.net; Website: catalacharters.net.

Codfather Charters Ltd., Box 2389, Port Hardy, B.C., V0N 2P0; Phone: 1-250- 949-6696; Email: codfthr@island.net; Website: codfather-charters.com.

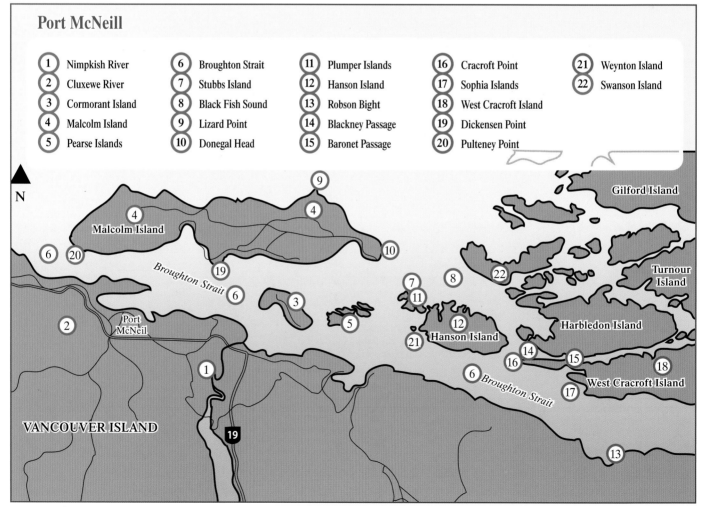

# Port McNeill

1. Nimpkish River
2. Cluxewe River
3. Cormorant Island
4. Malcolm Island
5. Pearse Islands
6. Broughton Strait
7. Stubbs Island
8. Black Fish Sound
9. Lizard Point
10. Donegal Head
11. Plumper Islands
12. Hanson Island
13. Robson Bight
14. Blackney Passage
15. Baronet Passage
16. Cracroft Point
17. Sophia Islands
18. West Cracroft Island
19. Dickensen Point
20. Pulteney Point
21. Weynton Island
22. Swanson Island

Reflecting the west coast's Spanish influence, the bay was named Port San Juan in 1790. Two years earlier a long boat set down from the Felice sought trade with the natives. They weren't interested as the boat was "furiously attacked by the natives and nearly captured."

About 60 miles (110 km) and 90 minutes west of Victoria on the twisty hilly Highway 14, Port Renfrew is the closest trophy summer fishery to a major city and airport. It is the start of the famous West Coast Trail that runs on to Bamfield.

Port Renfrew is the first of Vancouver Island's fishing grounds on the Juan de Fuca Strait that receives the full force of the Pacific Ocean. Consequently, this area is seldom fished in winter because of the frequent storms that blow in making for mountainous seas, as well as the fact that the very fishy Sooke area is closer to Victoria and easier to reach. Despite this, were a fisherman to find himself out on a calmer day, hardy locals say that 20 winter chinook days are the result.

Port Renfrew gives access to the truly stupendous Swiftsure Bank (24 miles (38.4 km) from Owen Point)—loaded with halibut and salmon—and the equally fantastic Nitinat Bar (15 miles—24 km—from Owen Point). Take care and full electronics before setting out to either because boats are lost every year.

## Local Winter Hotspots

If you were to be fishing, the winter feeders are in the area longer than areas closer to Victoria, the season being November 1 to April 30. These are larger than average fish, running 8 to 19 lbs (3.6- to 8.6-kg), with the occasional winter fish tipping the scales at close to 30 lbs. Tyee strip, anchovy and squirts are the lures of choice.

Winter chinook move in at 20- to 40-foot depths, i.e., deeper than summer fish, but far shallower than winter fish in inside areas of Vancouver Island. Draw a bead from Owen Point to the groaning whistle buoy and pick up the 120-foot contour.

## Winter Lures

Tyee strip is preferable in the winter in blue or white glow heads. Winter squirts include, green and white, Army Truck, and white.

## Local Summer Hotspots

Port Renfrew is one of the easiest places to fish for chinook on Vancouver Island. From the Gordon River estuary marina and gravel launching ramp near the bridge, a 15 minute run puts you on Owen Point.

Fish 15- to 30-feet deep on the downrigger on the 40- to 65-foot sandy ledge that runs down two miles (3.5 km) to Camper Creek, and then another mile (1.6 km) to nearby Cullite Creek. This is a dead simple pattern because if you move off the ledge your depthsounder lets you know right away. As you move out, Juan de Fuca Strait falls to 1000 feet deep.

Port Renfrew is where the incoming spawning chinook make first land fall and this may explain why the typical highest bite period is the last two hours of the flood tide as it moves the big fish home. You don't have to be up for the crack of dawn as you do for all places to the east of Port Renfrew, just get on the water

in time to fish the late flood.

The Columbians show in mid May, with the occasional 50 (22.7 kg) pounder taken, and followed by Fraser River chinook for example, the white, Harrisons in June and July.

In some years, in August, the Robertson Creek chinook (Port Alberni, Stamp River hatchery) and the Nitinat River (also a hatchery system) chinook, spill by their intended targets and swell the number of 20- to 45-pound (9.1- to 20.5-kg) chinook. In 2004, 8800 were taken—a phenomenal number—on this simple ledge west of the harbour. The San Juan River has a small chinook hatchery. It is common for the annual biggest chinook (to win the summer-long leader board run by Island Outfitters in Victoria) to come from Port Renfrew in September, often a plus 50-pound (22.7 kg) fish.

The only gremlin in the area is the prominent rock 300 yards south west from Owen Point—it is adorned with a lot of fishing gear.

The east point of the bay is San Juan Point, known locally as Cerantes Pt. It is not commonly fished for chinook because of its predominance of bottom fish. If tasty white meat bottom fish are for you, try this point.

Port Renfrew is the port of the DFO test fishery for Fraser River sockeye in late July. This alone should indicate the strength of this fishing spot. The chinook fishing is so strong that the other species are not actively targeted, but taken as incidental catches—some fishing hole. But if you do want to target the other species, move out half a mile to the tide lines and run between Owen Point and the whistle buoy in the mouth of the bay.

Pick up the 60- to 80-foot contour along the Owen Point shore and swing toward the whistle buoy until 120 foot depths are reached. The first coho begin passing through the tide lines that run parallel to the harbour mouth in July, 1- to 4-miles (1.6- to 6.4-km) off shore. Fish the top 30 feet of water. The flood tide also moves the sockeye and pink salmon by the harbour mouth, with the sockeye running 60- to 80-feet deep. By mid-August, most of the sockeye and pink for the Fraser (sometimes as many as a cool 30,000,000), and the Puget Sound rivers, for example, the Skagit have moved through.

A simple method of contacting sockeye is to run out from Port of San Juan keeping a bead on your fish finder. When you mark the 750- to 800-foot mark wait for the fish to hit the screen and lower you gear to their depth.

*Captain Peter Hovey urges on the newby fisherman in his battle with a wily halibut.*

Coho continue running through August and into September when the first local San Juan River coho arrive. For those wishing to get in on some saltwater shore action, fish below the bridge on the sandy beaches adjacent to a well-placed campground. Try the third week in September until the rains begin in earnest in October. A spinning reel, rod and a few Buzz Bombs and Blue Fox spinners are your gear. Be there in the dark—the first hour is the best fishing of the day.

The San Juan "northern" coho have the distinction of being, on average, the largest coho on Vancouver Island, at 15- to 22-pounds (6.8- to 10-kg) with some reaching almost to 30 pounds (13.6 kg). Once the rains have begun in earnest the San Juan River has two pools that you take to in flight because the in-river fishing for 20-pound (9.1 kg) coho can be furious.

## Summer Lures

Bait is always a good bet for chinook, anchovy in a blue or chartreuse teaser, with a 1- to 2-second flop roll on a 6- to 7-foot leader behind a Hotspot flasher. When the big Northerns show, use short fireplug cutplugs cut just behind the dorsal fin that have a fast tight roll when trolled quickly. You can dispense with the flasher if you wish and run a 6-oz. slip weight. Chum prefer anchovy.

Depending on current feed, the size of plastic baits can vary from year to year. When pilchards and herring predominate, use hootchies. When the smaller needlefish prevail, use squirts (gut a salmon and check the food content in its stomach). For fall coho, depend on blue or green combinations with Mylar skirts, a 36- to 42-inch leader behind a flasher and troll quickly.

In seasons when retention is authorized for sockeye lean to red or bright orange hootchies from which a few fronds have been pulled at random. Do not simply chop the tails off; this ruins the action. Remember that these fish are primarily plankton feeders and thus less is better than more.

Give a try to 5- and 6-inch Tomic plugs: the 602, 700, 158, 301 and 500. Try 7" plugs when the water is warm and mackerel have invaded.

For spoon lovers, the venerable Chrome Krippled K and Tom Mack still find use, but add to these with the 4" Wonderspoon, in half glow and half green, put out by many manufacturers but commonly known as a Coyote spoon.

When trolling quick with flies for coho, move as far into the bay as the current regulations allow. For traditionalists, use the venerable Cowichan Bay polar bear hair bucktail with a #3 abalone spinner early in the summer and a #4 abalone or nickel spinner later, trolled without a flasher. Colour patterns include: Pink Shrimp, particularly for the later larger coho, and the standard patterns: Grey Ghost, Ginger Jake, Coronation, Devil's Tail and Green Ghost.

If drift fishing is your thing, the fish are still so much in their feeding and fattening stage that they will bite any thing that moves, there are many of these lures including the Stingsilda, Buzz Bomb, Pirk, or any other heavy lead lure that is meant to flutter down when you quickly drop your rod tip. Be slow on the rise, so as not to rip the lure out of view of the salmon darting in.

**Launching Ramps:** The Pacheedaht First Nation has a gravel launch ramp on the left hand side of the bridge over the San Juan River. It's easy to find, but difficult to load on low tides.

The marina on the Gordon River estuary across the sand islands has a ramp, and gas taken down in plastic containers, as well as trailer and RV parking. While the owners are considering a fuel dock, it is best to fuel up in Sooke on the way out—by road. This harbour requires 3.5 feet of water.

**Tackle Shops:** Trailhead Resort has some terminal tackle items in the store. It is best to arrive with gear or book a charter.

**Access:** By Highway 14, 60 miles (110 km) west of Victoria.

**Accommodation:** Trailhead Resort and Charters, 1-250-647-5468; Email: info@trailheadresort.com; Website: www.trailhead-resort.com. This is brand new and a good job has been done in all respects. Try out the Coastal Kitchen Café for large, pub-style meals.

**Information:** Go to portrenfrew.com and you will find all the info you need.

Chamber of Commerce website: portrenfrew.com/chamber/.

**Fishing Guide:** Peter Hovey from Trailhead Resort has a new 30-plus foot metal boat that is state of the art for fishing Swiftsure Bank. He introduced a new halibut hole—Long Hole—in 2006 that only he has the boat to reach.

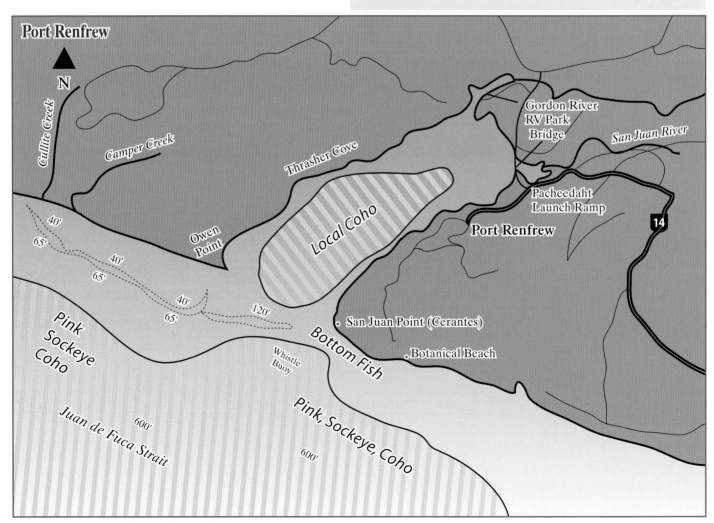

*A typical surfline rock pile on the west coast of Vancouver Island.*

Quatsino Sound takes its name from the older Koskino First Nation name, which has been variously translated over the centuries as, people of the north country, the downstream people and people who lived on the other side (of the island). And Quatsino does indeed offer the other side of the island, to such an extent that it stops only 12 miles short of cutting off the entire top of Vancouver Island.

Quatsino, the most northerly sound on Vancouver Island has six inlets and hundreds of miles of glassy smooth inside water, including Holberg Inlet, Neroutsis Inlet and Rupert Inlet with the main town connections being Coal Harbour on the east side, Holberg in the north, Port Alice in the south and Winter Harbour near the outside entrance to Quatsino Sound. Add two short inlets, Forward Inlet and Browning Inlet to the west of Winter Harbour and the slender Ahwhichaolto Inlet behind Winter Harbour.

Winter Harbour is a pretty little town reminiscent of Bamfield with the charm of its wooden boardwalk linking the houses, built before the road came in in the 1970s. The centre of sport fishing in the Sound, Winter Harbour, used to be the centre for the northern troll fleet and this lets you know its offshore fishing has to be great. And the area is even less crowded than the empty, but great, Kyuquot Sound farther south.

The Marble River Hatchery turns out some pretty large customers with the occasional chinook over 70 pounds (31.8 kg).

# Saltwater Fishing
## Local Winter Hotspots
Port Hardy, where most local guides live and fish, can receive full winter blasts down Queen Charlotte Strait from the open ocean. Consequently, to find good sheltered fishing, many bring their clients across the hump to fish in the protected inside waters of Quatsino Sound.

Most fishing takes place around Quatsino Narrows just a few miles from the Coal Harbour launching ramp. Troll also in front of Quatsino Village close by. The vast network of channels and numerous islands block gales from the open Pacific where at Kains Island and Cape Parkins it is too rough to fish. Fish behind the many islands and off the major points of land.

Winter feeders mill the inside markers in good numbers from December through the end of March.

Halibut fishing can be good early, as in March, on the shallow sand flats a couple of miles from the mouth of the sound. Few anglers fish here though, because Port Hardy also gets good early halibut and hence you fish there - there is little point going to the extra effort of 3 hours of haul, launch and run time on the Quatsino side.

## Winter Lures
Most anglers keep it simple, running the plain, old, white hootchie or white with a green stripe behind a flasher. Note that striped hootchies work better where needlefish abound. Add Wonder Spoons and other large spoons in 5- and 6-inch sizes.

## Local Summer Hotspots
Typically from Cliffe Point in is closed mid-season to protect local chinook salmon. You may still fish and may still retain coho and pink, but must release all chinook. This is not a problem because the outside waters are, as with all West Coast Vancouver Island waters, the marine highway for salmon runs from up and down the coast.

Fish the inside of Cliffe Point before the closure, fish along the wall for chinook. Mid-channel from Cliffe Point is where the coho and pink reside. Then Quatsino Narrows in September is big time coho fishing. The outside of Cliffe Pointe has to be considered prime real estate, fishing in 50- to 60-feet of water with the big springs high in the water column at 25- to 35-feet.

Also high on the list is behind Kains Point at the Forward Inlet mouth. On the flood the big springs get pushed into the back eddy behind Kains Island. Fish outside on the ebb.

In August when the Pacific is calm, shoot around the Quatsino Lighthouse corner for Lippy Point and Grant Bay. This is open ocean fishing close to the rocks. The chinook are 25- to 40-feet down and the sand flats out front are covered in halibut that inhabit the edges in contours from close in to 200 feet deep.

Peak fishing for big chinook is July 15 to August 15 and on the outside until September 15. Beyond Cape Parkins, at the light, fish the nooks and crannies in the kelp. September brings the biggest chinook and coho of the year.

The sound has great crabbing and prawning. Look for flat aprons of 60 feet for crabs and flat bottoms of 250- to 300- feet for prawns across from Cliffe Pointe. Surprisingly, you may find yourself almost alone. This is because the fishing on the Port Hardy side becomes so good that even the vast numbers of coho and chinook on the Quatsino side can't draw the anglers in. It is, after all, a 40 km run from Coal Harbour to the open Pacific. Too bad.

Fish on the west side out from Kains. Do so at 40- to 65-feet for coho and chinook. Find the bait and you find the fish—run your gear at the same depth. Move out to 4 miles (6 km) from Kains in 280 feet of water and you will find salmon at all depths down to 220 feet.

Halibut may be found on the shelf from Kains Island all the way to Lippy Point and out to 200 feet deep.

## Summer Lures

The big 20- to 60-pound (13.6- to 18.2-kg)chinook that are actively feeding prefer anchovy in clear or green teasers, whole herring or cutplugs mooched. Match gear action to the speed you prefer as action is more important than the lure. Move to the long-standing favourite 4.5 inch Tom Mack when mackerel or dogfish are present, trolled 48- to 52-inches behind a green Hotspot flasher. Other good spoons include the Wonders in chrome/brass, but without a flasher, and with large, 7/0 to 9/0, hooks to dissuade smaller fish. Other spoons include the green/glow Coyote or Devil's Tail, and a 6-inch Cop Car Apex.

For hootchies, use the Campbell River favourite, the Jack Frost with its green and yellow colouration. Carry other colours, too: the Green-glo Splatterback and the Purple Haze matched to a Golden Warrior Glow Flasher.

You can drift fish out front with Zzingers and Buzz Bombs on the apron beyond Kains Island at 40- to 65-feet as far out as 280 feet of water.

For coho flies, make up some green/white, chartreuse/white Clouser Minnows. Either cast where you see coho or skip-troll flies in the prop wash, two to five miles (3- to 8-km) off Kains Island.

Halibut average 15- to 60-pounds (6.8- to 27.2-kgs), with the occasional leviathan over 200 lbs (90.9 kgs). Use spreader bars, whole herring and 2 lb (.9 kg) weights. Bring your Mudraker jigs along in the fishy colours of chartreuse, any glow colour and black.

**Launching Ramps:** Winter Harbour's ramp is best only at high tide, so time your entry and exit based on the tide tables.

The Coal Harbour ramp is fine on tides above zero but it isn't good for big boats.

**Tackle Shops:** The Outpost at Winter Harbour.

**Access:** There is road, boat and air access to Winter Harbour at the mouth of the sound. Port Hardy is a 7 hour drive from Victoria. Then add the 12 paved miles (19.2 km) to Coal Harbour. If you launch there you have 21 miles (33.6 km) of protected water to Cliffe Point and then another 5 miles (8 km) to Winter Harbour with little more than the Gillam Islands to cushion the swell.

If you proceed from Coal Harbour by vehicle, it is 42 frame-shaking gravel miles (67.2 km) to Winter Harbour. But the harbour is calm and has ample moorage.

From Coal Harbour it is 24 miles (40 km) by boat to Kains Island on the open Pacific Ocean; about 6 miles (9.6 km) by boat from Winter Harbour.

Ask your resort for its air connection price.

**Information:** Port Hardy Chamber of Commerce, Phone: 1-250-949-7622; Website: www.ph-chamber.bc.ca; Email: phccmgr@cablerocket.com.

Salmon University Website: salmonuniversity.com. See the charts for summer fishing.

**Accommodation:** Eagle Manor Retreat, Toll Free: 1-866-273-5319; Website: eagleresort.com; Email: eagleman@island.net.

The Outpost at Winter Harbour, Phone: 1-250-969-4333; Website: winterharbour.ca; Email: winterharbour@telus.net. Suites, RV/tent park, fuel dock, moorage, general store.

**Guide:** Jim Witton, Box 526 6170 Hardy Bay Road, Port Hardy BC V0N2P0. Phone: 1-250-949-7560, or Cell: 1- 250-902-1031; Website: www.catalacharters.net; Email: info@catalacharters.net.

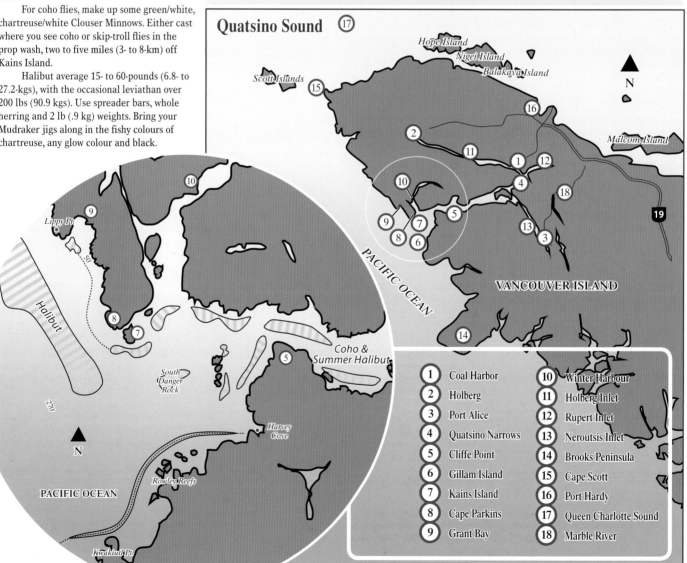

Quatsino Sound ⑰

1 Coal Harbor
2 Holberg
3 Port Alice
4 Quatsino Narrows
5 Cliffe Point
6 Gillam Island
7 Kains Island
8 Cape Parkins
9 Grant Bay
10 Winter Harbour
11 Holberg Inlet
12 Rupert Inlet
13 Neroutsis Inlet
14 Brooks Peninsula
15 Cape Scott
16 Port Hardy
17 Queen Charlotte Sound
18 Marble River

# Saanich Inlet

Home to the calmest saltwater in all of Canada, the 18 mile (28,8 km) long, 800 foot deep Saanich Inlet is a half hour drive from Sidney and Victoria. In the 1950s and '60s it had some of the best fishing on the coast, with plenty of stars and politicians, like Bob Cumming, John Diefenbaker and Lester Pearson catching the big ones on wire line and planers. Local guide Jimmy Gilbert once went 330 days without a skunk, a phenomenal record.

By the '90s though, fishing had declined, but is now returning, with work on the Cowichan River chinook underway. Because chinook salmon invariably follow the same patterns as preceding generations, there is purpose in knowing how to fish the Inlet for the days when its runs have rebounded. I cut my teeth here my first 12 years and credit it with making me much more particular about my tackle, leading to being more successful in areas where there were more fish.

Whether you fish summer or winter, the fishing pattern is the same: start at 25- to 35-feet on the downrigger, 50- to 75-feet on the Perfect Planer (a pink plastic rectangle that acts like an upside down kite to drag the lure down) at the crack of dawn, following the 75 foot contour. While tide changes sometimes produce results, once the fish have been in the inlet for a week or two, it is the crack of dawn and two hours before dusk if you want to catch a fish. That means putting your lines down in the dark in the morning.

After the first half hour methodically lower your planer lines 25 feet every 15 minutes and 15 on the downrigger until you reach 150 feet or 75 feet on the downrigger. At that point, pull in the downrigger and run two planers (and a third over the stern) down to 350 feet (147 feet down) for the rest of the day until about two hours before complete dark when you rise to 250 feet on the planer and 110 on the downrigger. You will catch 4- to 5-fish to 1 on the planer versus the downrigger in the day, and about roughly equal at dawn or dusk.

While you fish, send your wife to Butchart Gardens just down the road. It's world famous for flower lovers.

## Local Winter Hotspots
The chinook slowly circle Saanich Inlet in the winter. The best spot year-round is the Bamberton shore where the old cement factory used to be. You start by following the 75 foot contour and slowly work out to the 250 foot contour by noon. This pattern is consistent the year-round.

The winter hotspots ring the Inlet. Starting with Bamberton, the spots are: Jimmy's Hole, Sheppard Point, McCurdy Point, Stone Steps, Deep Hole, Glass House, Christmas Point, Sawluctus Island, Chesterfield Rock, The Wall, White Lady (Elbow Point), the V, Stick Reef, McKenzie Bight, The Boulder, Willis Point, Willis Point Wall, Tod Inlet, Slugget Point, Senanus Island, Henderson Point, Yellow House, Gas Station, Coles Bay Reef, Can Buoy, Ardmore Drive, Patricia Bay, Moses Point, and Wain Rock. You cross the threshold of the Inlet and pick up Patey Rock then move to the shore near Hatch Point, Whisky Point, Tanner and Tozier Rocks, the Mill Bay Ferry terminal, Bamberton Beach, the Destroyed House and the Silos at the north end of the Bamberton shore.

## Winter Lures
The best lure, year-round, is large strip in a Glow Green large strip teaser, without a flasher. Good winter lures include the 169, 225 and 417 Tomic Plugs in four inch models. In squirts, pick up the blue/green, Angel Wing, white and white/green. The tried and true silver/green Krippled K spoon works well and pick up a green/glow spoon, too.

## Local Summer Hotspots
For trollers, the summer hotspots for chinook are the same as those in the winter.

For drift jiggers, add in the flats off the south end of Senanus Island, the can buoy off the Dyer Rocks in Coles Bay, Wain Rock and Tozier and Tanner Rocks on the Mill Bay side. Fish 40- to 80-feet deep in these areas. Your fishing will be better where you spot new herring. The evening bite is usually between 7 and 8 p.m., a lovely time to be on the water.

Coho can be found where you find them jumping, which usually includes, the can buoy off the Dyer Rocks, Tanner Rock and Tozier Rock. They also hold 250 feet deep in Finlayson Arm in mid-channel. In late September and October, they hold off Whiskey Point and Hatch Point.

Remember that chinook can be 250 feet by 2 pm on a sunny day. So once you are past 350 feet on the planer, roll out the downriggers for your middle of the day fishing.

In April and May a run of 20- to 30-pound (9.1- to 13.6-kg) chinook come into the Inlet and the Coles Bay Wall, and the run from McCurdy Point to McKenzie Bight can be the hotspots.

*When you are done fishing in the Victoria area, hop a plane for the outback remote resorts of Vancouver Island.*

## Summer Lures

Drift jiggers use green or black Stingsildas bent in a slight C so they flutter down like wounded bait fish. White and grey Buzz Bombs work, too. Newly hatched 1.5- inch herring can be deadly when gathered with a herring rake and fished on size six hooks with a bit of plastic from a paper clip inserted behind to make a "false barb"—it is barbless hooks in B.C. these days. One small hook up through the lips and one through the body behind the dorsal fin, they are fished live, mooched and slowly row your boat to lift and drop the bait.

Trollers stick with large herring as the number one lure. But when the waters are open, anchovy on a Glow flasher in mid-channel Finlayson Arm at 250 feet in September finds the 30- to 40- pound (13.6- to 18.2-kg) chinook destined for the Cowichan River.

Use jigging lures off Whisky Point for chinook: the silver MacDeep; Pirkins; black Stingsilda; and, chrome Buzz Bomb. Pat Bay produces in the late summer and early fall. Try 6- to 8-ounces of weight, 50- to 100-feet of line at 3.1 mph. At the action end of the set up, try a 1 ½" Apex, number 75 to 77, in white pearl. White hootchies work all year round in the area.

Try a gold squirt or hootchie 170 feet deep in the day off the Yellow House in June. Some years it is a killer.

## Saanich Inlet

**Launching Ramps:** Tsartlip Indian Reserve launch. Come down Verdier or Stelly's X-road to the reserve and follow the signs.

Halls Boathouse up Finlayson Arm has a launch. Access via their sign on the Trans Canada Highway on the Malahat Drive as you head up-island from Victoria.

The Mill Bay Marina has a launch. At the lights in Mill Bay, take a right and follow the road to the water and marina.

**Tackle Shops:** Check the Victoria chapter for Robinson's and Island Outfitters. Most of the Marinas carry some tackle.

**Access:** Saanich Inlet is a half hour drive from downtown Victoria. Victoria has ferry and vehicle access from Port Angeles, Tswwassen on the mainland, and from Anacortes, Washington. Air service comes in at the airport near Sidney or via float plane in the Inner Harbour. The Heliport at Camel Point has scheduled service from downtown Vancouver.

**Information:** Tourism Victoria. It's Visitor Centre on the Causeway in the Inner Harbour is an excellent information hub. Address: 812 Wharf Street, Victoria, BC, V8W 1T3; Toll Free: 1-800-663-3883; Website: tourismvictoria.com; Email: info@tourismvictoria.com.

The Greater Victoria Chamber of Commerce,# 100 - 852 Fort St., Victoria, BC, V8W 1H8; Phone: 1-250-383-7191; Website:victoriachamber.ca; Email: chamber@gvcc.org.

**Accommodation:** There are more interesting places to stay and good places to eat than you can shake a stick at. See Tourism Victoria.

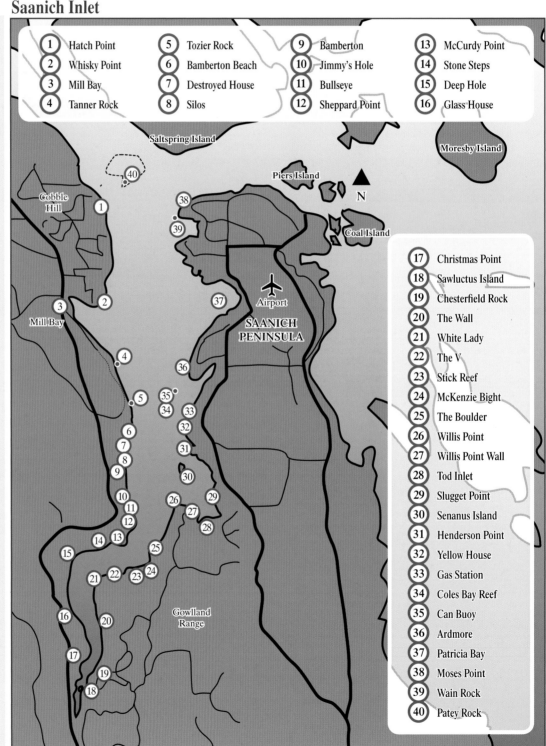

| | | | |
|---|---|---|---|
| 1 Hatch Point | 5 Tozier Rock | 9 Bamberton | 13 McCurdy Point |
| 2 Whisky Point | 6 Bamberton Beach | 10 Jimmy's Hole | 14 Stone Steps |
| 3 Mill Bay | 7 Destroyed House | 11 Bullseye | 15 Deep Hole |
| 4 Tanner Rock | 8 Silos | 12 Sheppard Point | 16 Glass House |

17 Christmas Point
18 Sawluctus Island
19 Chesterfield Rock
20 The Wall
21 White Lady
22 The V
23 Stick Reef
24 McKenzie Bight
25 The Boulder
26 Willis Point
27 Willis Point Wall
28 Tod Inlet
29 Slugget Point
30 Senanus Island
31 Henderson Point
32 Yellow House
33 Gas Station
34 Coles Bay Reef
35 Can Buoy
36 Ardmore
37 Patricia Bay
38 Moses Point
39 Wain Rock
40 Patey Rock

# Sayward, Kelsey Bay

The small towns of Sayward and Kelsey Bay are an hour's drive, or 38 miles (61 km) north from Campbell River and 6 miles (10 km) from the junction with Highway 19. They are where the Salmon River flows into Johnstone Strait, a river that is well worth the fish.

As for saltwater fishing, you can cast from the government wharf for coho in June to September and for pinks and chum into October. This land-based salmon fishery can be very successful. It's a good place for kids to spend the day.

The local attraction that is close to the junction of Highway 19 is the Cable Cookhouse, a restaurant built entirely of used logging cable.

## Saltwater Fishing
### Local Winter Fishing
Few people come to Sayward in the winter to fish.

### Local Summer Hotspots
During August and September all the coho, sockeye, chum and chinook destined for southern B.C. rivers pass by Sayward before hitting Campbell River. Thus there are many fish and few fishermen.

Try your luck a bit north west of town on The Shoal off Hickey Point, as well as both sides of Hardwicke Point on the island of the same name, across the channel from Kelsey Bay. You can actually troll the shoreline directly in front of Kelsey Bay across the harbour mouth to Petersen Island. Or move across to Hardwicke again and fish the shore all the way down and across to Helmcken Island. Fish Eden point on West Thurlow Island. Wellbore Channel deserves your time; focus on Bulkely Island as well as the run between Althorp Point, across Wellbore Channel to Thynne Point—the first reference to the mainland shore of British Columbia.

## Summer Lures
Anchovy in a green teaser head 4 feet behind a Hotspot flasher does the deed for chinook.

Sockeye and pink are attracted to lures, whether spoons, hootchies, apexes and others that have red in them.

**Launching Ramps:** The Kelsey Bay harbour is the only small craft harbour between Campbell River & Port McNeill. It has a new, concrete, all-tide ramp that will accommodate large boats and fuel. Phone: 1-250-282-3454.

The Sayward Fish and Game Club has a ramp, too. Phone: 1-250-282-3792.

**Tackle Shops:** Fisherboy Park, a campsite, store and has other facilities, including tackle; Address: Site 10, Box 1, RR#1, Sayward, British Columbia, Canada; Phone: 1-250-282-3204; Website: fisherboypark.com; Email: fisherboypark@telus.net.

**Access:** A four-hour drive north from Victoria.

**Information:** Sayward Tourism's website: www.sayward.com.
Village of Sayward, 601 Kelsey Way, Box 29, Sayward, BC, V0P 1R0; Phone: 1-250-282-5512; Email: office@village.sayward.bc.ca.
Sayward Business And Tourism Association, Site 10, Box 2, Comp 4, Sayward, B.C. V0P 1R0; Email: info@sayward.com.

**Accommodation:** See travelbc.ca for info on many activities.
Sayward Chamber of Commerce, PO Box 70 Sayward, BC V0P 1R0; Phone: 1-250-(250)282-3833

**Guides:** Bob's Fishing, 250 Spar St, Sayward; Phone: 1-250-282-3612
Hans Schuer, Phone 1-250-282-3618.

## Sayward, Kelsey Bay

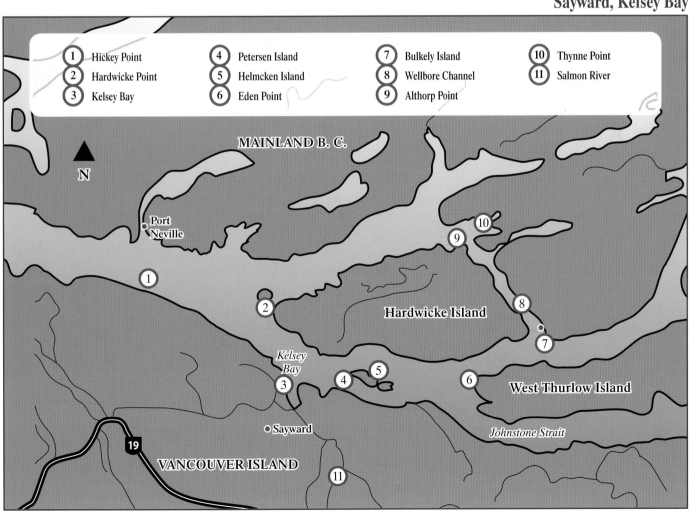

| | | | |
|---|---|---|---|
| 1 Hickey Point | 4 Petersen Island | 7 Bulkely Island | 10 Thynne Point |
| 2 Hardwicke Point | 5 Helmcken Island | 8 Wellbore Channel | 11 Salmon River |
| 3 Kelsey Bay | 6 Eden Point | 9 Althorp Point | |

# Sidney, Active Pass

Sidney is a charming, updated retirement community on the Pat Bay Highway as you come into Victoria from the Swartz Bay ferry terminal (22 miles - 35.2 km) north of Victoria (3 miles - 5 km) from the airport). You have to stop at the Sidney Bakery on Saturday morning as the stuff is spectacular—just get in the line up that stretches out the door and down the street.

Between Sidney and the ferry terminal, lie a half dozen quality marinas, so it is well serviced for boat access, including the Anacortes Ferry from Washington State that lands a few blocks from Beacon Avenue, which is the centre of town.

And, swimming among the islands off the water front, a resident pod of killer whales comes by every two days, making a circuit from Bedwell Harbour to Saturna Island and through the San Juan Islands.

## Local Winter Hotspots

Sidney is another area that could use chinook enhancement work for the Georgia Strait Van Isle Rivers. This said, there are many winter and summer spots to fish.

These spots include Coal Island and nearby Moresby Island, Miners Channel between Sidney Spit and Forrest Island, Gooch Island, the Powder Wharf, Cordova Spit, Fairfax Point to Seymour Point, Hambley Point, the 120 foot contour off James Island, Cordova Channel, Imrie Island, Colburne Passage, Knapp Island, Shute Rock, Shute Passage and the Swartz Bay Ferry Terminal—be aware of ferries!

April is the best month for winter feeders of 5- to 15-pounds (2.3- to 6.8-kgs). At this time, Nooksack spawners come through, too, that is, 30-pounders (13.6 kgs).

When fishing along Sidney Spit to the red can buoy, take care because strings of commercial traps have their floats disappear when the tide is running and are perfect for snagging downrigger cables. Danger indeed.

## Winter Lures

The area feed is predominantly needlefish, hence, smaller lures are the rule most of the year. In bait, the preference is for Tiny Strip on a 48 inch leader to a glow flasher. Drift jiggers work Coal Island with slender needlefish lures. Try anchovy in a green/yellow chrome teaser

## Summer Hotspots

Sidney Spit, James Island's Powder Wharf, and Coal Island are the hotspots. Fish the bottom in both summer and winter. This is primarily a chinook salmon area.

In May and June Columbians head through, reaching 45 pounds (20.5 kgs).

Cordova Spit holds chinook in its deeper waters. Work James Island on its 120-foot contour. Add jigging at the Powder Wharf on James Island with Stingsildas.

Move further afield in the summer to the Pender Bluffs in August and early September for sockeye and pinks at 90 feet.

## Active Pass

Active Pass, and its very strong currents, is accessed from Sidney. Fish the downstream ends of this very active pass between Galiano and Mayne Islands. Don't fish in the channel as ferries go through frequently, sending out 6 foot wakes. Try the Sansum Narrows drift jigs: Buzz Bombs, Rip Tide Strikers in green/yellow and red/white. Or power mooch with cutplug herring. Keep the line straight up and down, with the weight bouncing off the bottom. Try the drop off between the Cable and the Arbutus Tree. Use 10- to12-foot mooching rods. Wait for the rod tingling that means salmon testing your bait. The fishing is best on tide changes. Try the Galiano shore on the ebb, Salamanca Point up to the second cable, on the flood. Active Pass supports a year-round chinook fishery. Alternatively, troll teasered-up herring. Troll off shore on the outside, past the government store, up to the opening, and the Lighthouse Point. This is a big backeddy on an ebb. On the flood, mosey past the green can buoy and logging slashes.

Try the corny old trick of pulling the line a couple of feet and letting go to double your take of summer coho. For chinook, take the boat out of gear every now and then. Change directions frequently, particularly for coho.

Near Bedwell Harbour on Pender Island, fish the kelp bed off Wallace Point, Blunden Island and East Point.

## Summer Lures

Use cutplug herring at Active Pass, as well as the Coyote Spoon (half glow/half green) and Glow Below and Blood and Bones hootchies. Tiny Strip in a tiny teaser 42 inches behind a 120 O'ki flasher or small herring or minnows on a four-foot leader.

In summer or winter, the local squirts are: the J49, J79, Mint Tulip, green and white and Army Truck.

The plugs of choice include the 500, 232, 191, 158 and the 43.

During a sockeye and pink summer at the Pender Bluffs, fish fast and deep to 100 feet—rip out a few fronds of the standard pink hootchie and use black hooks. Pink fluorescent tubing on a single hook behind a flasher can be deadly, as can the Bubblegum squirt.

chinook catches come from the 70- to 100-foot mark, in front of Pane Island. Herring strip with a shortish 18" leader to a flasher has done the trick, as has the black and gold Buzz Bomb.

At Pender Bluffs use plankton squirts with ribs for pinks; Happy Hookers for sockeye. Fish the sockeye at the crack of dawn.

From the nicely-sheltered Montague Harbour on Galiano Island, try Gossip Shoals and Taylor Cove. Fish deep for chinook with Army truck hootchies or cutplug herring power mooched.

Launching Ramps: Island View Beach, Island View Road off Highway 17 at Keating Cross Roads south of the airport turnoff, concrete, limited use.

Van Isle Marina, 2320 Harbour Road, Sidney, BC V8L 3S6. Phone 604 656-1138.

Roberts Bay public launch, cartopper only, Ardwell Road, Sidney, BC.

Sidney Public Launch Ramp, McTavish Road to Tulista Park, adjacent Anacortes ferry terminal.

Tackle Shops: Harvey's Sporting Goods on Beacon Avenue. Turn in off the Pat Bay Highway, and you can't miss it.

Access: Pat Bay Highway for vehicles, two ferry docks and via air at the Victoria airport across the highway. Boat access into the marina's in the basin.

Information: Saanich Peninsula Chamber of Commerce, 203-2453 Beacon Avenue, Sidney, BC V8L 1X7; Phone: 1-250-656-3616; Website: http://www.spcoc.org/; Email: info@spcoc.org.

Try the Sidney Tourism website: sidney.travel.bc.ca.

Guides: Jay on Saltspring Island, Phone: 1-250-537-5464; Website: www:saltspring.com/rentals; Email: jaysmall@telus.net;

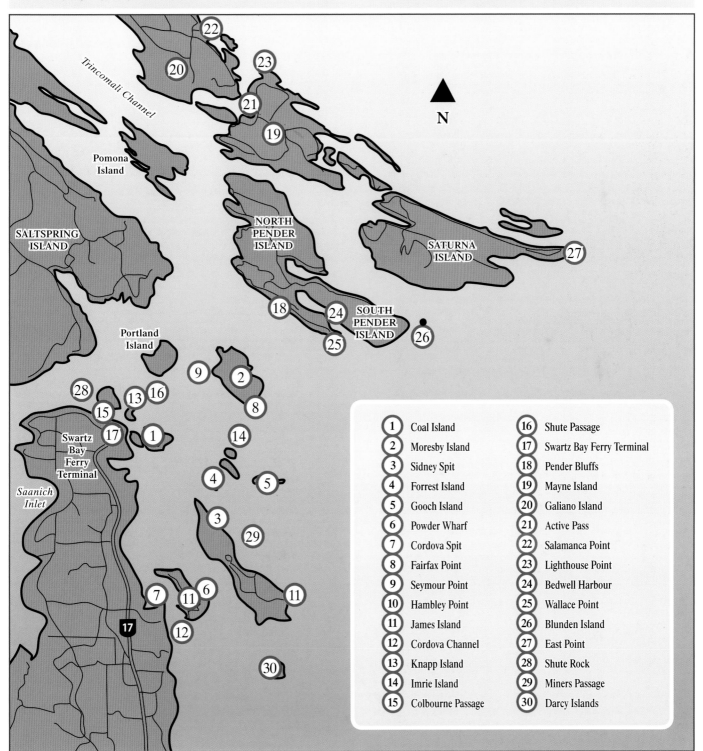

| | | | |
|---|---|---|---|
| 1 | Coal Island | 16 | Shute Passage |
| 2 | Moresby Island | 17 | Swartz Bay Ferry Terminal |
| 3 | Sidney Spit | 18 | Pender Bluffs |
| 4 | Forrest Island | 19 | Mayne Island |
| 5 | Gooch Island | 20 | Galiano Island |
| 6 | Powder Wharf | 21 | Active Pass |
| 7 | Cordova Spit | 22 | Salamanca Point |
| 8 | Fairfax Point | 23 | Lighthouse Point |
| 9 | Seymour Point | 24 | Bedwell Harbour |
| 10 | Hambley Point | 25 | Wallace Point |
| 11 | James Island | 26 | Blunden Island |
| 12 | Cordova Channel | 27 | East Point |
| 13 | Knapp Island | 28 | Shute Rock |
| 14 | Imrie Island | 29 | Miners Passage |
| 15 | Colbourne Passage | 30 | Darcy Islands |

# Sooke

On the western edge of the Victoria Waterfront lies Sooke, named for local aboriginals, who were "a most warlike and hardy race." Too bad for them, they irked their neighbours so much they were attacked by a federation of other tribes and almost wiped out circa 1848.

The Sooke fishery is adjacent to the Victoria Waterfront and extends west for 30 miles (50 km), a fishing ground too large to do in one day. Sooke starts at the William Head Penitentiary, passes west through Race Passage, on to Church Rock, thence to Becher Bay and Beechy Head, to Secretary Island, Sooke Bluffs and on to Otter Point.

The entire area is a far better winter fishery than Victoria, and recent years have produced exceptional fishing at the Sooke Bluffs and Trailer Park. The reason is that it relies less on Strait of Georgia chinook for its nursery fish and more on Puget Sound that has received more rehabilitation effort.

The winter fishery runs from November to the end of March for two- and three-year-old winter feeder spring salmon of 5- to 15-pounds (2.3- to 6.8-kgs), with the occasional plus 20-pound (9.1-kg)chinook. Limits of fish for every boat is common at the Sooke Bluffs and Trailer Park.

Unlike the Victoria Waterfront, Sooke can have an excellent summer fishery from May until October for coho, springs, pinks (every second, odd year, up to 30,000,000) and sockeye. Most of the fish are destined for the Fraser River system, with others for the Strait of Georgia and Puget Sound. In late May some boaters venture as far west as Sheringham Point to intercept the first big fish of the year, the Columbian chinook that pass through from then to late June— large fish up to 60 pounds (27.3 kgs). Halibut fishing is best in front of Jordan River in the 200 foot depths, a fishery 10 miles (16 km) beyond Sheringham Point.

## Local Winter Hotspots

Fishing West from Pedder Bay, the mouth of the bay is fished close to the bottom, following the 120 foot contour from William Head to the Navy Can Buoy and off the Deep Hole. Unless you are familiar with the area, do not continue fishing through the Race—it is shallow and as the name implies, the ocean rips right on through.

Pick up your downrigger balls and move on to Christopher Point, easily identified by the vertical wind turbine, an experiment in producing electricity. Drop your gear (best done on a falling tide) on the unnamed spire that rises to 40 from the surface. Often you get a fish before you put down the second rod.

The spire drops off to a broad mud flat that extends at 110- to 130-feet all the way to Church Rock, a good half mile to the west. This run is the best stretch in the Pedder Bay area and you should work it until the falling tide picks you up and pushes you around Church Rock where it has already deposited the fish in the rocky, but fishy backeddy extending to the Bedford Islands.

Exiting from Becher Bay, fishing can often produce lots of fish between the marina and Fraser Island in water, again a mud bottom, of 60- to 80-feet and fished as the guides say, "in the mud." This is particularly useful because this shallow spot can be the only area calm enough to fish in Sooke when the winter south easters blow in from Puget Sound.

Traveling out a little farther and turning west, Beechy Head is a major rock— keep your eyes on your depthsounder—that deposits fish on the down side of the tidal flow. As you move out, begin fishing in water 120- to 160-feet deep, keeping your gear close to bottom. The area from the Head to Secretary Island is productive but if you are really looking for lots of fish and the water is calm zip farther to the Sooke Bluffs, the Trailer Park and Otter Pont, fishing the 80- to 200-foot depths, close to the bottom.

## Winter Lures

As in Victoria, the best winter lure—always run one line with it—is anchovy or herring strip bait secured in a glow, chrome, Purple Haze, Army Truck or 602 colour pattern Rhys Davis Anchovy Special teaser head, a device for setting up a one roll per 1.5 seconds, 4- to 6-feet behind a flasher. Note that this distance means that the flasher is only bringing in fish by its sonic thump and flash of light, it is not imparting any action to the bait. Pick a flasher with one side of glow in the dark and other side a green Hotspot, Purple Haze or Army Truck. For squid resembling hootchies pick up Irish Mist, Army Truck, Purple Haze, Green/White, and Glow Below.

In spoons, try the Green/Glow, Army Truck, Cop Car, 4 inch Coyote, Blue Haze Devil's Tail, Titan, Gibbs Gator spoons, and the Tomic 402 spoon. Put these four feet behind a Cop Car, Boogey Man or Jellyfish flasher.

## Local Summer Hotspots

Sooke is a far better place to fish in the summer than Victoria next door. This is because the fish follow the northern shore or are as far as 12 miles out in the shipping lanes near the international boundary. Once they hit Race Rocks they move east all the way across Constance Bank and south of Trial Island by several miles. Few fish move into the near shore waters of Victoria Waterfront.

Summer spawning chinook tend to follow the rocky shore lines of Juan de Fuca Strait within a stone's throw from land. They are within 80 feet of the surface (usually in the top 45 feet), traveling in back eddies. They stop and

*The guys in the boat helping the guys on the rocks land a big spring.*

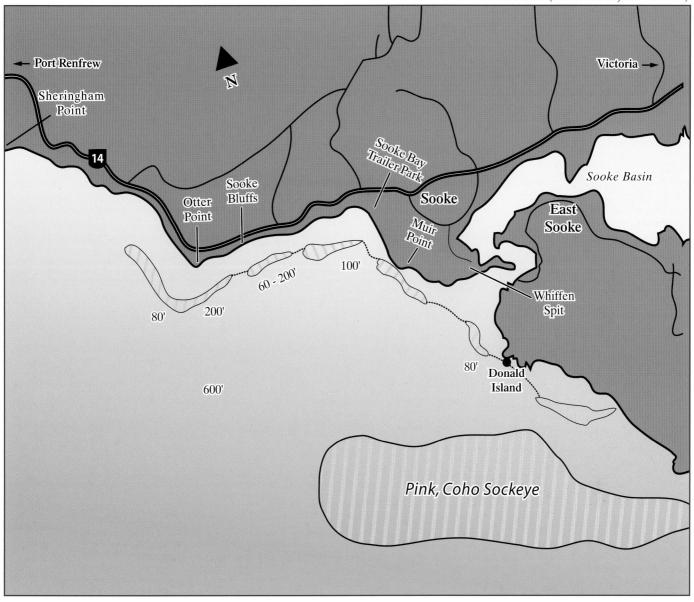

Port Renfrew →

Sheringham Point

14

Otter Point

Sooke Bluffs

Sooke Bay Trailer Park

Sooke

Muir Point

Victoria →

Sooke Basin

East Sooke

Whiffen Spit

80' 200'

60 - 200'

100'

80' Donald Island

600'

*Pink, Coho Sockeye*

rest on the falling tide and move forward on the flood.

Pick back eddies, including the kelp bed at the Deep Hole, the back eddy in front of Bentinck Island—the old leper colonythe back eddy tight to Church Rock and Sword Fish Island right in to 40 feet of water. You'll swear you could reach out and touch the rock you are that close.

Afternoon flood tides can be good too, with Many chinook 30- to 50-pounds (13.6- to 22.7-kgs) taken at Creyke and Aldridge Points. Beechy Head gives up lots of chinook too, but there can be hundreds of boats and I suggest moving on and working the Trap Shack, a local ripple that has ripped off more gear than anywhere else in the area. But you fish there because it is the hotspot as it holds lots of big chinook, usually at the crack of dawn. Keep that finger on the electric downrigger button to lift the gear when you get dragged over the rock.

The back side of Donaldson Island (known locally as Secretary Island) will often concentrate chinook. But don't fish between the Island and shore as it is too shallow. All along here you are fishing 30- to 80-feet deep. From here, pick up your gear and move down to the Trailer Park and fish Otter Point waters.

The many millions of pink salmon mosey through from July 15 to September 15 with August being the peak month. For lovely summer fishing pick a day

in the last two weeks of August featuring a flood tide that moves the pink along. Most days you can catch as many pink as there are licence limits on the boat. Like coho and sockeye, these fish are taken from the surface down to 85 feet—deeper than in the past.

Your best bet is to move offshore and fish the first, second or third tide lines as much as 5 miles (8 km) out into the strait. Some August days at the international line, Washington boaters fish up and down the one side with Canadians doing the same on the other side. All will be catching the summer fish as much as 15 miles (24 km) from land.

Jordan River, ten miles (16 km) west of Sheringham Point, produces some of the biggest halibut in April. Fish the spires and canyon edges 180- to 225-feet down.

## Summer Lures

The big girthy chinook want big bait and they want it trolled slowly. So rig up your larger anchovy and herring in the summer, 4- to 6-feet behind a Hotspot flasher or the old fashioned Pal No. 3 Dodger. The new hot flasher for all species is the Old Betsy from O'ki Tackle.

## Sooke (East Part, 15 Miles)

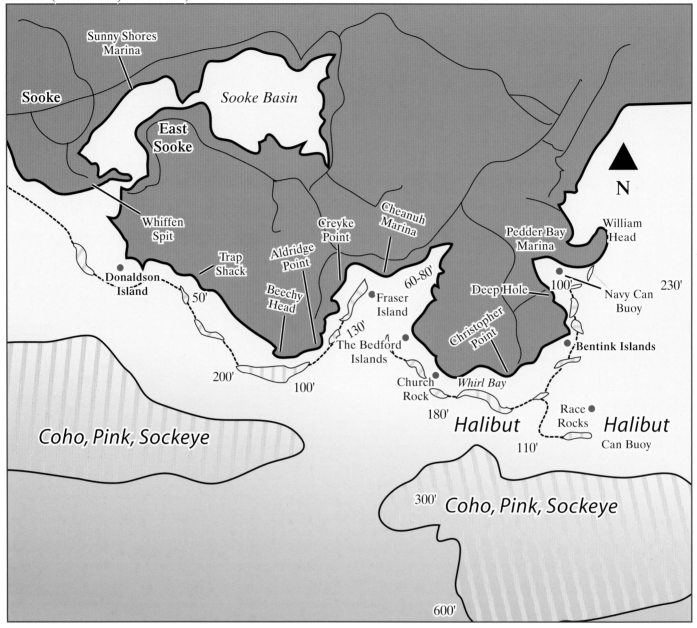

Don't bother with bait for the other salmon species, plastics will suffice. And they have an advantage, too; unlike bait that can be whacked and ruined, hootchies and squirts (spoons, too) continue fishing all the time, even when you change speeds. Buy every pattern of pink: Bubble Gum, pink with Mylar, pink with silver sprinkles and whatever.

The best, simple rigs you can buy at the marinas: a red or orange hootchie with one or two fronds removed and a honking 6/0 Kirbed Octopus-style hook. Along with these pick up some of Radiant's little spoons and those Slam Dunks. Having tried a half dozen on a particular day, I can tell you that colour is highly important every day out.

Bet on a Plaid flasher as they transmit much more light than flashers that are not 3-D, hologramatic. And a 34-inch leader. Leaders should be short for the intermingled sockeye, but if you speed up to take pink and coho, this has the effect of 'shortening' leaders. Move to 42 inches if seriously motoring in search of fish. Don't doddle in one spot if it does not produce.

Use the local favourite, Old Betsy, from O'ki, as a flasher for springs and coho as the summer wears on.

**Launching ramps:** Pedder Bay Marina, 925 Pedder Bay Road, 1-250-478-1771. Also boat rental and fuel.

Cheanuh Marina, 4901 East Sooke Road, 1-250-478-4880, also fuel. Sunny Shores Resort and Marina Ltd., 5621 Sooke Road, 1-250- 642-5731.

**Tackle shops:** Island Outfitters, 3319 Douglas St., 1-250-475-4969. Pedder Bay Marina.

**Access:** 20 miles (32 km) west from Victoria by car. Ask your hotel for a map.

**Information:** Sooke Chamber of Commerce, 1-250-642-6112; Website: sookeharbourchamber.com.

**Accommodation:** Stay in Victoria or in local resorts, as per Chamber information.

Sooke Harbour House is a lovely place for a couple. 1528 Whiffen Spit Road, 1-250-642-342.

**Fishing Guide:** Rollie Rose, Cell, 1-250-213-3055, Sooke Salmon Charters Ltd., fishingbc1.com, rrose@pacificcoast.net.

# Swiftsure Bank

Swiftsure Bank is known for its second-to-none halibut fishing. I have never been out there when everyone has not caught their limits. And there is more: Swiftsure is a nursery area for chinook and thus it has solid chinook fishing for as long as the weather will allow you to go out. In addition, all the big inside Strait chinook cross over in summer. It is remarkably fecund with coho in huge schools from July to late September. These have to be seen to be believed.

While filling the tub with meat is the primary goal of most anglers, Swiftsure will develop in coming years to be a major fly fishing spot for coho. As fly fishers let most fish they catch go, this is a good deal for all of us. The Bank lies 23 miles (36.8 km) south east from Cape Beale, or 24 miles (38.4 km) from Owen Point, west of Port Renfrew, or about 15 miles (24 km) off shore from the Carmanah Light House.

This is an extremely wild place where the tallest wave in the world was measured at 100 feet high. I have fished when the "chop" was 12 feet high, like houses coming at you from every direction. On other days it is so calm it is eerie unsettling.

The Bank, lying right beside the international fishing channels, is even more dangerous than it used to be, because the Juliet Buoy was moved farther out bringing freighters within a half mile of the bank proper. With most of August and September in thick fog, do not venture out without another boat and without radar and GPS. After all, a freighter cannot see its own bow let alone the blip that a boat makes in front of it. Very dangerous

The Swiftsure Bank is not a site to drop an anchor and float, and attach a line. The currents cross over it too quickly. On the Pacific side, the ocean rises from the black depths of 6000 feet and pushes a huge plume up and over the underwater mountains, raining nutrients dredged from the depths. This is the reason for their abundance: schools of baitfish half a mile across, feeding on plankton blooms; every run of salmon heading for southern B.C. has to cross these high plateaus to enter from the Pacific; 37 species of rockfish inhabit Swiftsure, along with halibut; and, trophy lingcod.

On charts it shows as three clover leaf shaped reefs at 120- to 170-feet beneath the surface in the choke point where the open Pacific meets Juan de Fuca Strait, the 40 mile (64 km) wide channel between Vancouver Island and snow-hung Olympic Peninsula in Washington State.

migration puts new halibut on the same spots every year. After you complete your drift—the tide can be so monstrous that the trick of backing up into the waves to keep the halibut lures on the bottom, won't work—motor back to the upstream waypoint and lower gear again.

The territorial nature of halibut is the key to catching them. As one fish is caught, another of these predatorial fish will move in. They have remarkable nasal and auditory abilities and thunking the bottom with something that smells good is your ticket to fish.

## Salmon

Because the Owen Point fishery near Port Renfrew is so solid, boats have no need of going out to Swiftsure to salmon fish. It is done as a secondary fishery once the main target, the halibut have been caught. Do note that the halibut hotspots are not the same as the salmon hotspots. Keep your eye on the guides and you will notice that they pick up their bottom gear and move to troll for chinook. Troll with them and make your GPS marks.

As a nursery area for 8- to 20-pound (3.6- to 9.1-kg) chinook, this factor pretty well assures you of a full load of salmon, too; because the fish grow here, they don't go anywhere else.

But the big summer runs include the Frasers, the Harrison River fish, Robertson Creek, Nitinat and so on, including Puget Sound chinook. You have to come out and experience a nursery area. It will astonish you with the amount of life. And the salmon behave in ways you seldom ever see. The coho for instance are so tame and close to the boat, you can reach over the edge and touch one with your finger. But you shouldn't do that because they are also in their last gorging phase and might nip it off. You don't need a depth sounder to mark these fish, you will see where they are by how many break the surface.

## Summer Lures
## Halibut

The simplest lure is the homemade pipe bomb. Melt a pound of lead into a copper pipe and attach a hootchie skirt on a wire cord with a treble hook on it. Alternatively, pick up 10-inch scampi tails and 12 oz. head weights. Bait hooks with a chunk of octopus because halibut nasal abilities are legendary: they will

## Local Winter Hotspots

This is far too rough and far too far from shore to fish in the winter. Don't go.

## Local Summer Hotspots
## Halibut

Swiftsure Bank is three clover leafs of mountain that present underwater plateaus. The canyon edges are where the migratory halibut come from as much as 1000 miles (1600 km) away to reside on gravel piles where they sort themselves out by size; big with big and so on. Hit one, then hit the GPS (before you play the fish) and you have found the place where another halibut of similar size will move in.

People come here to fill up on halibut and it delivers. Each time you mark a strike on your GPS you are mapping out the best fishable bottom for your future trips: the onshore May

*A typical catch of chicken halibut taken from Swiftsure Bank, the best Vancouver Island halibut spot.*

# Swiftsure Bank

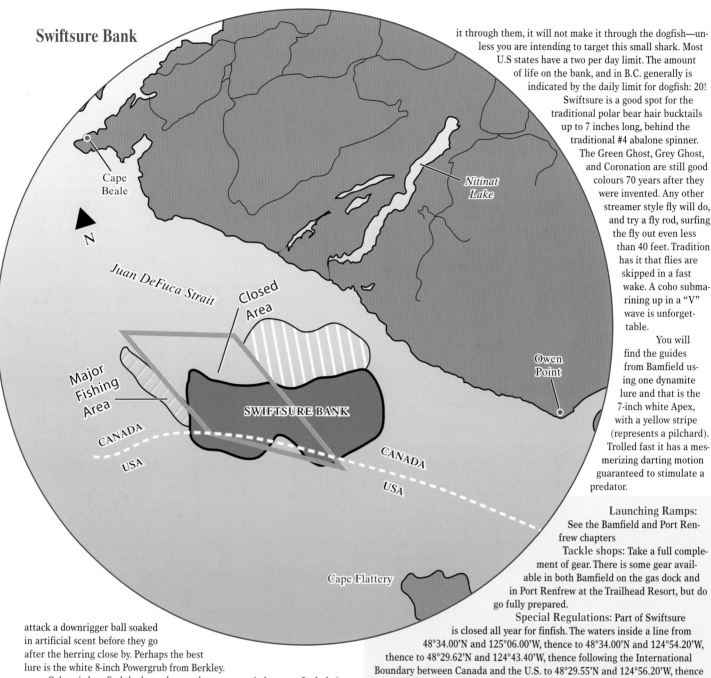

it through them, it will not make it through the dogfish—unless you are intending to target this small shark. Most U.S states have a two per day limit. The amount of life on the bank, and in B.C. generally is indicated by the daily limit for dogfish: 20! Swiftsure is a good spot for the traditional polar bear hair bucktails up to 7 inches long, behind the traditional #4 abalone spinner. The Green Ghost, Grey Ghost, and Coronation are still good colours 70 years after they were invented. Any other streamer style fly will do, and try a fly rod, surfing the fly out even less than 40 feet. Tradition has it that flies are skipped in a fast wake. A coho submarining up in a "V" wave is unforgettable.

You will find the guides from Bamfield using one dynamite lure and that is the 7-inch white Apex, with a yellow stripe (represents a pilchard). Trolled fast it has a mesmerizing darting motion guaranteed to stimulate a predator.

**Launching Ramps:** See the Bamfield and Port Renfrew chapters

**Tackle shops:** Take a full complement of gear. There is some gear available in both Bamfield on the gas dock and in Port Renfrew at the Trailhead Resort, but do go fully prepared.

**Special Regulations:** Part of Swiftsure is closed all year for finfish. The waters inside a line from 48°34.00'N and 125°06.00'W, thence to 48°34.00'N and 124°54.20'W, thence to 48°29.62'N and 124°43.40'W, thence following the International Boundary between Canada and the U.S. to 48°29.55'N and 124°56.20'W, thence in a straight line to the point of commencement, are closed.

The majority of halibut come from anglers fishing along the U.S. boundary just outside the southwest corner of the closure or find pinnacles. Check the closed area map at: www.pac.dfo-mpo.gc.ca/recfish/Tidal/area121_e.htm. You will note that sport fishers are within 800 yards of the huge ocean freighters. In fog you'd better be right on your GPS marks or you might be dead.

**Access:** By boat, one hour 15 minutes from Port Renfrew or Bamfield.

**Accommodation:** Trailhead Resort in Port Renfrew.

Tyee Resort in Bamfield, PO Box 32, Bamfield, BC, V0R 1B0, Phone: 1-888-493-8933; Website: tyeeresort.com; Email: infor@tyeeresort.com.

**Information:** Port Renfrew Chamber of Commerce.

Bamfield Chamber of Commerce, Phone: 1-250-728-3006; Website: bamfieldchamber.com; Email: info@bamfieldchamber.com

**Suggested Guides:** Peter Hovey, Trailhead Resort, Port Renfrew. Doug Ferguson, Westcoast Charters, Bamfield, 2530 Cosgrove Crescent, Nanaimo, B.C. Phone: 1-250-728-3217; Email: coastlinecharters@hotmail.com.

attack a downrigger ball soaked in artificial scent before they go after the herring close by. Perhaps the best lure is the white 8-inch Powergrub from Berkley.

Colour is key, find the hot colour and everyone switches over. Include in your gear chartreuse, red and black, yellow and green, orange and green and occasionally purple. Pick up ones that glow in the dark when charged with a flashlight and that have ultraviolet stripes. The bigger the hootchie, the better.

## Salmon

The only species intentionally targeted on the Bank is chinook, and they will be in the 100- to 130-foot range, visible on a good depthsounder. They are taken trolling, with big lures. In plugs, the 4- to 6-inch Tomics are the ones, such as the 500, 602, 158, 156 and 700. Use larger plugs when mackerel abound. For those who like plastics, use white or white and green hootchies.

Tomic's series of large spoons, the Roadrunners, are outstanding, including the pink over blue, Cop Car, Watermelon, 427 pattern, green and gold. They grab attention fished without a flasher, an added bonus for those who like unadorned fishing.

Don't bother with bait. It will not make it through the coho and if it makes

Tofino was the scene of a famous mass murder in 1811. After slighting the Indians during trade, the captain of the American vessel Tonquin and all but five of his men were murdered. The next day, the one injured man remaining aboard blew the boat, himself and boarding aboriginals into pieces of flesh and twisting bodies spread out on the calm waters, including a great store of blankets; these were rounded up by the natives and held in high esteem thereafter.

Tofino is also the home of one of the most unusual ports on the coast in that it is on a saltwater channel. Accordingly the tide smokes right on past the docks one way and when it changes, smokes right on by from the opposite direction. If boating, come into the docks with authority or you'll make an embarrassing mess of your boat and other boats.

Also on the continental shelf that stretches out some 25 miles (40 km) (not quite as far as in Ucluelet), Tofino has the same solid open Pacific fishing and is now the site of a well-known fly fishery for coho among the many channels and bays. Catface Bar is a classic mile-long (1.6 km) sand bar that comes within 12 feet of the surface and creates a vertical eddy on one or the other side depending on the tide direction, and traps the baitfish that attract the coho.

The Clayoquot Sound fishing arena has been designated a UNESCO Biosphere Reserve with 650,000 acres in the largest temperate rainforest left on earth. It's that large and that beautiful.

## Local Winter Hotspots

Like Ucluelet, Tofino faces the open ocean and winter fishing is limited by weather. Again this is a nursery area, so if you can get out, the fish will come. There are, however, inside waters where 7- to 15-pound winter feeders move in after bait (October to March), for example, Sydney Inlet near Hot Springs Cove. Both salmon and halibut follow and this presents a good fishery from December through May when the summer season comes once again. Troll 90- to 110-feet deep.

Note that, though not targeted, immature, 1- to 3-lb. (.5- to 1.4-kg) blueback coho call the coast home in January to March.

The inside waters of Clayoquot Sound present safe year round fisheries for the seasick-challenged among us. Local rivers such as the Bedwell, Megin, Moyeha, Clayoquot as well as Tranquil Creek all contribute chinook. Note that spot closures apply.

When weather permits, halibut fishing on the offshore banks proves successful 12 months of the year, with June to August being the prime period. Halibut move onto gradual dropoffs in the continental shelf 3- to 4-miles (4.8- to 6.4 km) off Portland and Rafael Points. 20- to 40-lb "chickens" form the basis of the fishery, with fish to 200 lbs. occasionally taken.

## Winter Lures

Troll anchovy or medium herring in glow teasers.

## Local Summer Hotspots

In the Tofino area, the continental shelf drops off gradually from land to 600 feet and fish tend to swim along the shelf lines or inhabit the various rock piles 1 ½- to 10-miles (2.4- to 16-km) out in the Pacific Ocean. It is not uncommon off Portland Point or Rafael Point to receive double headers of halibut and chinook at the same time in 140- to 160-feet of water. Like Ucluelet, La Perouse is the local bank with the Southwest Corner and South Bank consistent spots that boats from each area fish, and thus use some of the same gear.

Summer fishing begins in April with early chinook bound for the Fraser and Columbia Rivers. Weights average          The bulk of the summer fish are chinook from Robertson Creek, Conuma hatchery, Nitinat River and Clayoquot Sound's Kennedy River. These fish average 20- to 45-lbs (9.1- to 20.5 kg). Chinook fishing remains strong into September. Coho also run May to November in good weather years, the last fish being local ones.

Although millions go by, Fraser River sockeye and pink normally migrate great distances offshore and are not commonly encountered. Do note, however, that the local Kennedy Lake is home to sockeye that like to bite orange Gibbs spoons.

A recent El Nino induced change in baitfish species; long an area of needlefish and herring populations, now pilchards are increasing in numbers.

Although shaped like anchovy, pilchards are larger, like herring, and thus make extremely fishy cutplugs.

The surfline fisheries, not for the faint of heart, occur right on rocky points where the swell piles into the shore at Wilf Rock, Blunden Island, Bartlett Island, Kutcous Point, Glory Hole, Tree Island and other spots. July to September is the prime chinook period with coho fishing extending from May into November in some years at Kutcous Point, Chetarpe, Catface Bar and Wilf Rock.

Coho arrive early in Tofino, with good schools encountered as ravenous 5 pounders (2.3 kgs) in June. These commonly feed so heavily they grow a pound per week and by September reach the 12- to 15-lb (5.4- to 6.8-kg) range. Northern coho numbers strengthen in August and continue building through September. The Megin River and Tofino hatchery support good populations.

The most significant development in the past decade is the coho fly fishery developed by the Weigh West Resort. Don't worry if you can't cast. Often the least skilled angler has the best chance of catching a salmon. That's because they actually listen to the fish master tell them they can drop the fly to 30 feet beside the boat and hold it there to catch fish.

Early in the season, outside areas such as Catface, Tonquin Island, Wickanninish Island, Wilf Rock, Kutcous Point and Plover Reefs hold the migratory salmon rushing through to southern rivers. Inside areas, like Tsapee Narrows, Matleset Narrows, Indian Bay, Grice Bay and Tranquil Inlet, come into their own from August to the end of October. The vertical strip is often the most useful retrieve.

Many of the local rivers have good populations of sea-run cutthroat trout, to give fly guys another target, for example, Grice Bay close to the resort, and every trickle of freshwater in Clayoquot Sound.

## Summer Lures

For early chinook offshore from Portland or Raphael points, put your gear on the bottom, including anchovy or medium herring in a clear, chartreuse or Army Truck teaser, 4- to 8-feet behind a red Hotspot flasher. Fish large spoons. Cutpluging peaks in August.

Off Vargas Island in July, use gear when mackerel abound, for example, Octopus hootchies in Army Truck, chartreuse tractor-back or the locally-named "Tofino Dog Turd" a 6-inch brown squid on a 40-inch leader behind a Hotspot flasher.

Look at the Ucluelet chapter for plug and spoon numbers, including the best of the bunch, the 602. At Raffle and South West corner, use seven inch spoons, and pink mother of pearl plugs of 3- to 6-inches. Other spoons include

*Heading out into typical early-morning fog in Clayoquot Sound to fly-fish for coho salmon.*

the 4.5 inch, Devil's Tail and Gypsies in Silver Haze, Army Truck, glow white/glow purple, purple/gold, blue/silver, glow green/glow white and Glendon Stewart, Gibbs Gator spoons in Mud Pie and green/silver, as well as Krippled Ks in green and chrome and the frog pattern.

For halibut, add Mike's Glow Scent in Shrimp or Anchovy to hootchies, or try a fresh strip of salmon belly off a spreader bar and 2lbs weight (.9 kgs). Other baits include octopus, sardines and the 8-inch Berkley Power Grub. As this is not a snaggy bottom, use a large Spinnow for a weight rather than a 2-lb. (.9 kgs) ball.

Bring your favourite 8-weight fly rod and best anti-corrosion reel loaded with 200 yards of 25-pound backing line (11.4-kg). Bring both 325 grain and 425 grain sinking-tips and a Type 4 full sink line. For leaders, use 7 feet of mono, 8 pounds early in the season, rising to 12 pounds later. In June the four- to seven-pound (1.8- to 3.2-kg) coho feed on krill, so try small saltwater streamer patterns in orange, red or pink.

Weigh West has tested and perfected a whole series of flies: the Weigh Wester, Clouser Minnows (chartreuse is good all year), Monty's Zuma (pink, dark blue polar bear hair), Pearl Mickey (a variation on the standard Mickey Finn), Cat-face Streamer (chartreuse, dark green, red) Pink Streamer, Flashy Glow, a range of Deceivers, bucktails and streamers (in pink and chartreuse with silver bodies), etc. on quality saltwater hooks. For traditionalists, try pink bucktails, then, later, 7-inch Coronation and Grey Ghost patterns in polar bear hair. You will find these easier to cast on a Type 3 full sink line than a floating/tip combination, because a full sink line has so much weight, the fly does not result in hinging.

For drift-jig fishers: Magic Lures in green and white for both chinook and halibut, also Point Wilson Darts, Dungeness Stingers and Gibbs Minnows.

In November strong local chum runs return.

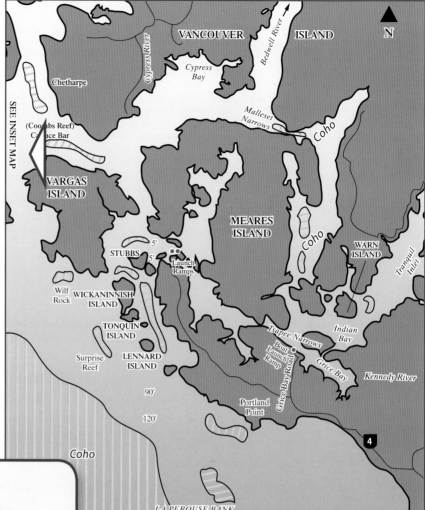

Grice Bay Road, 9 miles east of Highway 4. Need higher water as the entire bay can be a mudflat. Lots of sea-run cutthroat trout for fly fishers.

**Tackle Shops:** Weigh West Marine Adventure Resort, a Day's Inn on your right hand side on the way into town. You can't miss it. They have the genuine article in Clayoquot flies, being the folks who developed them.

Jay's Fly and Tackle, Box 652, 564 Campbell St., Tofino, B.C., V0R 2Z0; Toll free: 1-888-534-7422; Website: tofinofishing.com; Email: jay@tofinofishing.com.

**Access:** By car, a 4.5 hour drive from Victoria 190 miles (316 km), north on Highway 1 that becomes Highway 19 and then turn west on Highway 4, through Port Alberni and to the twisty mountainous section before the road drops to the Pacific Ocean level. Turn right at the T-junction for the half hour drive to Tofino.

Air flights from Vancouver or Seattle, via Atleo Air; Toll free: 1-866-662-8536; Website: www.atleoair.coml; Email: atleoair@alberni.net.

**Information:** Chamber of Commerce: Phone: 1-250-725-3414; Website: www.island.net/~tofino; Email: tofino@island.net.

**Accommodation:** Weigh West Marine Adventures Resort, PO Box, 634 Campbell St., Tofino, BC, V0R 2Z0; Toll Free: 1-800-665-8922; Website: weighwest.com; Email: info@weighwest.com. Visit their website for some truly outstanding prices on a range of activities.

Wickaninnish Inn and Pointe Restaurant near Chesterman Beach are considered among the finest accommodation and cuisine offered in pristine wilderness in the world.

See the Chamber of Commerce website.

**Launching Ramps:** Fourth St. Wharf, most commonly used launch and moorage, $10 per launch; Phone Tofino Harbour Authority: 1-250-725-4441. The Whiskey Dock, left of First St., free, used for kayaks and dinghies.

Ucluelet means "people with a safe harbour" in the local First Nation language and the town does indeed have a long safe harbour, something that is very useful because Amphritite Point, at the harbour mouth, takes the full force of ocean storms coming across the Pacific Ocean.

Ucluelet has the best "year-round" salmon fishing on Vancouver Island because it is a local nursery spot for maturing salmon. There are winter feeder chinook here 12 months of the year—the fish come but don't leave for years until nature pulls them home—and successive runs of summer chinook, the first being those passing in February for Springer rivers in Oregon, in May for California rivers, then Oregon, Washington and inside B.C. rivers all summer long, including Robertson Creek and, Nitinat hatchery chinook.

The banks stretch out more than 30 miles (48 km) before dropping from the relatively shallow continental shelf of 300 feet to the deep Pacific some 6000 feet farther down. The banks with their abundant bait supplies positively influence local fishing to such a point that the seasonal halibut (May to August) are taken as incidental catches while trolling "in the mud" for chinook. And from Tofino 30 miles (48 km) north of Ucluelet all the way around another 30 miles (48 km) to Swiftsure Bank (south east of Bamfield), is an enormous territory of relatively shallow bottom.

The Big Bank is a fall staging area for salmon of all five species. So loaded are Ucluelet's banks that in the time before coho and chinook were "reserved" for sport fishermen, commercial trollers—as in hook and line fisheries for coho and chinook—fished these waters for decades. In other words, this is prime time stuff.

Do not head out onto the ocean without a sound boat filled with safety electronics including, depth sounder, GPS Chart Plotter, radar, VHF, cell phone and a satellite phone when beyond cells. Add the humble compass and radar reflector. The foggy days of summer and fall feature ocean freighters crossing the fishing grounds for the shipping lanes of the 70 mile (112 km) across mouth of Juan de Fuca Strait, the USA point of which is Cape Flattery.

## Local Winter Hotspots

On winter days some adventurous souls move out to fish the banks on the Pacific. Most fish the various rocks that stretch southwest from Amphritite Point to the Starlight Rocks as they provide fair protection. On poor weather days, Barkley Sound with its dozens of wave-blocking islands is out this harbour's back door.

"Springer's," as Washington and Oregon state early chinook are known, go by in February and March, a time when most salmon fishermen are just dreaming about getting out on the water.

## Winter Lures

If you can get out to fish, go with the summer bait rig described below. Half glow/half green Coyote spoons 4 to 6 feet behind a flasher work, too. Irish mist and vermiculated greenish squirts work on most days.

## Local Summer Hotspots

Typically May is the most distant fishing, the Stinky Hole, named for halibut that without doubt have lousy breath. As the season progresses, the boats fish banks closer to port and end up in August right on the rocks for West Coast Van Isle chinook.

Local currents and channels formed by tidal flow veering off bottom structure, concentrate bait and thus chinook that relentlessly move after their meals. So filled with feed are these waters that a goodly portion of coho stocks stay close to Vancouver Island rather than migrate out into the north Pacific.

Named for a container's load of grapefruit lost off a freighter, Grapefruit Bay (Florencia Bay) is one that locals rave about. This June fishery, results from squid coming into the shallow waters to spawn. Big springs mosey in to get a good feed. Only 12 feet deep, the bay fosters great long horizontal runs and that spells fun. By August and September, the surfline is where the boats head for along Wya Point for Van Isle fish that are passing a stone's throw from shore. In August, grind those ledges and pinnacles, keep your depthsounder pointed forward so you see the bottom before your downrigger balls connect.

Another fishing pattern is to take a compass heading of 227 degrees from the harbour mouth 11- to 13-miles (17.6- to 20.8-km), and 45 minutes, to Southwest Corner. Chinook are usually in the 70- to 130-foot levels, but they can be right on the bottom 250 feet down.

Another late August pattern is to move 20 miles (32 km) off shore to GPS Marks in 300 feet of water and put down whole herring in teaser heads on spreader bars. Once you limit out you head back to Wya Point, Florencia Bay, Little Beach and grind the rocks with whole herring or anchovy 5 feet behind a flasher. Set a tight roll and fish the 35- to 45-foot level. Add Crow and Forbes islands in September,

Consider later in the season as well. In late August and for most of September, the Wreck and other shelf spots like the Rat's Nose, just like Swiftsure Bank, to the south east, can be filled with so many completely turned-on coho, it is hard to believe. This is corn cob pipe fishing, as I call it, because if you throw one out a coho would bite it. If McArthur won't let go, toss him out too. Turn in a circle and see fish jumping as far as the eye can see. The coho fishing is simply berserk and you fly guys bring along an eight-weight floating or Type 4 full sinkand big ugly flies, including poppers, that get engulfed in a gang. Or go light and use only a floating line – you'll be a believer when you do it.

*Darrick Dietrich and a handsome coho salmon taken on the fly in the open ocean.*

## Summer Lures

Due to the unpressured nature of the open ocean fishery, fishing tackle can be rigs of simplicity. In the bait department, utilize 7-inch herring in a Rhys Davis Super Herring Teaserhead or the Anchovy Special in clear, chrome or blue. One barb of a large 4/0 to 5/0 treble rigged on a 48" (or longer) leader inserts high on the dorsal flank, above the lateral line and behind the dorsal fin. The real tip is to extend the treble hook in a straight line from the fin on the teaserhead.

If you wish to fish "clean," the slightly iridescent 602 Tomic plug should be in your tackle box beside the 158. To save these expensive lures in break offs, pull the pins, string your mainline through the hole and attach to a gang of two trebles or a single treble behind a few 4-mm spacer beads. If the line breaks, the plug will float to the surface for retrieval.

Also add the 700 Tubby Tyee, and 432 Tomic plugs and fish about 40 feet at Wya Point, steering in and out of nooks and crannies along the surfline in depths of 60- to 80-feet. Other Tomic Plugs to consider are the: 111, 109, the always brilliant 602, 232(a good coho plug) and 700. Place them as much as 40 feet behind the release clip to give a wider range of action and to present the lure to more fish. Add the 49 and 722, 7-inch plugs in September.

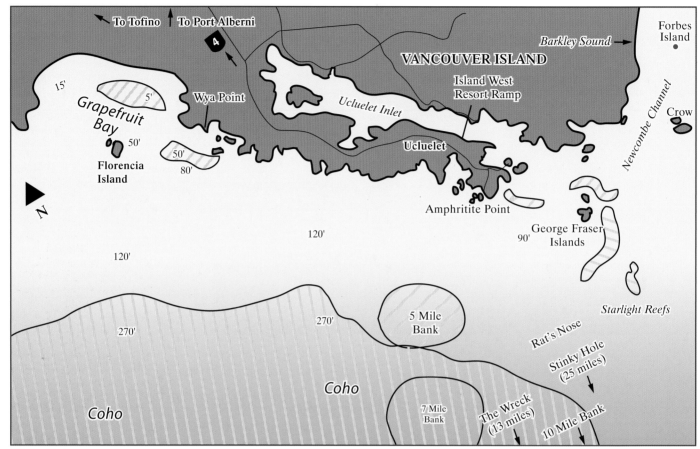

## Ucluelet

Hotspot Flasher colours in: 037, 181, 185, 481, 485, 956.

The Green Ghost and Coyote spoon have taken Ucluelet by storm. Make sure you have a few of these must-have lures from either Radiant or Luhr Jensen. Purchase the half green/half silver or half green/half glow. Utilize a 5 ½- to 6-foot leader, particularly on days when action slows down. Traditionalists use the long-time commercial spoons in half brass or half blue and half silver. But those new Tomic Roadrunners are big and fishy. Try the 203, 212,602, 512, and 700 (same colours as plugs)

In the plastic department, try from May on, a vermiculated blue-frog squirt, a Glow Below hootchie and any hootchie with a black stripe, the Purple Haze, for instance.

One final tip for halibut concerns Berkley Powerbaits. These squishy, scented plastic treats may be your best bet. They don't shred up like bait and last through fish after fish. In fact, if the halibut sucks them right off the hook, you can retrieve them for further use back at the dock during filleting. An octopus tentacle adds a tough natural bait to Extra Large Herring.

**Launching Ramps:** Island West Resort has a good ramp and owns another right next door. Stop in for advice and GPS marks as the whole La Perouse or Big Bank (along with South Bank, Stinky Hole, Seven Mile Bank, Ten Mile Bank, The Wreck, and Wya Point) and so on are on the chart hanging on the wall. There is a good fuel dock, Eagle Marine, 1-250-726-4262 five minutes from the launch ramp on your way out of the harbour.

**Tackle Shops:** Island West Resort, has an assortment of good basic tackle.

**Access:** Ucluelet is a 4.5 hour drive from Victoria. Drive north on Highway 1 that becomes Highway 19. Turn west onto Highway 4 that passes through Port Alberni and then becomes a twisty mountainous paved road before dropping to the Pacific shore. At the T junction turn left for the 10 minute drive to Ucluelet. Turn right at the T junction and the rolling highway brings you to Tofino in 30 minutes.

Alternatively, skip the long drive from Victoria (two hours from Nanaimo) and take a flight from Vancouver, BC or Renton WA. Connect with **Western Airlines** from the Vancouver Airport at an unbeatable $99 as we went to press and be dropped off on the Island West Resorts floats.

Westcoast Wild Adventures, drops visitors on the Island West Resort floats, and can be booked through the resort

**Information:** Ucluelet Chamber of Commerce, Phone: 1-250-726-4641; Website: www.uclueletinfo.com.
Fisheries and Oceans Canada, Tofino: 1-250-725-3468.

**Accommodation:** Island West Resort, a full service operation that has RV parking, Motel units and corporate buildings, along with a marine pub, laundry and on-site store, guides in Searay boats 24- to 30-feet long and has moorage for boats up to 50 feet. Phone: 1-250-726-7515; email: fish@island-westresort.com; Website: www.islandwestresort.com.

Canadian Princess, next door to Island West. Has on-ship or on-land accommodation and takes its fishing guests out in its fleet of 43 foot party boats, each taking upwards of 15 people and drift jigging for salmon and halibut. Its package prices are hard to beat, anywhere. Ask them about fly-in prices. Oak Bay Marine Group, 1327 Beach Drive, Victoria B.C. V8S 2N4; Phone: 1-800-663-7090; Email: info@obmg.com; Website: www.obmg.com.

**Guides:** Bill von Brendel, 3474 Hammond Bay Road, Nanaimo, B.C., V9T 1E6; Toll Free: Ph: 1-1-877-334-7466; Email: info@justfishn.com; Website: www.justfishn.com.

Salmon Eye Fishing Charters, Sam Vandervalk; Phone: 1-877-777-4344; Email: info@salmoneye.net; Website: www.salmoneye.net.

Island West Resort.

Canadian Princess.

On the southern tip of Vancouver Island, Victoria is the capital city of British Columbia. Known for its British architecture with the Empress Hotel, Provincial Parliament Buildings and quayside docks in the centre of town, Victoria consistently rates in the top five North America destination cities.

The waters lying between the south end of the Trial Islands on the eastern border with the city of Oak Bay, and Race Rocks, some 18 miles (28.8 km) to the west, comprises the Victoria Waterfront.

This area is primarily a November to March fishery for winter feeder spring salmon of 5- to 15–pounds (2.3- to 6.8-kgs), with the occasional plus 20-pound (9.1-kg) chinook, and secondarily a summer fishery, June to October, for fish intending on spawning in Georgia Strait, for example, the Fraser River near Vancouver.

## Local Winter Hotspots

Winter feeder chinook reside close to the bottom and are constantly feeding (not just at tide changes, sunrises and sunsets). Knowing this is the key to catching them. These are relentlessly structure conscious fish and all fishing is done either close to or on the bottom or deep on downriggers in deeper water. This is a nursery area for two and three year old Strait of Georgia and Puget Sound chinook before they move out to the open Pacific Ocean.

Follow the 110- to 120-foot bottom contour one downrigger ball bottom-bumping, i.e., sliding across the sand or mud bottom— and the other or others set within 10 feet of bottom. As the fish are simply staying in contact with lunch you are searching for needle-fish clouds close to the bottom or suspended schools of herring.

As you are searching for fish that are not migrating toward spawning, troll with the tide to cover more territory, thus increasing your chances of coming in contact with them. Once you find the school, circle the spot. Do remember that flood and ebb tides tend to blow fish along like wind does a cloud. And, of course, winter fish will take a faster trolled lure than summer chinook.

While most anglers would only fish part of the Victoria Waterfront, which is about 30 miles (48 km) long, here are all the hotspots starting from Trial Island on the eastern end. Its southern tip has a strong tide rip and concentrates the fish 120 feet down. Five hundred yards west lies a good rock. You don't want your balls—downrigger balls—on the bottom crossing this baby that rises to about 85 feet. This concentrates salmon on a flood tide.

The rest of the wide flat shelf of bottom across the Ross Bay Cemetery to Clover Point has little structure, because it is flat mud or sand. Salmon are picked up "scratching" as they say for fish that are not associated with good structure. Fish this on a flood tide.

Clover Point is another hotspot, with Victoria's outfall passing south for half a mile. Watch this obstacle; although good structure, it rips off downrigger balls from the unsuspecting. On a flood tide, curve into the 85 foot east side and then cross the Point at 110 feet, following that contour.

*Scotty with two typical winter springs taken near Trial Island.*

Off the Flagpole, a very visible land feature in Beacon Hill Park, is a mud reef that extends out for three quarters of a mile and the fish are often on the lee side of the tide. Passing further west you will encounter two very rocky bumps that you must be sharp to keep your downrigger balls near bottom but off them. Then there is a bit of a gap and then the Brotchie Ledge reef moves out for about 500 yards from the concrete marker. Both sides can give up fish but due to the number of boats, take care to keep your eyes on your downriggers.

Past Brotchie Ledge the bottom is again mud and about 115 feet deep and shallows to 85 on the run into the end of the Ogden Point Breakwater where shore anglers use Buzz Bombs and other heavy lures to cast out—and they do catch some salmon. This bank of mud drops off at about 120 feet on your left as you troll into the opening of the Inner Harbour. Follow this contour until it turns west at McCauley Point, past the Esquimalt Anglers launching ramp to Saxe Point where once again a mud shelf lies at about the 85 foot level. Fish the edge of the ledge, continuing west and the remaining waterfront structure at the Gravel Pit, Albert Head and finally William Head, the penitentiary also known as Club Fed, by jealous locals.

There is another winter trolling pattern that gives up lots of fish. If you don't want to keep watching your downrigger balls to keep them from getting stuck, you may move into 180- to 200-feet of water with your cannon balls set at 140 feet. You will catch fewer fish, but some days the deeper waters are better, particularly in the "pool" in front of the harbour entrance where the herring stage in 200 to 230 feet of water—in February. Fish this one after big tides push fish off shore.

The other local structure of note is Constance Bank 6 miles (10 km) south of Clover Point. The bottom rises from about 300 feet to as little as 60 feet across an area of perhaps four football fields. While some fish are taken by trolling directly across the shallows, most are taken by trolling the edges where the Bank drops from about 100 feet to 300 feet. On the north west end is a ledge of 140 feet. Fish this area on the ebb because the tide rounds up the chinook and deposits them in this verti-cal eddy as the tide progresses.

Constance Bank is usually a better bet than fishing the shores of Victoria, in both summer and winter. It is also the best halibut fishing on the Waterfront, using a large herring on a spreader bar, with 2 lbs. (.9-kgs) of weight. You anchor on the north west top edge of the bank and fish the 140 foot table on the ebb. Alternatively, you put down two spreader bars and float with the tide in areas of 200- to 280-feet deep.

## Winter Lures

There is a herring spawn in February and March in the inner waters of Victoria Harbour and these baitfish stop in the deep water off the water front—200- to 230-feet—and attract chinook like magnets for two months. Larger bait, usually 5- to 6-inch anchovy is the primary bait, rigged up in glow in the dark, glow green, glow 602 or Purple Chrome Scale Rhys Davis teaser heads rigged with a wire. Use 4- to 6-feet of 25-pound (11.4-kg) leader ahead of a glow in the dark flasher of green, red, Purple Haze or Army Truck hue.

For plastic baits, hootchies rule here, because the bait is larger, rather than the smaller squirts. Good colours, on a 34- to 42-inch leader include the Purple Haze, Jelly Fish, Army Truck. Mint Tulip, Irish Mist and Glow Below. In spoons, use the Purple Haze, green/glow, Army Truck, Mongoose and Cop Car colours in Coyote or Devil's Tail lines. While spoons can be used 42 inches behind a flasher, the clear waters of winter allow for running a spoon on its own.

Lures need be no more than 12 feet behind downrigger release clips in winter, presumably because you are fishing a greater distance from the sound of the engine.

## Local Summer Hotspots

Most of the five species of salmon do not come in close to the Waterfront shores with most taking a direct bead from Race Rocks to the south end of the American San Juan islands about 25 miles (40 km) east. However, the summer chinook that pass through, do so almost directly on shore. As all migrating chinook do, these 20- to 50-pounders (9.1- to 22.7-kgs) move forward on the flood tide and stop on the ebb in local backeddies behind land structure. They can be in as little as 35 feet of water. You have better fishing before the tide starts to flood, when the chinook are gone in an instant, during the late May to early September summer period.

McNeill Bay has a 60 foot trench about 800 yards long and with your lure, bait is best, you troll at 25 feet. Gonzales Bay has a very small back eddy right up on the shore of the Chinese Cemetery of perhaps 35 feet deep, here your downrigger balls are down a mere 15 feet.

The west side of Clover Point is perhaps the best spot for the big spawners on a summer ebb because over the roughly six hour period, all the chinook

from the Ogden Point Breakwater, three miles (5 km) away, will mosey up to the point and simply stop in 80 feet of water.

Coho and pink salmon are taken in the top 85 feet of water near the Quarantine Buoy a very visible bright yellow marker some four miles (7 km) south of the breakwater. It serves as a visual reference only to keep you in an area when the tide is moving you along smartly. Every second year on the odd year, as many as 30,000,000 pink salmon for the Fraser River will move through from July 15 to September 15, with August being the peak month, particularly an afternoon flood tide as staging schools are moved east by the tide. This includes sockeye which intermingle with the other species. Strangely, few chum are taken here, though millions pass by.

Put down your gear and troll smartly, looking for tide lines that concentrate bait and thus salmon. High speed allows you to cover more territory in a set period of time and thus you come in contact with more fish. Coho want a fast lure and most pink and sockeye will also speed up.

## Summer Lures

For the big brute chinook, place anchovy 6 feet behind a Pal No. 3 dodger or a simple red Hotspot flasher. For pink, coho and sockeye, any plankton squirt, squirt or hootchie in red or pink can be the hot lure on a day to day basis. Make sure to have two of each, in case you lose one. Colours include Mint Tulip, Army Truck, pink with silver sprinkles, Bubblegum, day-glo orange—rip out a few fronds for sockeye. Note that you troll slowly along shore for summer chinook, but fast for the other species in offshore waters, including the few miles (kilometres) from Race Rocks east.

Lures less than 50 feet down should be as much as 25 feet behind their release clips. In recent years, the summer salmon species have been as deep as 90 feet.

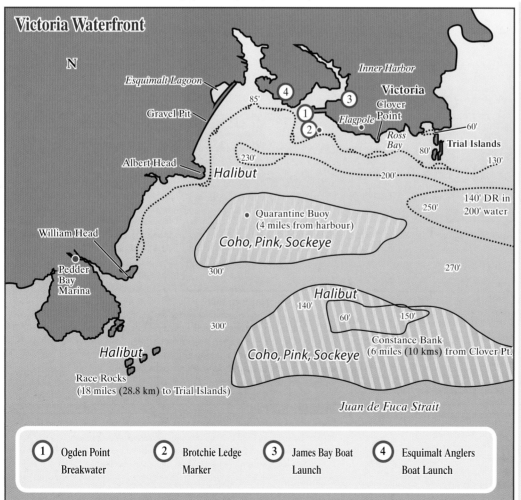

**Victoria Waterfront**

N

Esquimalt Lagoon

Gravel Pit

Albert Head

Halibut

William Head

Pedder Bay Marina

Halibut

Race Rocks
(18 miles (28.8 km) to Trial Islands)

230'

85'

Halibut

4

1

2

Flagpole

Inner Harbor

Victoria

Clover Point

Ross Bay

3

60'

80'

Trial Islands

130'

200'

250'

140' DR in 200' water

270'

Quarantine Buoy
(4 miles from harbour)

Coho, Pink, Sockeye

300'

Halibut

140'

60'

150'

Constance Bank
(6 miles (10 kms) from Clover Pt.

Coho, Pink, Sockeye

300'

Juan de Fuca Strait

1 Ogden Point Breakwater

2 Brotchie Ledge Marker

3 James Bay Boat Launch

4 Esquimalt Anglers Boat Launch

**Launching ramps:** James Bay Anglers Association,75 Dallas Road, 1-250-389-6123.

Esquimalt Anglers Association, 1101 Munro St.,1-250-385-9604.

Pedder Bay Marina, 925 Pedder Bay Road, 1-250-478-1771. (Also boat rental).

**Tackle shops:** Island Outfitters, 3319 Douglas St., 1-250-475-4969, Website: fishingvictoria.com.
Robinson's, 1307 Broad St., 385-3429; Website: robinsonsoutdoors.com.

**Access to Victoria:** Port Angeles Ferry to downtown Victoria
Anacortes Ferry to Sidney, 22 miles (35.2 km) north to Victoria
B.C. Ferry from Tswwassen to Swartz Bay, 28 miles (44.8 kms) north of Victoria
Victoria International Airport, 20 miles (32 km) north to Victoria. Car rental and shuttle bus at airport.

**Information:** Tourism Victoria, 812 Wharf St., 1-250-953-2033, Their website: tourismvictoria.com has a full list of accommodation. Chamber of Commerce, Phone: 1-250-383-7191; Website: chamber@ gvcc.org

**Accommodation:** For premium rooms check out The Ocean Pointe Resort, The Empress Hotel, and The Laurel Point Inn, all on the Inner Harbour. For inexpensive rooms check Traveller's Inn.

# Freshwater Introduction

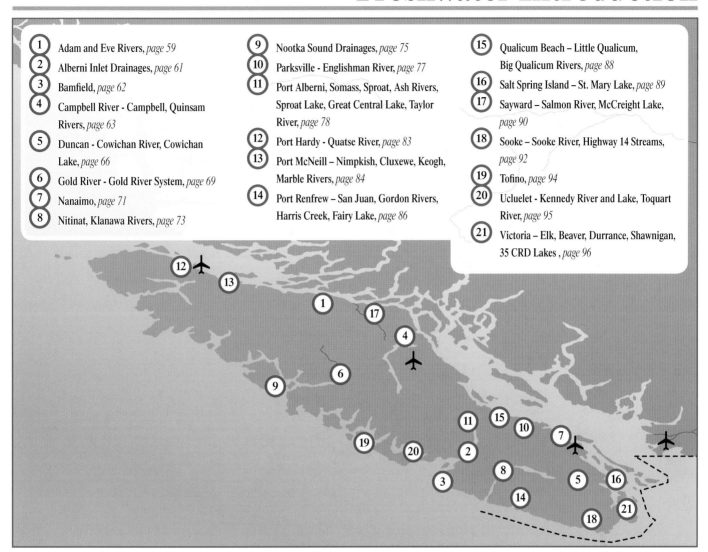

With thousands of lakes and 123 watersheds, Vancouver Island has more freshwater fishing than you can try out in a lifetime. There are hundreds of roadside lakes, most are near roads, many have free, lakeside campsites, and receive stockings from the Freshwater Fisheries Society of British Columbia. Each year about a million cutthroat, sea-run cutthroat, rainbow trout and other species are planted in easy to get to locations for campers and tourists. Other hatcheries enhance winter and summer steelhead and all five species of salmon in rivers.

When planning a trip to Vancouver Island, make sure to look at the freshwater stocking plans by visiting: gofishbc.com. Many lakes receive as many as a half dozen stockings per year from April to October, comprising as many as 30,000 trout over the fishing season. By looking at each year's stocking plans, you can plan your trip to arrive at lakes, and some rivers, within days of the fish being put in the lake, and thus expect good fishing and some nice dinners to have with your family.

Along with stocked fish, island rivers and lakes have other finny quarries, including Dolly Varden char, sea-run cutthroat trout, river-run and sea-run brown trout, bass, pumpkin seeds and yellow perch. Anglers who have been bitten by the steelhead bug will find some strong reasons to fish Vancouver Island rivers. For further information on summer and winter steelhead enhancement efforts on Georgia Strait waters, visit: http://www.bccf.com/steelhead/focus2.htm.

Vancouver Island has only a few paved highways, but is well-serviced by roads used for logging purposes. These are primarily gravel-based and can be dusty, muddy or rutty at times. Keep this in mind, particularly if you are towing something. The rivers and lakes in this book that are accessed by gravel logging roads usually lie very close to or right beside the road. Logging trucks have the right of way on logging roads. On approaching a logging truck, vehicles pull over to the side and stop to let them pass. Headlights must be used at all times.

The maps and text included in this book list the highways, major roads and some logging roads needed to get to rivers and lakes for fishing. There are, additionally, thousands of logging tracks that will not take you where you want to go. You should not venture down other roads until you are familiar with the major gravel roads in the area you will be visiting. On the route to the Adam and Eve river confluence, for example, on the South Main, there are almost twenty side roads that don't take you where you want to go.

Many island rivers have difficult access areas, even ones with easier sections closer to roads. The entire island is mountainous and thus rivers can and do have canyons, falls and other significant access issues. Some are water and helicopter access only. Do not attempt to find your own way in and out, except on well-developed trails, as forested areas can be very confusing. Go only with a local, knowledgeable person. Visit Catchsalmonbc.com and I can set you up with someone who is fishy and knowledgeable.

## Reading Tips

The freshwater sections of this book are a little different from the saltwater sections. Lakes and rivers, along with tackle and access are provided in this part of the book. For items like Chamber of Commerce listings, accommodation, tackle shops, etc. take a look under the saltwater write-ups as these are the same for an area's salt- and fresh-water fishing.

If there are other lakes and rivers that you want information on, drop a line to Catchsalmonbc.com or Amato Publications, as we will be updating with new editions from time to time.

## Crossing the Border

Since 9/11, you can expect greater security at borders and in airports and the Washington/B.C vehicle line ups can get long on special weekends. Canadian laws prohibit unregistered guns. Don't "fib" for if you get caught, they take the gun, fine you and can make you buy the gun back.

## Regulations and Licence Requirements

This book gives you the information you need to find and catch fish. As regulations change from time to time you need to refer to them to make sure that during the time of your trip the waters you intend to fish, are, for example, open for fishing, or allow the gear you wish to use, have retention limits and the other requirements for your trip.

You need a provincial licence to fish rivers and lakes. Typically, you buy a non-resident alien licence for short term—$20 to $50—or $80 for one year. Added to this are a mandatory steelhead tag of $60 if you intend to fish for steelhead. If you intend to retain salmon, a salmon tag of $30 is required. Add 7% Goods and Services Tax to the total.

The provincial website for freshwater licence matters is: www.env.gov. bc.ca/fw. Click on Fishing at the top of the page, and then on Licence Vendor Search, to buy a licence. In addition, a copy of the Freshwater Fishing Regulations Synopsis, available at most tackle shops, is the source for seasonal closures, gear restrictions and other matters to which you need to pay close attention. Do remember that in-season changes are made, even though they may not be in the Synopsis. This is particularly true of freshwater salmon openings and closings that are regulated by the federal government. See: http://www.pac. dfo-mpo.gc.ca/recfish/Freshwater/region1_e.htm.

## River Heights

The site for river heights in British Columbia contains very valuable information, particularly when there has been a lot of rain or snow melt into the river you want to fish. High rivers make for tough conditions. The site: http://scitech. pyr.ec.gc.ca/waterweb/formnav.asp?lang=0.

## Lake Diagrams

Lake diagrams for selected, stocked Vancouver Island lakes are included in this book. The 16 foot (five m) contour has been sketched in for your reference. The reason for its inclusion is that it is roughly the depth at which most vegetation stops growing from lack of sunlight, and corresponds in most lakes as the point where the bottom drops away into deeper, darker water. Most trout and related species spend most of their time in the top layer of the water, and in summer tend to cruise along at the level where plant growth stops, making detours into the shallows for feeding, particularly on insects in the cooler parts of the day. If you are a keener for detail, you can find out all the contours you want for hundreds of lakes on Vancouver Island, to help zero in on fish-holding habitat. The site for bathymetric charts for B.C. lakes is: http://srmapps.gov.bc.ca/apps/fidq/bath_images/pdf/00108401.pdf.

## Lake Fishing

Vancouver Island has lake fishing that most people from most any other place would like to have every day of the year. That is because more than 95% of local lakes do not freeze over in the winter. In fact, virtually all of them will not only offer up some trout every day of the year, but they have insect hatches everyday of the year, too.

When a lake remains unfrozen, it does not experience to the same degree the winter oxygen depletion and increased concentration of products of decomposition, ice-off and turn over events that ice-bound bodies of water undergo. In winter, while bass and related species tend to suspend over deep structure (usually 15 to 25 feet—6 to 15 m—deep), many trout and related species will continue on circling deep water looking for food.

Yes, there are lakes at different altitudes that turn on in the spring in sequential timing, allowing the angler to time the early bite akin to that after ice-off. But the three important things to remember about Vancouver Island lake fishing in the March to November holiday period are: insect eating trout bite in the shallows of lakes in the warming months of March, April and into

May, when big drone, flying ant hatches spur a feeding frenzy and in the fall when water temperature is declining in September, October and November; bass have their strongest bite in the summer period when trout are less active; and trout in lakes that eat mostly fry grow larger than their cousins in other lakes and spend little time in shallow water.

The annual pattern of lake seasons usually begins with ice-off, a time when the temperature of the lake from top to bottom, and thus density, is pretty uniform. The week after ice-off, trout feed massively after the winter doldrums. Then the turn-over phenomenon occurs. Wind blows surface layers aside allowing bottom water with its lower oxygen and higher levels of decomposition chemicals to rise to the surface and the lake contents mix; this is true to a lesser extent in lakes that don't freeze—they have been mixing all winter, too. In this period, trout go off their new feeding pattern and the lake looks cloudy.

Once the turbidity has settled down in a lake, the summer pattern establishes itself. Surface layers begin to warm, plant growth is stimulated by longer sunlight periods and hatches are cued by water temperature. Trout move into the shallows after the greater bounty. By the time summer has arrived, the lake has taken on its typical stratification: warmer surface waters to about 16 feet (five m) are warmer and less dense; then there is a middle layer of about six feet (two m) where temperature drops and this water is denser; the density difference is so great that the zone between the middle and bottom layers will actually float minor debris and marks the beginning of the much colder and denser bottom layer, which also has less oxygen.

Fish don't like to reside in the bottom layer of a summer lake and tend to not go deeper than the zone where the temperature drop is greatest; this is called the thermocline. What this useful concept tells a fisherman, and you can read the zone on a decent depthsounder, is that as much as 90% of the water in a lake can be ruled out for fishing: all the water beneath the thermocline, that lies usually somewhere between 30 and 50 feet (18.4 m and 30.6 m), will contain no fish. Knowing this makes it much easier to find fish.

Once summer temperatures are at their highest, trout spend time just above the thermocline and where the vegetation and thus insects peters out. They make forays into shallow water in the evening, remaining there all night and into the morning before seeking cooler more oxygen-rich water below. The rainbow and cutthroat trout, as well as the vast majority of stocked and native fish in Vancouver Island lakes, exhibit this pattern.

Bass do not follow the usual trout pattern. This makes for continued great fishing, for once insect eating trout move to deeper water, bass take up their places, usually in water less than five feet (1.3 m) deep, next to structure such as lily pads, and hold there waiting for hapless prey to plop into the water. So you are fishing very shallow water, indeed. In the hottest weather even bass will sometimes move off shallow water, and they are found suspended over structure (see your depthsounder) in 15- to 20-feet (five- to nine-m) looking for deeper running lures.

Trout that feed on fry—stickleback, sockeye, kokanee and salmon fry—also stick close to their dinners. In many lakes the most predominant feed is kokanee and sockeye fry. These species feed on plankton that grows in calm waters that receive the most sunlight. That means that the fish are usually found in deeper water cycling deeper and shallower in the day through night progression—that is, don't fish for them in shallow water. Both brown trout and large cutthroat trout feed almost exclusively on fry and small fish. That is why big flies like large Black Woolly Buggers and minnow patterns work well and why the thermocline and creek mouths (where salmon fry come from) become good places to troll for deep trout. Local rainbows grow larger where there are kokanee, too, though calcium-rich lakes with abundant shrimp also grow larger rainbows.

In the fall as temperatures cool, insect eating trout come back into the cooling, shallower waters and bass slowly move out to the deep structure they will inhabit for the winter. And the trout fatten up for the less well-endowed months of the winter. But, in well-stocked lakes, a surprising number of them will spend time in shallower waters all winter where, as noted, small hatches occur in the warmer middle part of the day. Put on your toque—a north of the border word for a shapeless, wool hat. Yes, they do look goofy, but they keep you warm—and get out there and continue catching the fish. In fact you can come to Vancouver Island 12 months of the year and fish for freshwater game fish 365 days of the year and the extra day in leap years.

# Adam and Eve Rivers

*Angler fishes for pink salmon in the Adam and Eve rivers estuary.*

The Adam and Eve rivers are seldom fished. Like most secluded rivers on Vancouver Island, the rivers have a diverse population of fish, both summer and winter steelhead, searun cutthroat- and brown-trout, Dolly Varden Char and a few residualized rainbow trout. Note that the presence of Dolly Varden is usually a sign that a river is seldom fished.

These are spectacularly beautiful little rivers in deep gorges that look like they were man made for a Hollywood movies, along with one waterfall that happens so quickly you only catch it out of the corner of your eye. Oddly, it falls at right angles to the road, then turns abruptly to flow under the bridge.

The Eve is the predominant steelhead spawning river, both summer and winter. Do note that the numbers of steelhead are not large and it has to be conceded that more experienced anglers will be more successful—and above the anadromous fish barrier, the Adam is artificial fly only. The barrier also means that the salmon predominate in the Eve River. And, because this system has all five species of salmon, it is one of the island's more diverse rivers. There is a good, free campsite at the major pool where the Eve and Adam join.

Think July through November for salmon. During the summer months, pink, sockeye and chinook salmon come back. For vacationers, who may want to be home after the Labour Day weekend, note that it is some time later that the coho and chum salmon return.

Brown trout devotees will find these fish above the barrier on the Adam River, and below, there is a population of sea-run browns, a very rare occurrence on the Island.

The Fisheries Society has put fertilizer briquettes in these rivers to stimulate the food chain.

Brown trout are the big cannibals in the crowd and so bigger is better in the lure and fly department. Large black Woolly Buggers are as complex as you need for them. Do consider that the other species will also take these patterns, and mix yellow, black, red, olive, wine, purple, pink, orange, chartreuse marabou along with black glo-brite chenille and schlappen for cutthroat and rainbows. Wriggly-legged nymphs are good back ups. Add simple Spey flies with a flowing mallard hackle.

Gear guys going after sea-run browns use the black with yellow dots Panther Martin spinner, and red Bolo spinners. Do remember that they tend to stay put by logs and under branches, where they are hard to reach, but where you will find them again and again—those caught and released, of course. For pink salmon use the Roostertail spinner in pink, along with pink marabou jigs. Try the mouth of the Eve River for pink salmon in July and August.

As the salmon come home, do run wool below a float, or simply with some split shot on the line. This is the number one chinook gear, as these big beautiful fish have no discrimination for class, though they have large preference for brighter colours in late summer.

Because salmon flesh becomes the number one food item as carcasses come apart, the brighter colours of late summer give way to the more neutral cream, peach, light pink and off-white bunny. Fly guys get into tying flesh flies and dead drifting them. Try using less bright colours, because you are imitating flesh that has decomposed and it is usually an off-white, light orange combination. In addition give a try, for a darker fly that is a Stamp River (near Port Alberni) sleeper: black tail, 3 wraps of bright orange, and dark brown over top, finished with bead chain eyes.

## Estuary Fishing

The estuary is a fabulous place to fish for salmon, down by the log sort. It is a wide gravel area in a classic example of a saltwater marsh and super for fishing for pinks and coho. It has a great bar at the ocean, a half mile down from where you encounter the estuary. You may find 20 people fishing there some days, with thousands of pink salmon crossing the six-inch-deep bar into a lovely slot 400 yards long. They will come in all day long, but most will move forward, and be very interested in biting, with the tidal push. As this is a saltwater area, gear can be used. Cast those good quality Gibbs spoons for springs. You may be entertained by killer whales chasing the salmon up onto the bar. This is truly one of the wonders of nature, close to Robson Bight where the killers rub themselves on the gravel. You get to experience their presence for free.

Fishing can take place on either side of the river. The slot lies closer to the left hand side where you come out of the trail from parking your car. It is often easier and better to fish from the opposite side of the river, meaning you catch more fish, but this entails wading across the river. Do remember that when the tide pushes up you need to cross the river before that happens or you will have

*A bright pink salmon hooked in the Adam and Eve rivers estuary with a fly.*

to sit tight several hours waiting for the tide to drop.

When the tide is rising, it will carry the fish over the shallow riffle and into a slot on the parking side that you can walk up to.

Fly-guys should think green flies, and chartreuse coho buggers with small bead eyes, drifted slowly. Don't retrieve, or only slightly, slowly, strip. This is basically a dead drift that begins with a cast to the far shore, and before the fly hits bottom, it is picked up softly—by pinks. The pinks just stop the fly most often, so that you need to strike more frequently than you would for other species of salmon. Another great fly is: size 6 saltwater streamer hook, calf tail, Lazer Wrap pink body, small bead eyes and with some small pink sparkle Globrite chenille wrapped figure eight style around the bead eyes.

**Access:** On Highway 19, about ten miles north of the right hand turn you took to Sayward to fish the Salmon River, Keta Lake lies on the left hand side of the road. Two miles past the lake, the highway runs parallel to the Adam River and it may be viewed from time to time for the next eight miles. Just after Rooney Lake (where there is a campsite), turn right when you come to the 260 km marker (roughly 20 minutes from the Sayward junction service station and pub) onto a gravel road that is a jolting half hour trip down to the estuary. This road is variously listed as the South or East Main on maps, but you will find that there is an East Main marker most of the way down, a few miles from the estuary. Take this right turn and five minute drive to a left turn where the rustic campsites are a few hundred yards down. This gives you access to the Adam and Eve junction pool. Gear guys tossing spinners and spoons will note that ones tinged with orange are whacked far more frequently by salmon than others. You can also walk down the river half a mile where there is a prominent rock on the far side.

I have seen as many as 10,000 pink salmon there. This is a better fly spot than the junction pool which has a huge backeddy, making sinking your fly and line next to impossible.

If you want to go down the Adam River fly-only section—all you brown trout addicts—take the first right once you have left the highway. This is a sketchier road than the main down to the estuary, and river access is limited to the occasional opening. The Adam River—and the Eve—is in a very rugged valley making the bushwhacking down to the river difficult and there are only a few spots where you can go down. But, these two rivers are typical of the in-a-canyon-dropping from pool to pool gems that are found on Vancouver Island.

This road system is typical of the logging roads out there, and as mentioned in the introduction, has about 20 tracks entering and leaving it, so you need to pay close attention to where you are going. On most backroads, the main gravel road you come in on, continues as the main road, meaning that when you have a choice, the more traveled road is usually the one you want to be on.

Below the highway, that is, to the north and east, the Adam and Eve rivers carry on the opposite side of the bluff for more than ten miles before emptying out and, as is fitting, join into one another before the river widens at the long estuarial reach. Several logging roads run along the rivers, including, among others, the Lower Adam Road, East Main, Montague and Naka Main Line. From time to time you will find easier river access by the roads.

If you carry on on Highway 19, it crosses into the next drainage area, the Eve River, and it runs along that river for a little less than 15 miles – the upper part of the Eve River. This is some distance beyond the logging roads to the Adam and Eve confluence that you access in the Rooney Lake area.

Check for the multiple regulations on this river system.

# Alberni Inlet Drainages—Nahmint River

Into the east and west sides of the Alberni Inlet that leads from Bamfield and the Broken Islands to Port Alberni, there are numerous small- and medium-sized streams. Most of these have small winter and summer steelhead runs, and are utilized most commonly by savvy locals. A lone fly guy eagle-eying the saltwater entrances will find sea-run cutthroat trout that most other anglers pass by; this is because the saltwater inlet is fished by boat for salmon. The steep rock walls rising from the sea provide limited road access, and the opportunities for freshwater fishing closer to Port Alberni, the town, are so good, that few take the trouble of cruising the difficult to reach short cascades of water falling into the inlet itself.

On the east side, these streams include Coleman, Franklin and China, right beside the gravel road that runs from Port Alberni to Bamfield. On the west side, these streams include Cous, Macktush, Nahmint and Henderson, but are considerably more difficult to reach by road, the last not having land access at all.

## Nahmint River

The Nahmint is the most interesting of the bunch, a river of diverse character and with a lake of the same name along its course. The river has both summer and winter steelhead and in the right conditions offers the rare treat of dry fly fishing for these wild beauties. Several miles above the lake are open to walk and wade fishing, for talented and fit individuals who fish the fly in this gear-restricted zone. Do remember that in clear water steelhead are so spooky you can put them down by just standing on the bank. Be crafty.

Nahmint Lake holds good quantities of rainbow trout that are distinct from steelhead and reside year-round in freshwater. The limited camping ground at the upper end provides access to this lake within steep mountain walls. Most use non-motorized craft to ply this clear water beauty. Do check the regulations for this system.

Some miles above the lake, the river changes character markedly and the bridge reveals a peaty river with slate runs reminiscent of the Atlantic salmon rivers of the eastern part of Canada. You may drive up a mile, take a seasonal creek entrance on your right and clamber down a good fifteen minute walk to some tremendous summer and winter steelhead water—that typical water of two to six feet deep comprising runs and boulder-strewn broken water. Do take care, though, as this section is as slippery as it gets with a large amount of didymo algae that is slicker than slick. You should also be a strong wader to make the crossings.

Where the river comes out below the falls below the lake one may fish from the falls pool down to the saltwater estuary on foot during the summer months when the river is low enough

to allow wading. The walk into this one is confusing and you should take a guide. It is worth it as it has a very neat side-hill trail that you will not soon forget. And the trout fishing is good and the fall salmon season memorable. The occasional jet boater comes up from Port Alberni—a sad thing for such a small beauty—to access the coho in October. The lower section of the river offers good coho fishing with size 3 to 5 large spinners and spoons.

Both a single and a double-handed rod come in handy, along with the local large stonefly nymph imitation with a gold bead head, black Woolly Buggers and leeches in purple and black. In summer you can take a full float dry line on your Spey rod.

*The author with a fly-hooked Vancouver Island winter steelhead.*

**Access:** The streams on the east side of Alberni Inlet are accessed from the gravel road that runs from Port Alberni to Bamfield and the Nitinat. Take Anderson Road out of town and fish where the road runs near the streams or crosses over them.

The streams on the west side of Alberni Inlet are accessed by logging roads. You are strongly advised to take a guide to these distant streams as the logging roads are steep and difficult. In addition, foot access to the lower Nahmint is both difficult to find and difficult to stay on track and the climb out from the river is even more so. Ugly!

There are two campgrounds, down the west side of the Alberni Inlet: Bill Motyka at Maktush Creek and Arden Creek Recreation Site. The route, turning left onto McCoy Lake Road on the way west out of town to Tofino, then picks up either the Stirling Arm traveling west and an SOB of a climb up, across and down into the Nahmint Valley (do not take this route) or turn right onto Stirling Arm Main and pick up Cous Creek Main that turns into Macktush Access. This is not quite as difficult a gravel road and takes you to the campgrounds and their boat launches into saltwater.

Do not go to the Nahmint without a guide. Port Alberni has so many good freshwater opportunities with good, easy access that there is no need to venture out into these boonies.

**Guides:** Nick Hnennyj, Toll Free: 1-866-839-8411; Website: westcoastrivercharters.ca; Email: nick@westcoastrivercharters.ca.

Bill von Brendel, Toll Free: 1-877-334-7466; Website: justfishn.com; Email: Info@Justfishn.com.

Dave Murphy, Toll Free: 1-877-218-6600; Website: murphysportfishing.com; Email: Murphy@island.net. Has accommodation, too.

*This angler had to pack a raft to access beautiful Sarita Falls on the Sarita River.*

all, have shorter mouths than the larger steelhead, meaning that longer-tailed flies receive taps on the feathers, but the trout does not hook itself.

In late spring there is good catch and release fishing for cutthroat trout that cruise up looking for salmon fry. This means small spinners for spin casters and minnow patterns such as epoxy flies with eyes in green and blue. Simple silver tape over a brass hook with a collar of brown saddle hackle or a Muddler Minnow will do the trick.

Summer time flow is usually so low that fishing isn't that productive, but the first rains of fall soon bring the river up to a fishable level.

In September, the rebuilt chinook run comes home and the handsome individuals may be seen thrilling you in the deep reaches along side the road. In October, there can be so many chum that you may encounter the odd situation that there are too many fish to fish. In this case, move up or down the river looking for fewer fish—some problem. The coho run is also coming back. Check out the Nitinat River for tackle.

The small Pachena River near Bamfield has winter steelhead and cutthroat trout, and a few salmon in season.

**Information:** Check out the local chamber website for accommodation, meals and fuel: www.bamfieldchamber.com.

**Access:** The Sarita River is almost three hours from Victoria. Past the T-junction near the Nitinat River, carry on until you reach the Franklin

The Sarita River drains from Sarita Lake, viewed on the right hand side of the gravel road that passes on to Bamfield. There is a lovely waterfall that is impassable to fish traffic and that doubles as a swimming hole on a summer day.

From the falls pool down to where the river access is closed below the confluence of the Sarita with its South tributary, the river is fishable provided you have a water craft of some kind. As with steelhead in other rivers, most of the winter steelhead (January to March) prefer runs of 2- to 6-feet deep. As you move down the river, stop at every place that has a run and plumb it thoroughly. There are also sea-run cutthroat trout in the river at all times. Opportunistic fish, the sea-runs move up and down the river a lot and may be found most commonly in softer water than the steelhead.

If you do not have a water craft, then your best fishing access is at the confluence where there is good road access. The Beanie Weanie pink worm fished below pencil lead and a dink float will motivate these steelhead easily. For fly fishermen, a short double handed rod is preferable, not because the river is broad, but because there is little back casting room and the roll cast that is the basis of the traditional Spey casts uses very little of it, particularly if your line is a short shooting head with line tips.

Winter flies might as well be big and beautiful. Don't be scared to use contrasting rabbit fur on big hooks with big bead chain eyes. Winter is the time for luminous flies and yellow, red, blue, cherry, black, orange and chartreuse all find use along with Krystal Flash and Flashabou highlights. Use shorter flies of the same type or tarted up Woolly Buggers for cutthroat trout that do, after

Camp log sort. Bear left and pick up the road for Bamfield. Alternatively, for the 1.5 hours trip from Port Alberni, bear right onto the Bamfield road, near Franklin Camp. River access is on the right, below Sarita Lake and then Bewlay Lake (it looks like an extension of Sarita Lake, though it is not)—both of which have some rough campsites, and spin casting can produce in the last hour before cocoa and bed. At the 54 km marker there is a rough track on your right that is suitable for trucks and four wheel drive vehicles only, unless you want to leave your muffler on one of the bumps. After more than a mile, park your vehicle at the end of the track.

From there it is almost a mile on a trail that you should take for the first time with a guide, as it is easy to get lost and this is a bad place to get lost as the forest is particularly confusing. The last 400 yards is a doozy of a drop, not for those afraid of heights, though some parties bring their children along. Be aware that this is a steep and difficult grade.

As river access from the falls pool can only be done with a water craft, you must carry in your vessel. The Water Master Kick Boats (www.kickboat.com) are the best bet because they fold down into a specially-designed packsack and, at 35 pounds (15.9 kgs) on your back, are the easiest craft to carry—a pontoon boat would be far too much trouble to cart in on this trail.

After fishing the falls pool, you have about three miles before reaching the bridge on Br 610 and then the confluence and run down to the water level meter under the power line where you must pull out, a total distance of about 4 miles (6.4 kms).

The Campbell River is one that travelers can really get to know because it is only 3 ½ miles long from the ocean to the John Hart Dam that is used for both power and drinking water. But this short, easy access river is one of the most historically significant rivers on the Island as its banks are where Roderick Haig-Brown lived and wrote his many wonderful books that although ostensibly about fishing are just as much about life and nature and man's place in it; he was an ecologist before its time.

One cannot talk of the Campbell without referring to the Quinsam River—a small, gentle, fertile river that enters the Campbell just before the Bishop Pool (aka the Confluence Pool). It is the river with the hatchery on it and produces pink, chinook, coho and some steelhead. The river also holds cutthroat trout and a very few Dolly Varden Char. It is the perfect place for a family to teach their children how to fish. There are high percentage spots where the river goes under the road and at the top where the hatchery gate is. You park on the right and go to the river on your left—many good spots on easy to follow trails.

The pink salmon are easy to catch and your child could catch his or her first fish in the Quinsam which is a real treat. Take your camera for this shady little river that can be stuffed with salmon from the second week in July right through October. In fact, most of the Campbell's fish originate in the Quinsam and thus you can find big hog chinook in the river, along with coho and chum as the season progresses.

And do note that the river has definite seasons for sea-run cutthroat trout, particularly in January when the first alevins emerge, as well as with the salmon in the fall when they station themselves just below a spawning pair and gobble up the drifting eggs.

The Campbell is a controlled flow river and so as the summer progresses, more water is let out of the dam to emulate a coastal river in the fall with increasing rainfall. The pool just above Haig-Brown House is known as Sandy Pool. It can be accessed from the highway or walking up the river. On the downstream side fly casters and spoon and spinner and wool tossers stand cheek

by jowl. While you are not supposed to tarry on the active logging bridge that divides Sandy Pool in two, a quick peak from it can sometimes reveal a dozen chinook of 40 pounds, a truly elemental sight. Expect Oohs and Ahhs from all.

The logging bridge is roughly the dividing point (the line is actually about 200 yards above the Quinsam Confluence) for gear and artificial fly. The latter means anything that constitutes a fly, including the wool/yarn that never had any connection with a bird. This zone is open to gear in the summer and is a nice shady spot to spend an afternoon—then find a spot in the sun for a picnic. Also, the various burger chains are five minutes back along the road you have driven from town.

Carrying on up the Campbell you come to the Power Line Pool. From the dividing line on up, it is fly fishing only—as in fly line, no added weight and a fly. The bottom of the island has a good run that can be packed with pink salmon from July 10 into September.

If you carry on in your car a little farther, you will come to a small parking lot on your right just before the B.C. Hydro Dam gate. Park here and take the path on your right down to the river. You will come out on an artificial spawning channel which is high interest if you have never seen one before. Later, the water may be knee deep and a succession of 40-pound springs will spawn here, then some coho and finally some chum.

Cross the channel to the two most historic pools on the Campbell: the Island Pool and the Upper Island Pool, so-named by Haig-Brown. If you see an article on the Campbell the accompanying photos will always show one or the other.

Find the white rock in the top third of the Island Pool and you have found the best spot to fish for salmon. Cast upstream at another white stone on the bottom with a Type 3 sink tip and let the river sink it. Oh yes, do remember that when fishing for salmon use a leader four feet in length or shorter. If the leader is longer the fly won't get down when using a sink tip fly line. The fly will come under connection just before the back rim of the bowl in front of you. Here the pink (and other salmon) will cover the bottom in a bluey-grey colour and your

*Marc and Jeremie Roy fish the Campbell River's Upper Island Pool.*

fly must bonk them on the nose for them to take it.

There are seven positions on this pool, from top to bottom, where you can take pink salmon, so if you are aced out of the best spot don't worry. The issue is spotting fish, marching a bit upstream and then hitting their zone on the bottom.

The wade to the Upper Island Pool has got to be one of the slipperiest in all of Vancouver Island river fishing, so take care, and a wading stick. The Campbell runs over a lip of stones that is set at a lazy diagonal to the current and in the crease below, the bottom is often covered with so many salmon, that the bottom looks black. That means many thousand fish waiting for you.

The best spot is half way up when you are across from a broken-headed tree. If you are not in this spot, you will notice that one angler consistently takes more fish than all the rest. Once that angler moves, try to sidle your way into the spot.

You can easily see, if you stop to take a look at the poolish run, what made this such a glorious spot for steelhead fishing in Haig-Brown's day when there were more steelhead in the Campbell. The river takes your cast and then swings your line in a semi-circle, depositing your fly right on the bottom among the waiting pink salmon—as though you are an ace caster. Then the writing is on the wall.

## Tackle

For gear anglers, a spinning rod with at least 10-pound (4.5-kg) test will work well. Pink Roostertail spinners are particularly effective for pink salmon. If you are going after chinook, you had better have a minimum of 20-pound (9.1-kg) test on a trigger-finger rod with a baitcaster style of reel, or you will not be able to stop the fish. In Sandy Pool, stopping a chinook isn't that hard, but fishing just above the Confluence, even this gear will not keep your chinook from turning downstream and going until it breaks your line. This is because the Campbell has a steeper gradient than most rivers and the water is running fast. Wool flies in pink, chartreuse, orange and peach will do the deed early in the year. Later, make combinations of colours, such as purple or blue with white,

and, using a dink float, run the current seam above the confluence for chinook on the bottom. You will lose lots of fish, but you will have a wonderful time trying to stop them

Fly anglers use a 6- to 8-weight rod and matching line which has a quad tip system to reach down into the faster runs on this river. Many flies work on pink salmon, particularly ones with pink in them, for example, pink shrimp, pink Woolly Buggers and sparse pink streamers (use eyes and silver hooks for new river entrants, to mimic the last baitfish feed). The most underrated fly in freshwater for pink salmon is a sparse, rolled Muddler, a minnow imitation, but many other flies will work, including a bead head black Woolly Bugger, or white Woolly Buggers on a dark day and a Robbing Hood streamer; and stop at River Sportsman tackle shop (located on the highway across from the Chevron station), for the local hot flies of the day.

Use egg patterns and glo-brite eggs in pink, orange and peach for searuns. Try a variation on the Coho Blue, Haig-Brown's best coho fly.

For chum salmon, pink and purple egg-sucking leeches are good. Try blue and white wool above an orange bead also. Try alevin patterns, with a good yolk sack, and fry imitations for the January sea run cutthroat trout.

## Echo Lake

Echo Lake is a small, fairly calm lake that is good for family visits with a small boat. It is stocked with a few thousand catchable—pan-sized trout that will make a meal, usually 10- to 12-inches (25.4- to 30.5-cm) that grow an inch a month—rainbow trout every year. There are also cutthroat and Dolly Varden char in the lake. This lake is restricted to paddling and electric motors.

A good deal of shallow water prevails in this lake and thus ample vegetation allows for lots of wriggly insects and leeches. Fish early in the morning, or after dinner when the fish will drift into the shallows from the deeper water.

A red and white bobber with a worm underneath is as simple a kid's rig as it gets. If you prefer to paddle around, a Wedding Band with a worm will work. Smaller gang trolls also allow for a worm to be trolled around where the bottom dips into the deeper waters of the lake. Black and silver-dotted Kwikfish also

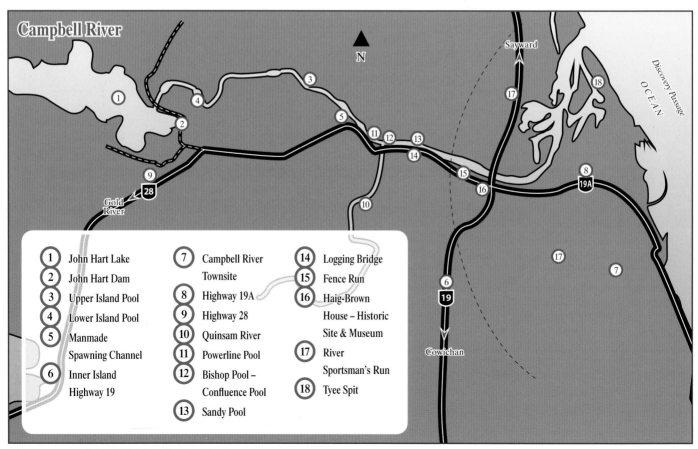

Campbell River

N

| 1 | John Hart Lake | 7 | Campbell River Townsite | 14 | Logging Bridge |
| 2 | John Hart Dam | 8 | Highway 19A | 15 | Fence Run |
| 3 | Upper Island Pool | 9 | Highway 28 | 16 | Haig-Brown House – Historic Site & Museum |
| 4 | Lower Island Pool | 10 | Quinsam River | 17 | River Sportsman's Run |
| 5 | Manmade Spawning Channel | 11 | Powerline Pool | 18 | Tyee Spit |
| 6 | Inner Island Highway 19 | 12 | Bishop Pool – Confluence Pool | | |
| | | 13 | Sandy Pool | | |

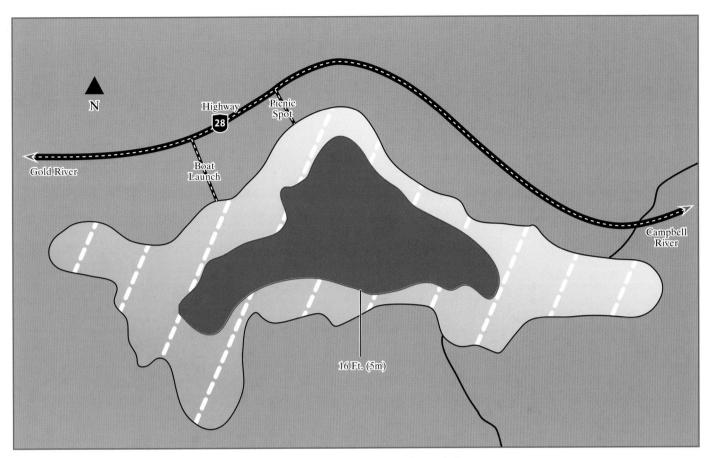

Highway **28**
Picnic Spot
Boat Launch
Gold River
Campbell River
16 Ft. (5m)
N

**Echo Lake — 1.5 miles (2.4 kms) long**

may be trolled. And you can cast the old stand by Len Thompson red and white spoon, along with smaller spoons in silver and orange, silver and silver and blue.

For those wishing to troll a fly, use a Type 3 full sink line and Carey Specials, red or black Doc Spratleys or a black or claret Woolly Bugger. Or match the hatch with pheasant tail nymphs, Tom Thumbs (a dry fly) and shrimp patterns.

*Marc Roy on a gentle stream with a sea-run cutthroat in its ocean colors.*

**Access:** A 3-hour drive north from Victoria on Highway 1 that becomes Highway 19 brings you into town on the north side of Campbell River and on the last light before crossing the Campbell River, you turn left. Once through the next set of lights, you will find the Campbell on your right and there are many spots for you to go through and fish, even at Haig-Brown's House that is marked as a heritage site—and open for pilgrims to take a look. His run is known as the Fence Run.

The Quinsam River is accessed just past Haig-Brown House by bearing left at the hatchery sign on Highway 28. If you do not turn, but continue on the highway, it carries on to Echo Lake and then Gold River, another hour down the paved road, and then to Nootka Sound, another hour on a bumpy gravel road to Tahsis. This road has a few doozy hills just before Moutcha Bay.

To reach Echo Lake, follow Highway 28 from the town of Campbell River for about 10 miles. You come around a right hand corner and swoop down. To your left and beside the highway is the small Echo Lake, with easy access along its length. It has a small boat launch and picnic site.

# Duncan—Cowichan River—Cowichan Lake

The Cowichan River has been synonymous with great fishing for more than a century. Travelers from Europe read regular reports of catches in London newspapers. They arrived in great numbers, taking steamship passage to Montreal and then by train to Vancouver and ferry to Vancouver Island, a leisurely trip of nearly 10,000 miles to dip a line in the 30 miles (50 kms) of Cowichan River water.

The Cowichan's fish fame arises from many sources, but two features stand out: Lake Cowichan feeds the river and the climate is warm. Lake Cowichan is more than 20 miles (32 kms) long and has more than half a dozen streams feeding it. This confers a prodigious flow that is regulated by a weir at the top end of the river in all but deep summer months, when low flow is common. The fish retreat to the big pools with cool springs to wait for the rains of fall.

The lake helps create a full 12 month fishery in the river because, unlike most island rivers, there are drop down and river-resident fish as well as anadromous fish. The resident fish are cutthroat trout that can grow to eight pounds (3.6 kgs) in the lake, rainbow trout to six pounds (2.7 kgs) and brown trout that have been recorded as high as 14 pounds (6.4 kgs). During their spawning season or when salmon are spawning the resident trout drop down into the river for extended periods, with the browns spending most of the year in the river itself.

The lake also has kokanee—landlocked sockeye salmon. They form the main food base for the lake fish and thus contribute to increasing their size.

The Cowichan valley is also known for its balmy climate in comparison with other island rivers, in fact, the aboriginal word, Cowichan, means: land of a warm sun. This helps make the river water far more fertile than the ultra-clear, nutrient-poor rivers that are the island norm. You can look at the water and see the richness in it, particularly in the lower regions near the town of Duncan through which the river flows to the ocean.

The climate has a positive effect on the river producing a much larger food base for fish production: insects, crustaceans and various types of worms. In the fall, the resident trout species further add to their girth by stationing themselves below spawning salmon and nipping up eggs until they can hardly move.

Three salmon species come back to the Cowichan River: chinook, chum and coho. Chinook have been recorded to 14 pounds (27.3 kgs). For a number of reasons, their numbers have dropped over the years and in some autumns, a fall closure of all fishing can be brought into effect as early as August to protect the chinook.

Chum salmon can be in such great numbers that angler arms fall off after a day of fishing from the Silver Bridge in Duncan and the half-mile run below—a very easy access spot. These fish are friskier than most chum and their range can extend above Marie Canyon and Skutz Falls, through Lake Cowichan and into the streams flowing into the lake, for instance, Little Shaw and Nixon. The same is true of Cowichan coho salmon.

The Cowichan River can remain high after rain for three weeks before dropping. The upper end above Skutz falls remains clear in all water levels, but the clay banks downstream but above Stolz Pool now leach into the river on high flows and can make the lower river unfishable for weeks—a winter phenomenon—though river bank rehabilitation has improved the situation.

Winter steelhead begin to enter the Cowichan by the middle of December and exit by the end of April. Early fish spawn higher in the river while later fish spawn in the lower reaches.

The number one issue in terms of fishing the Cowichan is finding access if you are on foot. The river has lots of private property which results in limited river access. The Cowichan River map sold by the Haig-Brown Fly Fishing Association clearly shows the main access roads, which are Greendale, the former CN Railway right of way (lots of hiking on this one, bring a bike to follow the logging roads—these have gates that prevent car access) off Skutz Road, Stolz Road near the provincial park of the same name and Riverbottom Road, though there are others on the north side of the river.

On the south side of the river, turn off the Island Highway, left, at Allenby Road, with a quick transit on Miller Road to Glenora Road that will shunt you to Vaux and Robertson Road where the Duncan Fish and Game Club is situated. This is the start of the 10 mile (16 km) trail system to Skutz Falls.

For those who want an easy fish that is close to lunch at most recognized burger chains, try right beside the Silver Bridge in Duncan. It's very simple and you can also take an easy walk a half mile below, fishing as you go. Along with winter steelhead, try in November for large chum salmon that average 15 pounds (6.8 Kgs) and rise to 25 (14.4 kgs)—big fish and non-stop action.

The Cowichan River is best fished by drift boat. Add the limited foot access, to the long walks, to the canyony sections and you come to the conclusion that a guide will serve you well. And, happily there are good people on the river to help you. Do not launch your own drift boat until you are familiar with the many rock walls and sweepers that can make navigation difficult and dangerous for the uninitiated.

But once you have taken a good boat and long-term guide down the Cowichan it reveals itself to have many very scenic, lovely drifts that will have you singing its praises. You may find yourself coming for the winter steelhead, but hooking into the brown trout that made the river famous will have you back in spring with a 6-weight fly rod.

Add one plus: there are no jet boats on the Cowichan and thus the beauty of the river can be enjoyed in peace.

## Fishing for Winter Steelhead

Cowichan winter steelhead average 5- to 13-pounds (2.3- to 5.9kgs), with the occasional monster tipping the scale at 20 pounds (9.1 kgs). These are obliging fish that will whack pretty much anything fished properly. The issue is finding the fish, not getting them to bite.

Gear advocates rule. With the high water of winter, gear is the preferred option because the water forces shore anglers back into the trees. The B.C. rod of choice is a 10.5 foot trigger-fingered rod with a baitcaster, levelwind style reel. For those who like the sleek feel of a centre-pin reel, fish any spot that gives you enough room to get these machines up to speed with a side arm cast. Mainline should be 15- to 20-pound (6.8- to 9.1-kg) test for the snaggy bottoms, with 10-pound (4.5-kg) leaders of 20- to 30-inches, depending on water clarity.

A float, typically a dink, foam float, is pulled up the mainline to get the lead, usually pencil lead, to touch the bottom from time to time in the straight line runs that float fishing affords so well. Plumb those slots and pools in two foot slices and then move on.

Terminal tackle includes pink worms, aka, Beanie Weanies, threaded onto a leader, with a red sequin below and size 1 to 4 single barbless hook. 'Lil Corkies and tandem 'Lil Corkies in orange or pink and those with glitter work well, too. Add a bit of wool above the lure. Spin 'N Glos in scaled patterns, red, orange and pink, and red Gooey Bobs find common use.

In-your-face tactics are sometimes employed in slow water and tailouts. A spread of Hot Shots in blue or hot pink are back trolled over the gunwales of a drift boat rowed against the current just enough to get the rod tips throbbing.

Winter brings tough conditions for fly anglers—deep fast water and low clarity in the lower sections of the river. But Spey anglers have a distinct advantage as current rods and lines require little back casting room and the heavy tips you can pick up do a better job of dredging the bottom.

Fly casting is much easier in March and April when flow decreases and fish move into the slower tailouts.

## Fishing the Cowichan from Top to Bottom

The Cowichan offers a number of drifts and your guide will pick where the most fish are holding. Do try to commit to memory the tailouts, rock ledges, boulders and slots that are fished as these consistently hold fish from year to year.

Foot access at the top end is good where Greendale Road touches the river at the Road Pool, a spawning spot (for salmon and trout) that then drops into a nice deep slot on the left. For the nimble this is either a boat launch or egress point.

Following the footpath below the Road Pool leads you past Joe Saysell's house, a local guide, and the run is called either Saysell's or the Home Run.

Between Golding Brook and Josiah Creek there is a path on the river side that is difficult to find, so drive slowly. If other fishers have beaten you there, there will be vehicles parked on Old Lake Cowichan Road (joined by Greendale). The walk down to the river is about half a mile, but once on the river, a path leads for five miles along the river, and the changing river course to Skutz Falls.

If you wish to proceed directly to Skutz Falls you will gain foot access along the CN Railway right of way and on gated logging roads to the same territory that you can reach from the Golding Brook entrance. The 70.2 Mile Bridge is the current fly fishing only bottom boundary. This is the area to fish when the lower river is blown.

Skutz Falls is a necessary boat pull out and very tricky for the uninitiated. If you miss the very short swing in, you go over the falls and are never heard from again. So don't miss it.

The Marie Canyon is a good 100 feet deep and best viewed from the bridge (part of the railway grade) that crosses it. Once on the south side of the river, you may follow the trails the 8 miles to the Duncan Fish and Game Club, or go back up the south side of the river to the bridge below Skutz Falls.

Driving toward Duncan (east) on Skutz Road, you will meet Stolz Road and enter Riverbottom Road that provides many close encounters with the river, the first of which is Stolz Pool Provincial Park, the Cable Run, Washout Pools, the Powerline Run, Bible Camp, Sandy Pool and a number of good slots down to the Cedar Log Pool.

Vimy Road provides a flattish bar to pull your boat across and then a real good pull onto the trailer and up the steep exit.

The Pumphouse run has good holding water. As noted, the Silver Bridge in Duncan provides an easy-access half-mile wade that produces early in the winter and late in the spring.

*A beauty of a 12-pound winter hen taken on the fly in February.*

**Fly Tackle:** Eight- to ten-weight single handed rods along with quad-tip systems are the gear of choice for winter steelhead. This is a broader river and distance comes in handy.

The current approach to west-coast winter Spey casting is to the Rio Skagit style lines with a full set of tips used on a shorter Spey rod. The rule is 2.5 times the rod length to equal the head length. With a Rio head at 27.5 feet this suits an 11- to 13-foot Spey rod.

**Flies:** Black and pink are the best colours. Make up a box of Bunny Leeches, Egg-sucking Leeches and Woolly Bugger variations, black for the browns. In the October to December period, egg flies do double duty for trout and steelhead. Do remember that big chum can be in the system as late as January and they take a variety of Deceivers, streamers, emphasizing chartreuse and orange. Dries include Royal Coachman, brown Wulffs and mosquitoes.

**Lures:** For murky water, add the simple gold wobbler to the list above. They send out more flash than other lures and colours.

**Regulations:** The Cowichan River is one of the most highly regulated bodies of water in the province, hence, you have to really understand the regulations if you will be fishing on your own. On the other hand, if you fish with a guide, he or she is responsible for knowing them.

On the plus side, the regulatory regime helps ensure that there is a quality fishery year round.

Find provincial regulations at: www.env.gov.bc.ca/fw/fish/recreational.html.

**Guides:** Bucky's Tackle Shop; Toll Free: 1-800-667-7270; Website: www.buckys-sports.com/fishing/index/htm.

Dave Gunn, River Quest Charters; Phone: 1-250-748-4776; Address: 5650 West Riverbottom Road, Duncan, BC, V9L 6H9; Located on the upper Cowichan River; Website: riverquest.ca; Email: dgunn@islandnet.com. R748-4776

Kenzie Cuthbert, Kenzie's Fishing Adventures; Phone: 1-250-749-3594; Website: www.kenzies.com/; Email: k&kcuthbert@telus.net;

**Accommodations:** www.cowichanriverwildernesslodge.com, overlooks the Cowichan River, e-mail: k&kcuthbert@telus.net

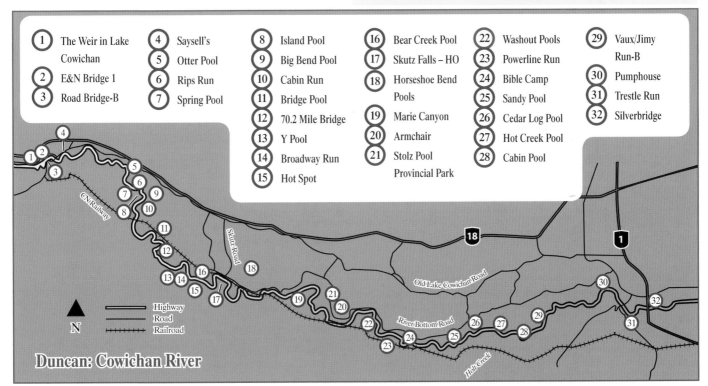

| | | | | |
|---|---|---|---|---|
| ① The Weir in Lake Cowichan | ④ Saysell's | ⑧ Island Pool | ⑯ Bear Creek Pool | ㉒ Washout Pools | ㉙ Vaux/Jimy Run-B |
| ② E&N Bridge 1 | ⑤ Otter Pool | ⑨ Big Bend Pool | ⑰ Skutz Falls – HO | ㉓ Powerline Run | ㉚ Pumphouse |
| ③ Road Bridge-B | ⑥ Rips Run | ⑩ Cabin Run | ⑱ Horseshoe Bend Pools | ㉔ Bible Camp | ㉛ Trestle Run |
| | ⑦ Spring Pool | ⑪ Bridge Pool | ⑲ Marie Canyon | ㉕ Sandy Pool | ㉜ Silverbridge |
| | | ⑫ 70.2 Mile Bridge | ⑳ Armchair | ㉖ Cedar Log Pool | |
| | | ⑬ Y Pool | ㉑ Stolz Pool Provincial Park | ㉗ Hot Creek Pool | |
| | | ⑭ Broadway Run | | ㉘ Cabin Pool | |
| | | ⑮ Hot Spot | | | |

Highway
Road
Railroad

N

Duncan: Cowichan River

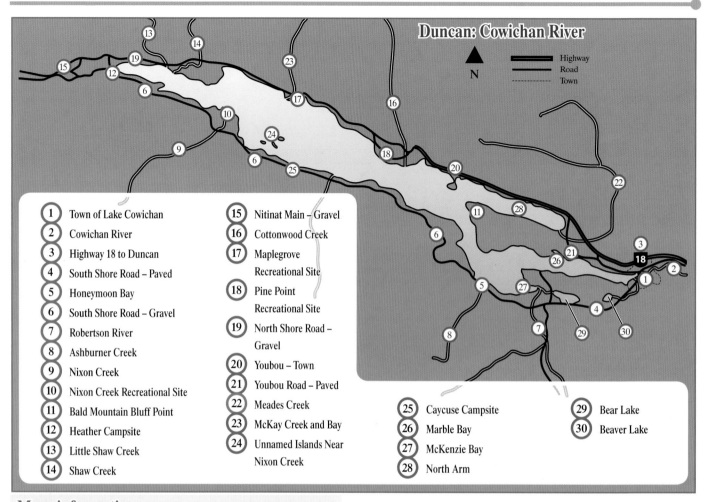

**Duncan: Cowichan River**

Legend:
— Highway
— Road
---- Town

N

| | | | |
|---|---|---|---|
| 1 | Town of Lake Cowichan | 15 | Nitinat Main – Gravel |
| 2 | Cowichan River | 16 | Cottonwood Creek |
| 3 | Highway 18 to Duncan | 17 | Maplegrove Recreational Site |
| 4 | South Shore Road – Paved | 18 | Pine Point Recreational Site |
| 5 | Honeymoon Bay | 19 | North Shore Road – Gravel |
| 6 | South Shore Road – Gravel | 20 | Youbou – Town |
| 7 | Robertson River | 21 | Youbou Road – Paved |
| 8 | Ashburner Creek | 22 | Meades Creek |
| 9 | Nixon Creek | 23 | McKay Creek and Bay |
| 10 | Nixon Creek Recreational Site | 24 | Unnamed Islands Near Nixon Creek |
| 11 | Bald Mountain Bluff Point | | |
| 12 | Heather Campsite | | |
| 13 | Little Shaw Creek | | |
| 14 | Shaw Creek | | |

| | | | |
|---|---|---|---|
| 25 | Caycuse Campsite | 29 | Bear Lake |
| 26 | Marble Bay | 30 | Beaver Lake |
| 27 | McKenzie Bay | | |
| 28 | North Arm | | |

## More information

**River Map:** Haig Brown Fly Fishing Association, Address: Box 6454, Depot 1, Victoria, B.C. V8P 5M4; Website: www.hbfa.ca. This association puts out a must have map of the Cowichan River, $8.95, with its 89 named pools, runs and features.

Use the Cowichan River with caution. It has 130 rapids and numerous small waterfalls, along with a major canyon section.

**Access:** By car from Vancouver airport or by car crossing the border at Blaine, take the Tswwassen Ferry to Victoria, Vancouver Island. Drive 1 hour 20 minutes up the Island Highway #1 to Duncan and turn left on Highway 18 to reach Lake Cowichan about 20 minutes and 20 miles (32 kms) west. Alternatively, fly into the land-based Victoria airport and pick up a car for a slightly shorter drive on the same route.

**Camping:** Both the Skutz falls and Stolz Pool Cowichan River Provincial Parks have camping facilities. And there are more than a dozen campgrounds in the surrounding areas. Check out: www.cowichanlake.ca.

**Non-fishing Attractions:** Wineries! If wine is your thing there are 12 local wineries that do daily tastings within 10 minutes of Duncan. For a map, look at: www.vancouverisland.com/Maps/?id=83. Then have someone else drive while you enjoy yourself.

## Cowichan Lake

At 20 miles (32 kms) long, Cowichan Lake is among the larger lakes on Vancouver Island. Almost a dozen streams and small rivers empty into this lake that reaches 400 feet (120 m) deep. In most areas of the lake, the bottom drops rapidly from shore, leaving little of the magical 16 feet (5 m) area where vegetation grows and thus sustains good numbers of insects. Small aprons of shallows exist near Heather and Nixon campsites, along with the islands in that area, as well as in Honeymoon Bay and brushy areas of North Arm and the run into the weir for the Cowichan River. The channel to Beaver and Bear lakes in the 10- to -15-foot depths can be good in November for large cutthroat on Flatfish and with big black leeches that dredge the bottom.

Because the lake has little shallow water, fishing concentrates in front of creek mouths and on downriggers in central parts of the lake. The other major stimulant to fishing is the hapless few-inch-long kokanee. In this and other lakes where these small "land-locked" sockeye salmon reside, kokanee become the main feed for the trout population resulting in far larger fish than in lakes where trout are restricted to insects, which are much smaller. That is why Cowichan Lake resident cutthroat can exceed 8 pounds (3.6 kgs), the rainbow grow to 8 pounds (2.7 kgs) and brown trout exceed double digit weights.

Shore anglers trundle out on the logging roads that parallel both sides of the lake and look for the various streams that drain into the lake. Other hotspots include, Honeymoon Bay, Bald Mountain Bluff Point, Marble Bay, McKenzie Bay, Maple Bay and Gillespie Bay. Mepps and Vibrax Blue Fox spinners are constant companions for gear anglers. In later months, fish the streams as underfed cutthroat will often sit in them long after the salmon have spawned and gone.

Trollers in boats frequent the stream mouths, and the bays noted on the map, fishing with Apex lures, Coyote spoons, jointed Rapala lures, or Tomic plugs trolled at 50 feet in central lake areas and at 30- to 40-feet near creek mouths. Keep an eye on your depthsounder for drop-offs and work these, too. Gang trolls and worms will always work. Or try small green frog Flatfish and Kwikfish. There is good structure from Nixon Creek to the far end of Cowichan Lake—fish reefs, ledges and structure.

Fly fishermen use fry patterns because of the salmon fry in the lakes, larger streamers because of the kokanee, leech flies and Muddler Minnows. Nymphs and chironomids find good use at stream mouths, particularly in March and April. Stand on a dock in the Lake Cowichan town area and Honeymoon Bay on a summer evening and when the fish begin touching the surface, begin your casting.

At the far end of the lake are the Caycuse Campground, Heather Campground and Nixon Creek Campsites that offer launching. There is also plenty of shore camping along the north shore of the lake in rough, free sites.

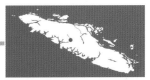

The town of Gold River serves as a hub for fishing the area's mountainous setting west of Campbell River. The Gold River system (includes the Muchalet and Heber) is famous for its winter and summer steelhead, being the number three river on Vancouver Island. But in season there are also runs of sockeye, chinook and, later, coho and chum salmon in the fall.

Though well known, the Gold has less traffic than one might expect in the December to April period when the winters hold in pools and tailouts. Your percentage is high provided you pay attention to a few key points: winter steelhead tend to hold stations belly to bottom; water colour influences fly and lure size; and, the colder the ambient air temperature the greater the precision required in presentation—or many casts in the same run.

## The Runs

As the Gold River winter season progresses through February, March and into April, steelhead drift back into tailouts where they lie. As these are usually conditions of slower water flow, a 225 tip in the now warmer water will put your fly on fish more inclined to move and attack. Take care to stay out of sight upstream, beneath the 10 degree above-water angle in which water will not refract your image to the waiting steelhead.

By June, the first of the sockeye run begin their streak up the Gold to the Muchalet River. These fish have the delightful trait of being "biting" sockeye; most anglers will know that sockeye have the reputation for being decidedly close-mouthed in freshwater so that a strain with the genetic trait for biting is not to be overlooked.

For sockeye in July and August, your best bet is to fly fish for them in the Muchalet River, even above the lake of the same name. The key for these fish is precision in the cast. Sockeye are not curious in the way that coho salmon are. They prefer the fly, for example, any marabou creation, such as the Popsicle pattern or even a small orange yarn fly, tied directly onto the tippet using a sliding knot on a #1 hook, to come directly at them from upstream.

Sockeye will not chase a fly more than a few inches, thus, the zone is extremely small. If you find the black streak that indicates stacking sockeye, be patient, altering your drift until you receive your first bite. Then deliver the same cast on target for the rest of the day. Sockeye, like their chum confreres, seem less bothered than other salmon species when one of their numbers gets zipped out by an angler, and this makes up for their reluctance to bite.

In July and August, summer steelheading reaches a peak. Find those deep pools and concentrate on the seams that run across them from the head of the pool. Steelhead invariably station themselves beneath these. But they may be found elsewhere, too. Pocket-water behind big boulders usually secrets a steelhead or two. Also, straight line runs of 3- to 6-feet in depth provide the classic conditions for Gold steelhead.

Along with the summer steelhead and sockeye that peak in July and August, the first of the big chinook begin nosing the Nootka Sound canyon runs below the town of Gold River in later August. Add coho in September, October, and chum in October, November to finish out the calendar cycle and begin the next.

The Gold River has many easy access pools and runs near the town of Gold River. The lower end of the Heber has an easy access run and then, where it joins the Gold River is a large pool that can be fished from three sides, depending on which road you take, in other words, it's easy to get to and worthwhile driving the short distances that will give you other water to work, all the way down to the tailout (Gravel Bar) and then either side of the next pool that has a humdinger of an unusual ninety degree bend, Big Bend. You can fish by water craft or by car access to water visible from the highway just below town. The river continues down to Muchalet Inlet below, but don't be tempted to go below, from the campground on your left (left from the highway, right from the river), because the river falls into a canyon and it will seriously ruin your day.

The Gold River is a rated white-water river and not suitable for first timers. Take a guide or walk to the easier pools.

Some of the local lakes that receive an annual seeding of trout include Antler, Crest, Darkis, Drum and Star.

Saltwater access rivers include the Burman (off the Muchalet Inlet boat launch) which makes it a good bet for summer steelhead and sea-run cutthroat trout.

*A late-winter shot taken on the Gold River.*

**Tackle:** Nine to 9.5-foot, 8-weight fly rods well equip the fly fishermen to match his skills with these 5- to 18-pound (2.3- to 8.2-kg) steelies. Take along fly lines capable of cruising the fishy zone—right on the bottom. These include exchangeable tips in the 225 to 525 range (depending on a specific pool) and floaters (easy to see) with tips in the 425 grain range. A Type 3 or 4 sink line will also dredge the zone, however, most are drab and thus difficult to follow. When fish hold a station and exhibit "passive bites," that is, do not move following the bite, the ability to visually see flyline drift deflections becomes crucial.

Another Gold technique is to use a sink tip with a strike indicator and stack mend floating line on top of it. Your guide can give you good clues as to the precise zone where you want your fly sunk, line stacked and mended so as to come under control just prior to making fish contact.

Winter steelhead take the usual lures fished below a float and lead, including: pink yarn flies, Pink Gooey Bobs, Jensen Eggs, Pink Worms (for both summer and winter steelhead) and pale pink and orange Spin 'N Glos. In April, steelhead congregate to spawn in tailouts. At this time they will take single pink, red, or orange plastic "eggs" that have been stuck to size 6 or 8 hooks that have been heated to melt the plastic. Try home-made gold or silver Colorado Blades. For those who prefer casting a lure, give the common, and inexpensive, generic gold wobbler a first try. Then move into Wobblers, Vibrax Blue Fox spinners, Len Thompson spoons and similar lures from other manufacturers.

Place that foam float (commonly called a dink float) 3- to 8-feet above a pencil lead crimped to a short piece of mono and tied to a #5 Crane swivel. Below this, attach a #7 Crane swivel to the end of the main line (15- to 20-pound (6.8- to 9.1-kg)). Add a 3-foot leader in the 4- to 12-pound (1.8- to 5.5-kg) range (go lower in lower and clearer water).

Flies for steelhead include simple egg patterns, pink and purple bead chain or dumbbell eyes or copper beads for Woolly Buggers, leeches, pink and blue Egg-sucking Leeches. For summer steelhead try some of the traditional Spey flies including a Green Butted Skunk, Purple Peril, Babine Special and Silver Hilton. Other flies include the General Practitioner and orange Comets, the latter of which finds double duty for sockeye. For chum, include pink and white and pink and black Egg-sucking Leeches with big bead chain eyes. And make up some garish leechy things in black, orange and chartreuse with dumbbell eyes.

*A summer steelhead taken on a pink worm by Morgan McLean.*

**Access:** Gold River is four hours north and west from Victoria by car. Once you have traveled the three hours to Campbell River (Highway 1 and then Highway 19) and turned left onto Highway 28 you have an hour drive on a very scenic road that moves you through the very pretty Buttle and Upper-Campbell lakes where you can stop and fish for rainbows—look for dimple on the surface in the morning or evening. These lakes are set in rising rock walls that as you continue west become mountains that exceed 6000 feet, before you drop down into the almost alpine setting of Gold River itself.

Pools on the Gold that are easy to find, include easy access spots on the road (turn left at the only Stop sign in town) down to the ocean where boats are launched for fishing Nootka Sound—do not however get yourself down in the canyon, it's not safe.

Just after you pass over the Gold River (before going to the lower river) there is also the confluence pool for the Heber and Gold. Bear left through the light industrial businesses and you will find yourself at the confluence, where you can walk down river for about half a mile.

The opposite side of the river confluence, that is right beside the school, is reached by a left turn before the Gold River bridge onto Matchlee Drive. This is a small town, so if you lose your way, there are few streets to choose from before you find yourself on the right one.

If you decided to carry on straight through the stop sign the road angles to the right until it comes out on a bridge over the Gold River above a bouldery run, called the Railway Pool. This is a good spot to fish below the bridge on the near side. Below this is Peppercorn Park and it has a trail down the Gold to just above the Confluence Pool.

The other easy access spots are on the Gold River East Road. It gives you the opportunity to view an interesting spot where the aboriginals have a weir to trap sockeye. Above this point, bear left for Muchalet Lake where there are a number of campsites. Before coming to the lake, you will come to a clear cut. Stop your car just before it and pick up the steep slope to the Muchalet River below. There are cutthroat trout in the lake and river.

The other access points for this gorgeous river system are more difficult and you should take a guide. Do not take a water craft down this rated white-water river on your own until you are familiar with it.

**Guides:** Courtney Ogilvie, Website: ogilvieoutfitters.com
Matt Guiget, Website: www.murphysportfishing.com.

# Nanaimo

anaimo has its fair share of lakes stocked with cutthroat and, especially, rainbow trout. These lakes include Blackjack, Brannan, First, Second and Third Collieries, Diver, the four Nanaimo Lakes, Shelton, Westwood and others. Long Lake right beside the old highway in Nanaimo itself receives stockings of thousands of catchables (that is, edible size) each year.

The area has lakes at different altitudes, so it is quite common that you can have a succession of lakes coming on strong sequentially for long periods of the spring and summer. When one goes flat, you go higher or lower, avoiding turn-over events or higher water temperature. Remember that Vancouver Island does not have an ice off period—because residents passed a law forbidding ice and snow and it's proven quite effective in keeping Camelot a paradise!

Both gear and fly anglers can catch their fair share at the amenable lakes around town. Anglers with spinning gear do their best to spy trout on the surface. If you do, then fling out the red and white bobber and put a worm some feet below on a snelled size 8 hook. Alternatively mold some Powerbait, either pink or chartreuse, around the hook, but when using this kind of artificial bait you will require some split shot on the line beneath the bobber, because Powerbait floats.

The alternative to casting is plunking, and one uses the standard technique of an egg sinker on the bottom with a snelled size 8 some feet above, or snelled on the bottom with Powerbait, and a rubber-core weight a couple of feet above so the bait floats up; this is the easiest way to plunk anyway, so it might as well be the first way you try.

Standard casting spoons and spinners will work on these willing fish, Panther Martins in yellow, black and green. Use small gang trolls, with worms behind—so their action does not impede the enjoyment of the fight. A Wedding Band in red, pink or black, is a good alternative, as it has an attracting spinner and you can adorn the hook with a single worm. Trollers also give small Kwikfish and Flatfish a try in green or frog patterns. Blue Fox spinners in size 3 and smaller will also work for casters.

Fly guys and gals have a whole arsenal of weapons, too. For dry flies try the standard Tom Thumb, Parachute Adams, Royal Coachman and Elk Hair Caddis for surface hatches as well as when you see fish rising. If they aren't rising, switch to wet flies, the Doc Spratleys in red, water boatmen in black, nymphs in black with bead heads, both damsel and dragon fly and humpy style flies. The island-wide favourite Woolly Bugger also takes these lake fish and don't just limit yourself to black. Claret, dark olive, and wine are good alternatives.

April, when the lake warms, brings the bite on for hungry, lean, winter fish. May arrives with huge black ant hatches and thus switch to a floater pattern and get in on the action. In the hot months that can put fish down, fish higher elevation lakes or cruise the creek mouths and where cool springs enter the lake. The trout will be here. September and especially October can be terrific trout months, when the water has cooled from its summer high temperature.

## Long Lake

If you opt to take the 'old' highway—19A—on the way into Nanaimo from Victoria (straight ahead, rather than exiting right) you will drive through the downtown district with its pretty water front on your right hand side. Once you climb out of the centre of town, you will pass a long strip of malls and franchise restaurants, and come to Long Lake that lies right beside the highway on the right. You'll even notice a nice hotel that rents paddling boats so you don't have to bring one along.

Try Emerging Caddis, Pheasant Tail nymphs and Muddler Minnows. Gang trolls and worm produces the best results but light tackle guys like Panther Martin spinners because they are light. If fish are on the surface use a float and worm, remember to put some split shot on the line if you use Powerbait—it floats. If not, make a loop in the line, a couple of feet above the hook and slide it through the swivel on top of an egg weight, then around the weight and snug the Martingale knot on the top of the swivel.

On hot summer days, troll the deep trough down the centre of the lake. In winter, most of the bigger fish are usually caught here, too. Keep your eye open for adjacent weed banks as they are also good fishing, particularly in the spring and fall. Key in on the shady parts of the lake in the morning.

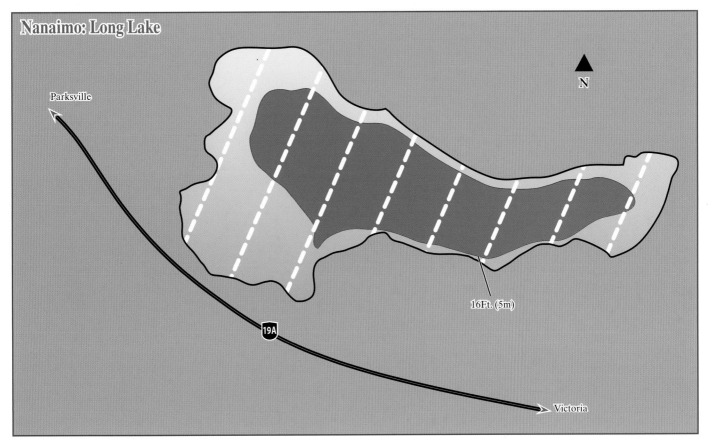

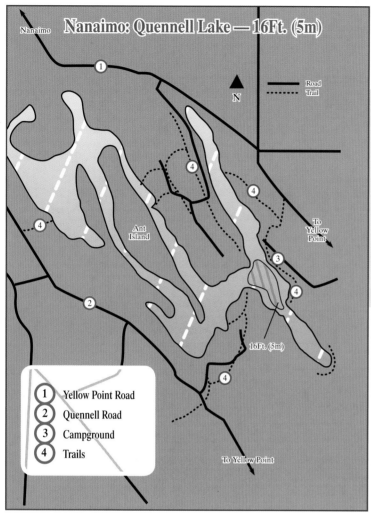

**Nanaimo: Quennell Lake — 16Ft. (5m)**

Nanaimo

N

Road
Trail

Ant
Island

To
Yellow
Point

16Ft. (5m)

To Yellow Point

| ① | Yellow Point Road |
| ② | Quennell Road |
| ③ | Campground |
| ④ | Trails |

around. They are hanging near structure and shoot out explosively to whack a hapless prey found within a couple of feet of where they lie in wait. That is why your lures need to plop and whir and create commotion and they need to drop down right in front of cover, be it a rock, log, dock or simply overhanging branches. Leave it a second and then twitch the lure to stimulate the strike.

**Access:** When driving north on Highway 1, you will be prompted to take the Duke Point Ferry Terminal exit. Turn right at Cedar Road that eventually turns into Yellow Point Road that takes you by Quennell Lake and deposits you at a campground where you can access the lake.

Regardless of the side of the lake you drive in on, there are many trails to most parts of the lake. The alternative is a quiet paddle on this narrow lake that presents a great deal of possibility.

**Interesting Hotel:** Stay on the road of the same name and follow it to the Yellow Point Hotel. It is only for adults, has no locks on doors, has ocean cabins without water (main lodge rooms do), and has an otherwordly atmosphere that adults need to experience. I am not a classical music buff, but it plays all day long as the only electronic activity—no phones here—and with libation hour out on the unusual sedimentary rock formations near the saltwater pool makes an evening complete. Surprised even me.

## Nanaimo River

An east side river on the way back up, the Nanaimo has one of the few—and very small at this time—spring time (March) runs of the big kings, as in spring "springs," where the name came from. In the fall there are small runs of springs and coho and a growing number of pink salmon. This is a highly regulated river.

**Access:** Nanaimo is a 90-minute drive north, 60 miles (100 km) from Victoria on the Trans-Canada Highway, 1. For the Nanaimo Lakes, take the turnoff in Cassidy, south of Nanaimo, from Highway 1. There are campsites on each of the four Nanaimo Lakes which is paid to the timber company en route through their day-time entry gates.

For the lower end of the Nanaimo River, take the Duke Point Ferry turnoff and pick up Baines Road just on the other side of the river.

There are six traffic lights on the "new" highway in Nanaimo (nobody who drives it everyday can figure out why) and you will see lakes on your left as you drive north. For the old highway, go straight ahead on your way into Nanaimo, and it will take you to Diver and Long Lakes; left on Jingle Pot Rd. for Westwood Lake; Doumont goes over the highway, but gives round-about access to Brannon Lake; Aulds Road light grants access to Green Lake.

## Quennell Lake

One of the strangest shaped lakes you will ever fish is Quennell Lake a few miles south of Nanaimo, out on Yellow Point. This shape, however, lends itself to mighty production of smallmouth bass because there are more miles of shoreline on this lake than any lake of its size on the island.

Here, as well as in other island lakes, bass were stocked by anglers and are considered by the fisheries folk an alien fish. That didn't stop anyone from stocking them, though, and now they can hardly wipe the grins off their faces when they angle over to the shallows that are pretty well everywhere you look.

Add to the bass fishing with 10,000 rainbow trout a year and you have an instant fish Mecca secreted in the rolling farm hills east of the Nanaimo airport. Like other lakes with good populations of bass and trout, there is a definite pattern to the fishing. Trout fishing is best in the March to May period and then in September to October (you can catch fish here all winter, too) as the water cools. In the summer when the shallow lake is too warm for trout (they tend to move into the only deep water and hang there waiting for fall), bass fishing is hot. As you will note on the accompanying lake map, the deep part of the lake is very small. That means that it will have a high concentration of trout in the heat of summer and is thus a good place to target with deep rigs.

Remember that bass tend to hole up near structure. They are not followers and they are not actively moving

*Typical winter gear used to catch steelhead on Vancouver Island.*

# Nitinat & Klanawa Rivers

The Nitinat River (pronounced Nit-nat) is a very good river for salmon in September to November because the hatchery is one of the largest in Canada, releasing millions of coho, chinook and chum fry. The river also has very small populations of winter and summer steelhead along with searun cutthroat trout throughout the summer.

Although the river may be fished from Parker Creek (the upper fishing boundary), some 20 miles (32 kms) from the saltwater lake, most salmon fishing takes place below the bridge on the Nitinat River. The only easy access pool above the bridge is Worthless Creek and this is a good coho pool beside the road, where you first come to the river on your journey from Duncan.

The Nitinat River in its lower sections has many easy access spots for anglers and many rough and free campsites. Just above the bridge, is a right turn for a boat launch and take out that has some campsites. In a recent fall, the largest log you are ever going to see—120 feet long and ten feet in diameter, must be 15 tons— came down in a flood, wiping out all the trees and breaking bedrock before coming to rest precisely in the launch and thus it is no more. But intrepid campers squeeze underneath to plonk their tent at stream side.

Walk above the log and stand on the rock that gives access to a good back eddy in the "boat launch." Below, the pool under the bridge is closed in salmon season, but is a good spot to try for trout earlier in the year.

Farther down the river, left from the T junction, you come to the Road Pool right beside the road, a good one for coho, again, in the deepest part of the soft water. Past Red Rock Pool (a boat launch spot), closed in salmon season, is a small bridge, a culvert, really. Park here and walk down to The Seam a well-utilized spot for all species of salmon.

The other good access spots for salmon are, past the Nitinat River bridge (there is only one bridge), take the road on your left to the Nitinat River Hatchery and where it branches, bear right and immediately find yourself on a bridge over a very pretty canyon. This is the Hobiton Main, a decommissioned logging road over the Little Nitinat River (and it's slowly falling apart, so take care). It is not suitable for trailing a boat or trailer.

Down the Hobiton Main there are three access points close to the road: No Fish Pool (so-named by me because I have never caught one fricking fish here— that doesn't mean others can't catch 'em, only me), Glory Slough and Sturgeon Pool, accessed across Poison Slough where the road is decommissioned and you park your car before going down the hill and across.

All three pools are good for salmon, and in a retention year, September gives you a good chance of catching a 30-pound (13.6-kg) chinook to take home. Do remember that big springs are heavy to carry more than a hundred yards back to the car and that there are more bears on this river than you will ever see anywhere ever again. Sturgeon Pool is a one mile lug back to the safety of your car.

For salmon, while some anglers use cheap spinning rod and reels, do treat yourself to a step up and procure a baitcaster rod and reel with 17- to 20-pound (7.7- to 9.1-kg) mainline. Do not use lower pound test, thinking it more sporting, because the salmon will simply break it and a hundred feet of line will end up on the river bank or fouling the fish.

Most gear chuckers use wool in pink, peach, orange, chartreuse, white, or four mm orange or green beads above a size 1- 3/0 Octopus style Kirbed hook. Tie a sliding knot along the hook shank, push a loop through the eye and put an inch of yarn through, pulling the leader to snug it along the shank. Finish by trimming the wool to a small ball And, from time to time, re-trim the wool—it tends to straggle back during fishing.

The 20- to 30-inch leader is tied to a size five to seven Crane swivel, that is tied to the mainline, leaving a three-inch tag end onto which a piece of pencil lead is crimped. Surprisingly, chinook are not discriminating other than some days preferring other colours, like blood red, burgundy, tan and will take hold of the fly as it swings past them. They will usually not move for the fly therefore you must be very aware to set the hook when the line firms up. If you miss the connection, the salmon will just let go of the lure or fly and you will have to reel in and try again.

chinook will also take, occasionally, the larger casting spoons, like the Illusion and Ironhead in silver, gold, green, and do so particularly when the lure is falling. Coho are taken mostly on metallic lures. Vibrax Blue Fox, Bolo and Mepps Aglias in sizes three to five are the best lures, emphasizing, silver, brass, gold and then chartreuse as the season progresses, along with the newer glow in the dark surfaces that will also take a few chum and the occasional chinook. Body colours include blue, red, chartreuse and green.

Chum, like springs, are less choosey and you can rig up with your yarn offerings and some days, take into the double digits because chum school in large clumps on the bottom and are notoriously indifferent to the fate of their brothers that get zipped out of the group all day long. Figure out the indentation that they lie behind or below and you are into a day of fishing you will not forget.

Fly guys utilize a good 8-weight single-handed rod for most salmon fishing with a quad tip-exchange system offering from floating to quick sink. A quad system with an 8- or 9-weight Spey rod will let you plumb distant waters that few other anglers—gear or fly—can reach.

chinook flies can double as chum flies and can include diverse and different styles of flies, from a four inch bunny leech in black, to tiny orange egg patterns with glow in them, the others include the Nitnook, a chartreuse Woolly Bugger with holographic tinsel, the Needlenose, a chartreuse rump with lead along the shank, and the Tutu, a fluff of wool behind a palmered white front end. White Woolly Buggers with hot pink thread (the thread colour glows through once the fly is wet) are effective early in the day and late, and in rain. Try black Woolly Buggers in the sun.

Coho flies need metal or shiny surfaces in them. So bead chain eyes or gold bead heads are mandatory, tied into streamer patterns with blue, chartreuse, pink, purple and red as the predominant colour, but with lots of tinsel. Try blue Angel Hair, too; my Blue Coho is a funny looking fly but it catches a lot of coho and a few springs up to 42 pounds (19.1 kgs) every year.

**Nitinat River Access:** As below, a 2.5 hour drive from Victoria to the T junction in the Nitinat valley. Turning left takes you to Nitinat Lake and the boat launch for the saltwater fishery at the Nitinat Bar. Turning right takes you to the bear left for the Nitinat Hatchery, as well as to the left turn across the Little Nitinat for the Klanawa. It is a one hour drive to the Nitinat Bridge from Port Alberni, as noted below.

**Flora Lake:** This small tree-lined lake is typical of the thousands of little bodies of water out there in the forest and mountains of Vancouver Island, and that is the reason for including it in this book. It will take you a lifetime of holidays and more to reach the small, stocked lakes on the island.

*A group of fly fishermen share a shore lunch.*

Situated on the route to the Klanawa River, and a short drive from the road to Bamfield, Flora Lake is a quiet little spot to enjoy with the family and get away from it all, including other people at the major resort-style lakes. There is a small boat launch and a few rough, free campsites right along the north side of the lake.

Every second year the lake is stocked with 1500 yearling rainbows and these, along with self-sustaining natural cutthroat trout, form the basis of the fishery. As the road-side shore drops into deeper water you can fish from shore, sending out small spinners in the Mepps or Panther Martin style. The silver/ orange should do you, or the venerable black with yellow spots.

Flora is a good spot for float tubers as it is set in trees and this makes the lake calmer and thus easier to fin around and sit where you want to fish. The inlet stream on the west end flows into some good structure in the lake and is a good spot to toss an attractor style fly such as a Doc Spratley or Mickey Finn style of sparse streamer. In the evening look to the lower end of the lake as it has more extensive shallows where the fish mosey around looking for insects hatching off the surface.

Access: From Port Alberni or from Victoria, as described for the Nitinat and Klanawa rivers, turn onto the Flora Lake Main and the lake is three miles (five km) from the junction of the two routes. This junction opens immediately onto the Little Nitinat River, a real beauty here, and on hot days, picnicers sometimes swim in the run above the bridge. Do not go below the bridge as it soon falls steeply into the Little Nitinat falls.

## Klanawa

The Klanawa is a jewel of a little river that has been ruined by clear-cut logging. A few summer and winter steelhead remain. You can walk up from the bridge to the confluence, of the Klanawa and Tsocowis Creek or down.

Consider this one to ramble for sheer beauty alone. The trek downstream from the bridge gives way from a gravel section to one of large boulders on a classic steelhead run, and turns a corner, goes over a low waterfall into a pool at least 20 feet deep where you can see every pebble on the bottom. Continue on and then the river falls away into a canyon. Beyond Blue Creek you are on

a serious canyon hike, not suitable for children or those who are out of shape, down to the West Coast Trail Cable Car near the mouth of the river. There is no trail.

Access: The Klanawa Bridge is reached in a little less than two hours from Port Alberni by gravel road. Take the turn off on Highway 4 into Port Alberni for Bamfield and it will put you on a good quality gravel road. At Franklin Camp, you carry on through the log sort and past Darlington Lake and Francis Lake, and then right, across the bridge over the beautiful Little Nitinat River. This is Flora Lake Main and the lake will be on your left, stocked with rainbow trout. Bear left on the Klanawa Main, left on the Newstead Main until you reach the bridge over the Klanawa on your right.

From Victoria, travel north on Highway 1 through Duncan and turn left onto Highway 18 that takes you through Youbou and the start of the gravel road to the Nitinat Valley. In another 28 miles (45 kms), you will find yourself at the T junction, turn right or left and you will find the Nitinat River. In total, this is a 2.5 hour drive.

For the Klanawa, turn right at the T and carry on until you can turn left to cross the Little Nitinat River onto the Flora Lake Main, then the Upper Klanawa Main, and finally the Newstead Main. There are a couple of rough campsites beneath the bridge on the Klanawa. This is another hour, so count on more than 3 hours from Victoria to reach the river.

Information: There is no good source of information as there is no urban centre with a chamber of commerce. The Ditidaht First Nation (pronounced dee-tee-dat) has a small hotel in their little town. Website: www. ditidaht.ca.

The Ditidaht manage the windsurfers campground – the Nitinat Lake is among the top 10 in north-America with good 30 mile (50 km) an hour winds almost every day.

Guide: Catchsalmonbc.com. Send me an email , and I will take you, or refer you to a good fishy guide.

Check out my book: *A Man And His River*, for more in-depth information on the Nitinat River.

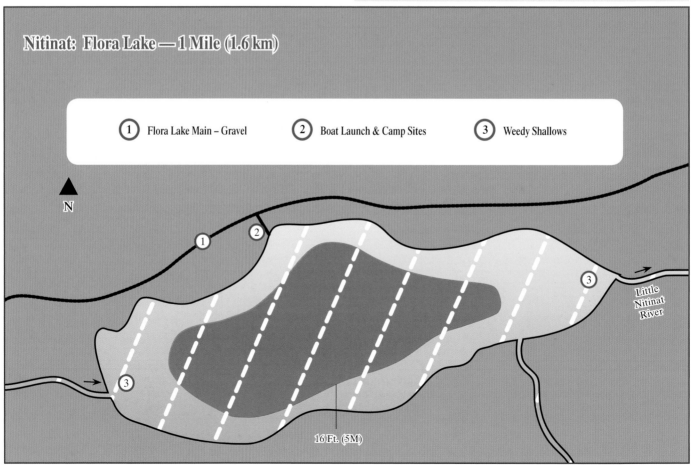

**Nitinat: Flora Lake — 1 Mile (1.6 km)**

① Flora Lake Main – Gravel  ② Boat Launch & Camp Sites  ③ Weedy Shallows

N

Little Nitinat River

16 Ft. (5M)

The main rivers of the Nootka Sound region are the Burman, Houston and Gold up the Muchalet Inlet, the former two being water access only. Up Tlupana Inlet are the Conuma and Sucwoa rivers, accessed by gravel road. The Conuma's hatchery is what makes this area a prime saltwater fishery for chinook. Up the long Tahsis Inlet are Tahsis and Leiner rivers accessed by gravel road. And, up Zeballos Inlet is the river of the same name that is accessed from the water or from a long and winding gravel road.

The Houston is a seldom fished river, and, as with all the various rivulets in the astonishingly large area of Nootka Sound, will have searun cutthroat trout around its entrance. And you must prospect for these with binoculars in the morning or later in the day when waves subside and you can see them cruising the shallows for food. The particularly large Tsowwin River estuary is a prime spot to look. And who knows, later in the season, you may even catch a 30-pound (13.6-kg) spring while looking for 2-pound (.9-kg) trout.

The Conuma River raises primarily chinook, but also some coho. There are also summer and winter steelhead in this river and in some summers the summer run can be quite surprising in size. There is about four miles of river above the hatchery turn off and the upper access is from the bridge where the Conuma changes from being a flat coastal river to a steep gradient impassable stream.

You can fish from the hatchery as well and move down toward the estuary. That direction often reveals big log jams in the river, making the bushwhacking a medium level affair, above the ability and interest of most children.

The Conuma River may be accessed from the ocean from Moutcha Bay RV lot or from the gravel Head Bay Road that runs from Gold River. In some pools you will find as many as 5,000 chinook in a black school. Very impressive. Later in the season, coho come home.

These large springs will actually take a dry fly—something very uncommon on Vancouver Island. Other usual flies include small, size 6 chartreuse streamers with glow properties and critter-sized eyes. Coho, as always, favour metallic colours and metal itself in both gear tackle and flies. Do consider that the Conuma is as clear as air and if you can see the fish, they can certainly see you. Usually, this means you will catch nothing. So, either you want to cast from considerably upstream to downstream and across positions, or take a walk through the streamside vegetation, staying out of view and espying your quarry in downstream positions and then staying out of view as you walk back up to cast down stream to them.

It always surprises me when I see anglers not taking the precaution of

*Morgan McLean fishes the far side of this run on the Gold River.*

being invisible. Some of Vancouver Island's rivers are air clear. I have spied summer steelhead, crept 100 feet above them and, on my knees, cast a light fly on a straight line 40 feet above them. Then the interested fish has seen the fly from 40 feet away—think of what that means in terms of how good their eyesight and motivation is—zip forward to inspect the fly, then move forward another 50 feet to where I am on my knees hiding behind a six inch daisy, look at me, saying, "Nice try, turkey," then drift back the 90 feet to settle in among its buddies, all of which are now too spooked to come forward.

Summer steelhead are indeed the ghosts of summer, so you had better be clandestined. You can imagine my frustration one day, when I plopped a small stone in hoping it would cause the big steelhead lying on the bottom and thumbing his nose at me to have to move, when from under a ledge an 8-pounder (3.6-kger) moseyed out and whacked the stone! Grr. So the rule is: stay out of sight.

The Conuma is one of those very clear Island rivers at its lowest flows in the late summer and early fall when the spook potential is at its highest. Stand by the runs accessed from the hatchery and look at the schools of springs. You can almost count the teeth in their mouths. So, do yourself a favour and land that spoon or fly lightly, above the fish and let what current there is, move your offering down into the fish. Gear anglers have the advantage of using mono that is more-or-less invisible. Fly anglers should consider this and use a floating or intermediate clear "slime line" tip or a long leader and weighted fly.

The Sucwoa River just down Head Bay can often have fishing restrictions in salmon season to protect its run of chinook as it is the closest wild-chinook river to the Conuma River. But it, as all the rest do, will have coastal cutthroat trout in the river and in the estuary.

The Leiner River has a run of sockeye near the campsite that many visitors will pound in hopes of a hook up. Good luck. Sockeye are the most close-mouthed of all five species of salmon, even more so when pooled up in the rainless sunny days of summer and fall. But it is a good biology and behaviour lesson for the kids, the advantage being that they can actually see the couple of hundred fish on the bottom of the run and this alone can be the arresting image they remember for the rest of their lives.

The Tahsis River has a coho run that is building. Like all the other rivers, it receives chum salmon in late fall, after the salt approach-water closures and thus casting with spoons and spinners will work for coho. For chum, the issue is to creep up on a raft—usually spotted by a bit of nervous water or the

*Angler Spey casting on a typical Vancouver Island stream.*

appearance of a few stick-like dorsal fins. Typically these are over a few hundred chum and you cast just in front and fish through the school. A pink and purple Egg-sucking Leech is all it takes in saltwater, but you can pound your heart out with Buzz Bombs.

Further away, along Esperanza Inlet, an area of great Spanish influence, the Zeballos River flows into the ocean at the town of the same name. A few miles from the ocean the road crosses the river and the logging road follows both sides of the river into the town. Just above is a canyon and waterfall worth stopping to view. Stop to fish where you see access, and the pool with the house-sized rock is a spot to give a try for large cutthroat trout in the spring and late summer before the salmon come home. Note that it is a very typical pattern for cutthroat to enter island rivers in the week or two before the salmon do—late August or early September. Just below the falls is a good slow pool that holds coho and chinook in the late August to October period. Move down to the town swimming hole and fish when no one will be swimming and hooked accidentally.

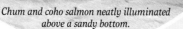

*Chum and coho salmon neatly illuminated above a sandy bottom.*

**Access:** The Conuma River is accessed about 45 minutes west from Gold River on Head Bay Road. There is a sign that you will not miss on your left side. The Sucwoa and its beneath the bridge pool is 15 minutes beyond the Conuma after you have come out above Moutcha Bay.

The town of Tahsis is another 10 minutes beyond the Sucwoa and the road passes over the Leiner River giving you access to the river. The Tahsis River flows on the west side of the village of Tahsis and you take the last right and follow it up to the gated road that you walk up toward the refuse site, the river at all times being on your right, with side paths here and there. This, like other coastal streams, fill quickly in the rain and you should always keep in mind your exit plan from the river.

The Zeballos River is so out in the middle of the wilderness that it is accessed either by boat or the much longer route, north of Campbell River on Highway 19. The turn off on the left is just past Steelhe Creek about 15 minutes north of Woss and well marked. Alternatively, turn left before Woodengle Creek for the 26 mile (42 km) bumpy rutty ride on to River Main that will soon cross the Nimpkish River and, bear right, and turn left onto Atluck Road. Near Mukwilla Lake you will pick up Pinder Main for a long, rutty ride down to the Nomash Main. Keep right and you follow the Zeballos River down to the bridge that you cross and Gold Valley Main takes you into the town of Zeballos.

# Parksville—Englishman River

Renowned for its huge Rathtrevor Beach and equally huge migratory bird populations, Parksville's local river is the Englishman that you pass far above on the new Island Highway 19 or lower, on the old Island Highway 19A, right in town. The river has winter steelhead, cutthroat trout and searun cutthroat trout as well as chum, coho and chinook salmon in the fall.

The Englishman's steelhead run has seen better days but from time to time it surprises with the reward of a bar of silver. Do note that good portions of the river are fly only and seasonal in opening.

You will find that walking up from the Highway 19A bridge or down from there gives gives you good fishy water, and with the added bonus of peace and quiet. From the Highway 19 turn off for Parksville (when driving south) and take the first right. As the Fisheries Society stocks the river with many thousand sea-run cutthroats trout most years, your chances of catching a hatchery, i.e., marked and thus keepable trout are fairly good.

Do take the time to meander around the estuary as well. It is an interesting niche in its own right, particularly for migratory birds, and, of course, a focus for sea-run fish as they spend a good part of their lives in saltwater, in very shallow beaches, seldom more than three feet deep. If you see them, you will catch them; if you don't, mosey on.

Sea-runs gang up on the river mouths during fry migrations. As chum go to sea right from the gravel in April, this is a good time to fish the saltwater beaches in the estuary. Chinook and coho fry typically migrate out after an extended period in freshwater, during the summer months. Chinook fry tend to reside close to their river of origin and this makes for an extended summer season for sea-run fish.

Your gear will be minnow imitations, epoxy flies in blue and green with big wide eyes, and in lures, little spinners that sea-runs seem unable to resist. Do remember to wash them when you have finished fishing in saltwater.

Salmon season can be rewarding in the fall. Plummer Road that runs beside the river in its lower reaches grants you good access to a broad flat river. You will find that if you stand there for ten minutes before fishing you will begin to see the salmon, much more so than if you waded in and went to it. Keep your eyes on the far shore under branches or in the creases that form. This structure will be the key for all species of salmon.

In flies, egg patterns, sparse pink streamers, green and white shrimp with bead eyes, and glow in the dark chartreuse flies, Silver Thorns with green tails, standard Mickey Finns and blue on green Mickeys and Muddler Minnows will all take salmon.

As with other rivers, Englishman coho and sometimes chum will take Vibrax Blue Fox spinners in green, blue and red and the much cheaper Colorado blades that you make your self in silver, brass and gold. Chinook will also pick up the heavier Illusion and Kit-A-Mat spoons in blue and green over silver.

## Lakes

Spider and Horne lakes often receive 15,000 cutthroat in a year. Try green and black Woolly Buggers and ant patterns on warm May days. Key on shorelines and their structure in the morning and evenings with poppers for bass, give it action for the bass in Spider.

**Access:** There are two easy access points for the Englishman. If you take the last bear right just before crossing the bridge into the main part of Parksville, this little road runs beside the river for more than a mile, granting good access to day fishers. The road, Plummer, takes you through a small, pretty subdivision where you can get access to the broad estuary. If you choose to walk upstream under the Highway 19A bridge, there are access trails to give you a hand.

The other easy access is reached by passing under the Island Highway 19 and taking the first right. Stay on this road until it comes out at a lovely craggy park with the river below. There is a trail and in places, boardwalk down the near side of the river that gives access to the south side of the Englishman River.

*Spey casting on the lower Englishman River near Parksville; the casts are beautiful.*

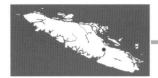

# Port Alberni—Stamp, Sproat, Taylor

Port Alberni is one of the best hubs for freshwater fishing on Vancouver Island. The town has full amenities for travelers, a good tackle shop, and several lakes and rivers within an hour's drive.

The important lakes are Sproat, Great Central and Cameron lakes. The rivers include the Somass which begins at the confluence of the Sproat that flows from Sproat Lake and the Stamp, the latter river flowing from Great Central Lake and gathering up the Ash River on its way down the large valley. Into the top end of Sproat Lake flows the Taylor River, the prettiest river on Vancouver Island.

Put and take, stocked lakes include: Gracie, Summit, Turnbull, Turtle and others.

## Stamp River—Vancouver Island's Greatest River

Sent to Canada by his doctor in 1913, Brigadier General Noel Money brought with him his two-handed Wye rod. His graceful double Spey arced across the waters that would some day bear his name. Although he called the shimmering pool of uncertain windows below his cabin on the Stamp River The Great Pool, today it bears his name and is known by anglers as Money's.

The Brigadier was raised on Atlantic salmon and brought with him his leather-bound game book that recorded his days and years on the Somass system. Similarly recorded is his penchant for sinking red or orange flies in high water as well as his preferred low-water dressings offered on the end of a floating line.

General Money fished with the young magistrate, Roderick Haig Brown, who regarded him as a mentor. Neither lived to witness the changes that time has laid upon the Somass: the Robertson Creek hatchery; and, a much wider range of gear and technique, including the zoom of winter jet boats.

Since the mid '70s, the Robertson Creek hatchery has become justly famous. First built to enhance pink salmon runs, the facility branched out into steelhead and left the pink behind. In an average year, 150,000, 8- to 10-inch summer- and winter-steelhead are released. With an average of 3- to 6-percent return (pretty darn good) that means 4500 to 9000 steelhead and the reason that the Stamp is the most heavily fished river on the Island. And it's busiest in winter!

Chinook salmon were the next for enhancement. They were—and are—the famed 20- to 40-pound (9.1- to 18.2-kg) Robertson Creek chinook. Although typically averaging 50,000 fish over the years, this run reached a staggering return in 1991 of 292,335 fish. In the fall of 2006, a healthy 100,000 chinook swam the river, along with a slightly low 40,000 coho. Sixty to 100,000 coho is more the average, when ocean survival is good. And these are bity fish.

But the Somass system has other species of equal or greater importance to sport fishermen. Originating in the large central lakes—Sproat and Great Central—the Sproat and Stamp rivers funnel Vancouver Island's greatest sockeye run from the Somass to spawning gravel along the shores and in the streams above the lakes. With an optimum escapement of 350,000 sockeye, these two rivers have felt the weight of runs as large as 1.2 million sockeye.

Seldom mentioned by Stamp anglers, just prior to the annual cycle of fishing seasons renewing itself in early winter, 20,000 chum salmon rise into the Somass on a flooding tide. Few of these fish make it as far as the Stamp and Sproat River confluence, preferring, instead to spawn in the lower reaches of

*Nick Henny with a typical summer steelhead that he caught with a Blue Fox spinner.*

the Somass. Then in mid-November, the winter steelhead begin drifting in while summer steelhead are still entering. This marks the beginning of the fishing calendar as the Stamp system is primarily considered a winter steelhead river.

## Fishing the Stamp System

Only a very few anglers take themselves up to the Stamp River weir at the Arc Resort on Great Central Lake and that is perhaps because it's a river of boulders and a difficult, slippery downstream wade. Too bad. The May to June period is a delightful time for beautiful lake rainbows that drop down to spawn. A 6-weight single-handed fly rod serves useful purpose on these beauties. Pass through them first with a "greased line" technique: cast, upstream, mend the fly, a Courtney (a tarted up Woolly Bugger) and let it pass butt first down the river. Then after you have worked down river for the morning, come back and hit them again with a different fly and technique: a dead-drifted bead head nymph.

You will be pretty much alone up top because angling pressure will be focused far below. Paper Mill Dam is considered the saltwater boundary and thus saltwater rules apply. In a usual year, this can mean a four sockeye a day limit and a possession limit of eight fish. Locals are meat hunters and thus they will be found in large numbers at the "Dam," Gun Club, Stamp Falls Pool, and above the Hatchery in predictable months: June at the Mill for sockeye; December to February for winter steelhead—with jet sleds zooming up and drifting through the slots; and, in September to October for chinook and coho.

June means fishing the "Dam," once the site of an ill-fated factory to change weeds and chips into low grade paper. Your dink float is placed—brace yourself—10- to 13-feet above two ounces of pencil lead inserted into surgical tubing. A simple swivel inserts itself and three feet of leader ends in a 1/0 steelhead hook onto which an orange or chartreuse yarn fly is tied. The extremely sticky bottom demands 15- to 20-lb. mainline (6.8- to 9.1-kg).

From the most downstream angler, fishers cast in turn, aiming to extend the float, weight and fly in a straight line from the rod tip. As one float hits the water, the next is cast. The in-a-wave procession of rods and floats is sheer ballet to watch, but difficult to perform. Woe be he who crosses lines or casts out of turn, for he will be thrown over the water fall by the skilled but irascible locals. During run peak, every angler hooks his limit.

And then the meat hunters go home. In fact, though the system has a 12-months-of-the-year calendar, large numbers of anglers are encountered only in five of those months. In other words, the river has lots of opportunity for on-your-own fishing and for those willing to hike a bit or take to the water in portable water craft. Note that for most of its length the Stamp system—also including the Sproat River and the Somass below the confluence—has trails on both sides of the river.

Some of the under-utilized sections of the river, include Swanson's and the Farm just up from Somass Park, an absolutely gorgeous set of boulder runs and broad river, that in low water is just under your ribs and there is only you and your double-handed rod working your way down the river—the best kind of fishing.

The untapped also includes the Sproat River sockeye that stack up at the Confluence Pool in tens of thousands. The reason they receive virtually no pressure, is, again, because locals fish only during retention periods. The section just below is also known as the Miracle Mile because it has been the site of steelhead plants in the past and thus they tend to congregate between Somass Park and the Confluence before progressing—try the good weather month of July; you'll be the only one on the river for the ghosts of summer. Also of interest, the hatchery people truck steelhead back down to Clutesi Marina so they provide further sport in the week it takes them to migrate back up to and above the Hatchery. With both hatchery summer and winter steelhead in the system 12 months of the year (noted by clipped adipose fins), your chance of taking home dinner is great.

In the winter though, intrepid anglers claim their share of the Confluence pool—now risen ten feet and producing a great back eddy—before first light and wait for sun to slither over the mountains. The winter steelheaders' gear of choice is a baitcasting reel mounted on a 10 1/2' rod. Terminal tackle includes a dink float, split shot (or pencil lead) and Gooey Bobs or Jensen Eggs. Ghost shrimp or roe compete as natural baits—when and where authorized. For backtrollers, deep diving hotshots or huge flatfish are lowered to the fish behind the drift boat. Colours of choice include blue, green, red, chartreuse and the Pirate combination (blue, green and red). Two other time-tested tips include: using smaller bait and hook in low, clear water; and, fishing closer to shore with bigger gear in high, cloudy water.

Note that the same colours prevail for chinook in the early days of fall. They reach in and nab those high-weight-to-volume spoons from Gibbs Nortac, the Illusion, Kit-A-Mat and the rest, lures that endear themselves because they cast a mile. The biggies gather in the runs and pools, for example, the deep-water Russian Meadows and The Meat Hole (now you know why) can be wall to wall flesh.

Remember that September and October brings the best coho fishing. Cross your fingers and hope for rain, because, without a doubt, if you are prepared to get wet, you will experience the best coho fishing of the year. The Stamp Falls Pool (also a consistent summer- and winter-steelhead spot) can astonish you for coho in two inches of rain. A memorable day for me was a pack of cards worth of coho—all on the same knubbly, half-blue, half-silver old-fashioned spoon. I caught one fish four times.

When the section above the Ash River is opened for coho, above the Hatchery can be rewarding. You walk in from the Hatchery, and its only down side is that you have to be out by 4:00 p.m. when the gate is closed—and no exceptions.

But those for whom history rates high, consider Money's Run in September. It was here that the Brigadier, in low water summer conditions, waded from the Ash to Money's proper, crossing back and forth for the creases each side affords. This morning or afternoon wade, gives one time to try and figure out how Money and Haig-Brown would have fished the 800 yards of water. Truly a spot of legend in B.C. fishing

The west side of Money's – the pool itself - is the better side for fly fishing; the run slowly tails off into deep water and then large steelhead-hugging boulders fill the tail end. This is one of the Stamp's nice features: it is a river of freestones, ledges and large boulders, some larger than cars and its beauty and the adrenaline factor that boulders are for steelheaders makes for a lovely day. Do recall though the larger rocks make for more difficult wading, and expect sore feet by the end of the day. Consider bringing your kick boat (particularly those rubber craft with the hole in the middle and proper oar guides). The white water sections will be as satisfying as the sections you fish. And if you catch one of Money's cutthroat trout, consider yourself extremely fortunate. These fish have had years to inspect thousands of flies and lures, and saying they bite short understates their wariness.

Do note that one campground, above Stamp Falls, offers summer, fall and winter fishing, so you can set up the tent or back in the RV and have the fish right at your door. The runs that look good to you, will be ones that are good. Some of the better ones are on the side of your tent and some will change depending on river level. Keep your eyes on the guides; they plumb only the best runs.

Fall is the time of change. Nature turns itself inside out with colour and anglers match the low angled sun with spinners, K3s and Colorado spoons. With either brass or silver spinners, these lures in red, pink, green or blue, can be seen by the angler all the way through the shifting viscosities. Don't be surprised to see a diligent fly fisher plumbing the stacking fish with a chartreuse or pink fly on an intermediate sink line. Glow-in-the-dark Flashabou in orange or green provides a nicely visible fly in the low light conditions that prevail with the coming rains of winter.

Give yourself a day at Swanson's or at the drop off below Somass Park. Chum though soon macabre in colour and firmness, provide action most in-the-know anglers prize above other salmon. There is always a trick of water hydraulics to figure out, but once you have found the way to present the fly at eye level, you can work the same school all day long and result in much more than a 10-fish day.

Even with the rain and rising water levels of winter, the Somass system remains relatively clear and fishable. Almost a century ago, General Money would poke his head from his small cabin and muse that it was a fine day to fish. With satisfaction he then hauled, once again, his long cane rod brought from the family estate, Culmington Manor in Shropshire England. Although remembered as a fly fisherman, Money also knew practicality. Days when the river had him standing in the trees he moved to gear and let that float float down a seam

Once away from the parks and campsites on the river, the Stamp reveals its great character and you feel as though you are in a wilderness that no one has ever seen before you. There are long drifts in the upper river where no houses line the banks, and equally long drifts below the falls – take care at The Bucket, though. This is a moderately difficult river and a pontoon boat or kickboat are very useful in the big long boulder stretches of the river that fairly well scream steelhead to longtime anglers.

*Bill von Brendel with a prime salmon. When it rains it's time to river salmon fish.*

# Stamp River

**Needed Equipment:** Waders and belt, boots, $CO_2$ inflatable vest, sun glasses, hat, raincoat.

**Fly Tackle:** 8-weight single-handed rod, with a tip system allowing clear and floating tips for summer, up to Type 8 sink for winter. Type 4 full sink for fast sections. 9-weight, 13 foot double-handed rod. Scientific Anglers XLT for summer, Hardy Mach 1 line series. A tip combination for winter, for example, the stellar Skagit from Rio, or add up to Leadcore.

**Flies:** Summer steelhead take black leeches, both bunny style, and Woolly Bugger style, gold bead-heads, Glo-brite chenille, red, olive, maroon, purple marabou/bunny, bead- head nymphs with rubber legs.

Winter steelhead take Winter's Dream, bunny leeches with three colours for contrast, pink, red, black, white, chartreuse, pink Krystal Flash, Holographic Tinsel, bright yellow, big flies that get attention, lead on shanks.

Sockeye will go for the simple, humble yarn fly in any colour, or the Popsicle and Tequila Sunrise. Coho want metallic finishes, but will nab Haig-Browns Coho Blue, or my Blue Coho, chartreuse Woolly Buggers with holographic tinsel, Christmas tree Icicles, silver bead eyes, purple over pink marabou flies, silver bead head and etc. For chinook try white Woolly Buggers with chartreuse yarn rump and chartreuse Needlenose. Chum bite the same as chinook plus four inch black leeches in tailouts, bright yarn below a dink float. Some days, tiny orange or pink Glow Bugs do the deed, though they are so small, using egg hooks, you need to hook a lot to land a few.

**Lures:** Summer steelhead will take the straight ahead gold wobbler. Winter steelhead take roe (check the regs for bait openings), Jensen Eggs, Gooey Bobs, Spin N Glos, 'Lil Corkies, pink worms, in pink, peach and red. For coho try Bolos, Vibrax spinners in gold, silver, red, blue, green and chartreuse. Gibbs Illusion, Kit-A-Mat, Ironhead, silver, gold, Colorado blades in silver, brass, gold. Chinook like Gibbs Illusion, Kit-A-Mat spoons in blue/silver, green/silver. Chum will take a range of soft yarn colours over a Jensen Egg and will occasionally bite a Vibrax or Bolo spinner or Colorado Blade.

**Regulations:** Retention opportunities for salmon and steelhead vary every year. Check with Fisheries and Oceans Canada for chinook and coho retention (as above). Sockeye, up to 4, retention allowed up to saltwater border, Paper Mill Dam. Retention for hatchery steelhead summer and winter.

**Access:** Expect medium-level bushwhacking. East side trails, parks, and camping are accessed from Beaver Creek Road. West side trails and etc., are accessed from the Great Central Lake Road. Stop at Gone Fishin' in town for directions to the smaller tracks.

## Sproat River

The short Sproat River drains the lake of the same name. After the fall closure, you may spot steelhead and coho just where the river begins and they may be fished with bait or other lures/flies.

In the spring find Hector Road near Highway 4 below the lake. Take yourself down until you find river access—a more difficult spot than most. You will find rainbow and cutthroat trout.

## Taylor River

The Taylor River is my choice as the prettiest, easy-access (right beside the highway in several locations), free-stone river on Vancouver Island. It's a perfect spot for the family to have a picnic and do a float down on a raft.

Flowing into Sproat Lake, the Taylor provides temporary home to cutthroat trout, rainbow trout, sockeye and coho salmon and steelhead, a few winters and summers. The river is catch and release only and fly fishing only.

The fishing calendar begins in March when large, 2- to 7-pound (.93.2-kg) lake cutthroat trout begin massing under the estuarial drop off where the Taylor flows into Sproat Lake. Use a Type 3, full-sink fly line, with blood worms, chironomid pupae and black nymphs. Anchor your craft on the Taylor gravel bank, cast out and let sink to 30- to 40-feet, then inch up, the hand-crank method, taking four inches at a time, and repeat—slowly. Wear your woollies as this time of year is cold, and snow is a definite possibility. Use standard black leeches, or match the hatch in April.

In April and May, the river can be popular, so get there early in the day. The cutthroat and rainbows move into the river for spawning and are arrayed out in tailouts. Stand on the decommissioned bridge and you are usually looking down at more than a dozen or two large fish. These are ultra-spooky in the clear water. Wave your arm from the bridge—you are at least 100 feet away—and watch them take notice. Hence, when fishing, you want a low profile: stand in the water and cast beyond where you can see. Your best chances are in 3- to 5-foot-deep runs and

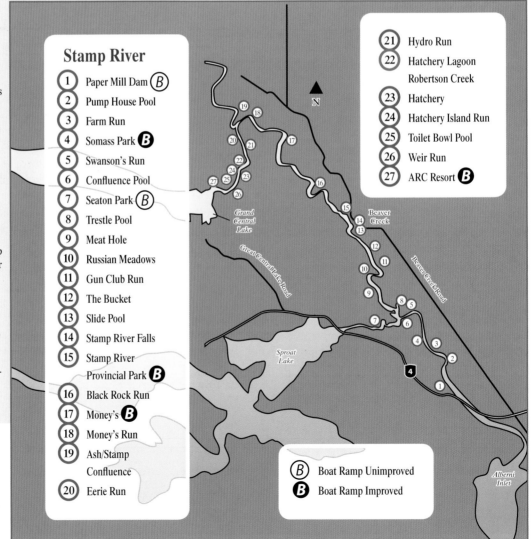

**Stamp River**

1. Paper Mill Dam **(B)**
2. Pump House Pool
3. Farm Run
4. Somass Park **(B)**
5. Swanson's Run
6. Confluence Pool
7. Seaton Park **(B)**
8. Trestle Pool
9. Meat Hole
10. Russian Meadows
11. Gun Club Run
12. The Bucket
13. Slide Pool
14. Stamp River Falls
15. Stamp River Provincial Park **(B)**
16. Black Rock Run
17. Money's **(B)**
18. Money's Run
19. Ash/Stamp Confluence
20. Eerie Run

21. Hydro Run
22. Hatchery Lagoon

Robertson Creek
23. Hatchery
24. Hatchery Island Run
25. Toilet Bowl Pool
26. Weir Run
27. ARC Resort **(B)**

**(B)** Boat Ramp Unimproved
**(B)** Boat Ramp Improved

in tailouts. Slime lines—clear—rule, particularly floating ones. Cast well above the fish and let your fly be drifted back into them. Light pecks are the bites from these wary fish, so sharpen those hooks before you fish.

You will also see some winter steelhead among the other fish. These are more bold than the other fish until fishing pressure puts them down. Add larger leeches with bead chain eyes in bright colours, such as red, yellow on black, olive, and add some pearl Flashabou.

Fish the deep pool at the decommissioned bridge from above with sink tips. Get someone to creep to the edge of the bridge—the person must stay out of sight—and direct your casting. Great fun.

During summer, you can carry Rabbit Leeches, Woolly Buggers, standard wet flies and large stonefly nymphs—Gone Fishin' on Johnston Road has some real dandies—and wade or raft your way down. In slots, around roots, rocks and where streams enter are your best spots to connect with some very lovely rainbow trout.

Late in the fall, even through December and into January, there are coho salmon in the Taylor River. These willing fish key in, like their confreres in other rivers, on metallic or flashy surfaces. Think blue, green and red, with a smidgeon of purple. During this period, a few winter steelhead may be found in the river, and consider using some of the high-glow flies now being developed, that use orange, purple, claret, pink along with stinger hooks on big beautiful marabou creations, with a rump of orange glo-brite chenille that adds the attraction of looking shrimpy.

**Access:** Roughly 20 miles (32 kms) west of Port Alberni on Highway 4 (the highway that leads west to Tofino and Ucluelet) there is a Smokey the Bear sign on your right. Look to your left and turn left onto the gravel road; left again takes you to the top end of Sproat Lake where the Taylor flows in; going straight takes you down to where the road has been decommissioned at the one bridge that crosses the Taylor below the highway crossing another 10 miles (16 kms) up Highway 4 (that is, you don't turn off the highway until the upper end).

Anywhere along the highway that you come to the river can be an access or egress point. Where Highway 4 crosses the Taylor, there is a viewing site on the right, just above the highway. This is a good place to park for the day. Do note that above this stretch that the river flows through a canyon and you should venture upstream only with a guide.

**Accommodation:** There is a small, well-used campground at the top of Sproat Lake. Camping is also done informally on stretches of the river, including two sites at the decommissioned bridge. If you are camping in the rain, take special note that the Taylor can rise dramatically in a short time. The hundred yard gravel banks on either side give evidence of this fact. Take care.

## Great Central Lake

This very large lake receives less pressure than others because few roads grant good access. But there are large cutthroat trout in the lake as well as rainbow trout and larger Dolly Varden char.

Troll the creek mouths in spring and fall. Remember to use minnow pattern flies and lures because hundreds of thousands of sockeye salmon spawn in the lake tributaries in the fall and even in the lake shore gravel. As sockeye fry may spend as much as two years in the lake before seeking saltwater, Flatfish and Kwikfish plugs will do the deed. These fry can be two inches long so large, attention-seeking lures should be high on your list.

Shore fishing spots include the well regarded Scout Beach recreation site that is a good 20 minute drive from the river mouth of the Stamp River. Fish also on points of land or where there are shallows—very few indeed.

**Access:** Take Highway 4 west until you see Great Central Lake Road on your right and turn onto it. This is also the way to the Robertson Creek Hatchery, signed on your right. The road then comes to Ark Resort, the end of Great Central Lake. If you miss it, the road goes across the Stamp River and you simply back up and go down to the resort. This large lake more than 20 miles (32 kms) long is poorly accessed by road. And thus it must be accessed if you are fishing by boat, by launching at the resort. Afternoon winds can be strong, so take care.

## Sproat Lake

Also a large deep lake (as in more than 15 miles long (24 kms) and 650 feet deep), nestled beneath high cliffs, Sproat Lake sees tens to hundreds of thousands of sockeye for a fall spawning in the lake tributaries and in the lake gravel itself. The fry comprise a large portion of the feed for larger cutthroat and rainbow trout. Hence troll where you see fry in the morning. They will sink in the day as they are plankton eaters and thus do not key in on the hatches. Try also the creek mouths. More than a dozen streams fall into the lake from the steep-pitched rock faces.

There is next to nothing in the way of shallow, weedy shoreline on Sproat Lake, except near Taylor River on the west end, and even this one drops off from the river mouth steeply. You can see 40 feet down here in March and April. Anchor on the gravel bar and drop on a Type 4 full sink fly line over the edge with a chironomid pupae fly. Let it sink 30 feet and retrieve four fingers at a time—so slow it takes several minutes to bring it to the surface. The large cutthroat, rainbows and steelhead migrate into the Taylor in April and May for spawning and cruise the river drop off for a month before. While most people fly fish, trolling with plugs and jointed lures should put you on fish, too.

Various islands dot the length of the lake and these also provide structure to be fished, as well as shallow light-filled water conducive to insect growth. Do note that you will need a boat with significant horsepower to move you to and from them, and to the creek mouths that have only water access.

There are also some near shore shallows in Klee-Coot Arm that bear fishing as does the Sproat River mouth—it is where all anadromous fish enter the lake. In any given year, this means hundreds of thousands of sockeye, coho and steelhead, in that order.

As this lake is deep,

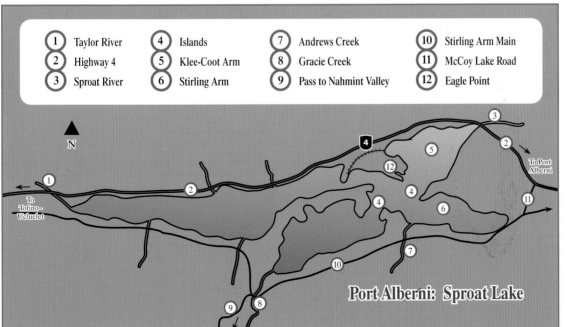

| | | | |
|---|---|---|---|
| ① Taylor River | ④ Islands | ⑦ Andrews Creek | ⑩ Stirling Arm Main |
| ② Highway 4 | ⑤ Klee-Coot Arm | ⑧ Gracie Creek | ⑪ McCoy Lake Road |
| ③ Sproat River | ⑥ Stirling Arm | ⑨ Pass to Nahmint Valley | ⑫ Eagle Point |

**Port Alberni: Sproat Lake**

keep your depthsounder on to try and spot the herbivourous kokanee schools as you troll. Once you find them, fish the thermocline, where surface waters meet the frigid deep water—usually within 50 feet of the lake surface. The large cutthroat and rainbows will be found here in the summer. There are many sharp points of land in the eastern half of the lake and these, for example, Eagle Point, represent good places to focus your trolling efforts.

**Access:** Cross the silver bridge over the Somass River on the west side of Port Alberni and drive on Highway 4 for 15 minutes and you will see signs for the resorts on the lake on your left, along with a boat launch. Highway 4 then rises above the lake for its length, perhaps another ten miles (16 kms), and then returns to river level for five miles (eight kms) of the Taylor River.

There are campsites dotted along the highway side of the lake and near the Taylor River entrance. Many are free. You may spin cast with spoons from the shoreline. Look for points of land jutting out and put your effort in there.

## Cameron Lake

A deepish (140 feet) and windy lake, Cameron lies between high cliffs below the summit of the pass to Port Alberni. Highway 4 winds along its shores. The Little Qualicum River drains the lake and you may fish it beside the highway for brown trout and drop-down rainbow trout. It is a catch and release water.

The browns, and these can reach more than ten pounds (4.5 kgs) (the largest on record is a gargantuan 32 pounds (14.5 kgs)) are chiefly caught by trolling the lake on the shore opposite from the highway, accessed from the resort on the Little Qualicum River end of the lake. Fish the browns deep with plugs and big saltwater spoons off downriggers because they tend to sit in deep water during the day. But in the morning, consider trolling shallow with big U-20 Flatfish with one ounce of weight. These large plugs will dive as much as 15 feet and they are visible from long distances. Angel Rock is a good spot. There are also huge cutthroat in the lake with a monster weighing in at an almost unheard of weight of 20 pounds (9.1 kgs).

Remember that the browns move into the top end of the Little Qualicum River in late November for spawning. Thus you may catch a very big brown

indeed in shallow water with big—browns are not shy—spoons and big black bushy flies.

The shallows in front of the sandy beach (east end of lake) where swimmers come on warm summer days are beside the highway. It often features trout rising on hatches in the early morning and later in the day when the lake has calmed. Row out and cast to them or troll a light spinner, when you see fish. There are several natural access points for those with pontoon boats or lighter craft that you can carry, along Highway 4 where it winds almost right under the rock walls of the crowding mountains.

Although some years the lake is not stocked, Cameron can receive as many as 20,000 yearling cutthroat and rainbow trout in some years. And they have to be big, because browns (and cutthroat, too) become fish eaters when they become large fish. The rainbow trout strains raised by the Freshwater Fisheries Society are insect eaters, thus the fish you see rising must be rainbow and/or small cutthroat. The hapless, plankton eating kokanee become feed for the big fish.

At the upper end of Cameron Lake, you may park in the spectacular Cathedral Grove where huge Douglas fir trees loom up seemingly higher than you can see. The highway crosses Cameron River twice and on the far side of the first one, there is a pull off on the right where you may park your car and fish down to Cameron Lake. Take care in rain as this snaggy creek can rise very quickly. And it is too rough for children.

The west end of the lake has good shallow water spots, by the highway and near the creek mouth, trout will rise onto in the evening and spend the night until morning, supping on the chironomids that such waters offer. Hence Black Woolly buggers for the browns and the standard wet flies along with, when they are hatching, May Flies, as dries.

**Non-fishing Attractions:**
• Cathedral Grove on the highway into town for 1000-year-old firs.
• An interesting day trip aboard the period *M.V. Lady Rose* to Bamfield and back, www.ladyrosemarine.com, 1-250-723-8313.
• Good local history, steam mill, railroad museum, www.alberniheritage.com/.

**Lodging Camping:** There is a full range of lodging, B&B, camping and RV opportunities. Check with the information centre, 1-250-724-6535. You pass the Timberlodge, 1-250-723-9415 on the way into town, just before the information centre. The Coast Hospitality Inn is downtown, 1-250-723-8111. Arrowvale Campground – 1-250-723-7948.

**Tackle Shop:** Gone Fishin, can give you a hand with directions and current lures/flies; Phone: 1-250-723-1172. Go down the the main drag to the bottom of the hill and just before the T-junction, the tackle shop is on your right.

**Guides:** Dave Murphy is the best local guide operation, serving fresh-, salt-water, and providing meals and accommodation. Has fly guides. www.MurphySportfishing.com Phone: 1-877-218-6600. Email: Murphy@island.net.

Nick Hnennyj (rhymes with penny) knows the Stamp system cold, a fishy guide, West Coast River Charters. An all-around good guy. Phone: 1-250-723-0136.

Bill von Brendel, the man with 42 fishing rods, is also a long time guide. Phone: 1-877-334-7466; Website: just-fishn.com; Email: info@justfishn.com.

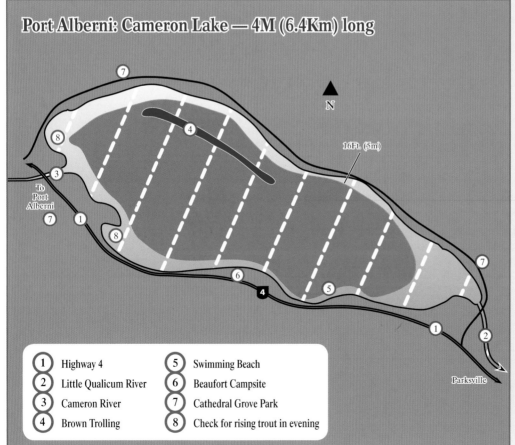

## Port Alberni: Cameron Lake — 4M (6.4Km) long

16Ft. (5m)

To Port Alberni

Parksville

| ① | Highway 4 | ⑤ | Swimming Beach |
| ② | Little Qualicum River | ⑥ | Beaufort Campsite |
| ③ | Cameron River | ⑦ | Cathedral Grove Park |
| ④ | Brown Trolling | ⑧ | Check for rising trout in evening |

*All five species of salmon, summer and winter steelhead, along with sea-run cutthroat and Dolly Varden migrate through the Quatse River's broad estuary.*

There is a well subscribed salmon fishery on the Quatse River where it joins the ocean just south of Port Hardy. There is ample room for both gear anglers and fly anglers for the good run of pink salmon, as well as the coho and chinook that are also enhanced by the local hatchery.

Spin casters use Roostertails, and other spinners, along with small Stingsildas, Buzz Bombs and spoons in the requisite colour: pink. Fly fishermen use sparse pink streamers.

The river has both wild and hatchery winter steelhead that are best fished in February and March. Pink is also the steelhead colour, including the found-everywhere pink worm below a float. This is a tea-coloured river and pink just stands right out.

Cutthroat and large Dolly Varden call the river home as well.

**Access:** From Byng Road (the right turn for the airport and the Keogh River), it is one mile until Highway 19 crosses the Quatse River at the estuary. There is a good campground here and another down Byng Road. Port Hardy, itself, is another mile from the beach, so, if you are so inclined, you could just amble down from your hotel room in Hardy for another day of—life's tough—fishing on the beach.

The Quatse River may be accessed from Highway 19 by turning left onto Coal Harbour Road, either before or after the river. There are four miles of easy access to this small river. The hatchery is also on this road.

Port McNeill, on the Broughton Strait, has easy access to both saltwater and freshwater fishing. In fact, it is in the centre of some terrific Vancouver Island rivers and river systems.

## Nimpkish River

The largest drainage on Vancouver Island gives rise to the largest river, the Nimpkish. Above Nimpkish Lake (which is 16 m—26 km—long), three rivers combine to form the Nimpkish proper: the Davie River from Schoen Lake; The Nimpkish River from Vernon Lake; and, the Woss River from Woss Lake.

The rivers are home to both summer- and winter-steelhead, cutthroat trout and rainbow trout. Turn left off Highway 19 through the town of Woss, cross the upper Nimpkish and the road will take you to the Woss Lake Recreation Site that has camping. The Woss River starts here and the stretch close to the lake has good access for a mile and then drops into canyons.

This is a good area for dry fly fishing in July and August, with an elk hair caddis, Haig-Brown's Steelhead Bee, waking bombers and a truly ageless pattern: the Royal Coachman.

The Nimpkish River is accessed a mile below Woss at Gold Creek where Highway 19 runs along the river. There is good drift and foot access for the next five to six miles (8- to 19-km). In the dry Vancouver Island summers, there are occasional wading crossings which are always a treat when they are found, but seldom suitable for children—and deeper than they look. Take care.

The power line 1.5 miles (2.5 kms) past Gold Creek has vehicle access and you can drive right down and bear left to a lovely slot that has trout and steelhead. Above, the river braids in this flat area and if you can reach the channel on the far right, it has a classic run that will hold both steelhead and large cutthroat trout. Fish back to the slot where your car is, taking care to fish the water absolutely at your feet where it tumbles into the slot that fishes well on both high and low water. Salmon will also hold up here, sockeye, chinook and coho. If you plan to tackle the salmon, look to put your gear down with pencil lead as the run is quick; a dink float set up with wool flies or Colorado blades will do the trick.

If you continue on down the power line, instead of bearing left, you will come to a shallow back channel and a good spot for a picnic, and a pool below on the right hand side for the angler.

Where the highway rises up on your route north, the Nimpkish pulls away across the valley and falls into another canyon that is best taken with a guide—there is a portage section that should only be taken with an experienced person. The river canyon is a stunning beauty and of vastly different character from the flat, high, open free-stone section north from Woss. You will cross the Nimpkish again several miles from the lake, perhaps 150 feet high on the Zeballos turnoff road. It is a very impressive boil through slate canyon walls. Just before the bridge is a steep scrambling bushwhack down to the river, best taken without children.

Trout that follow the sockeye up and shadow them for eggs provide good sport, with egg patterns or a trusty 4mm orange bead for gear anglers. Surprisingly, for sockeye are usually as tight lipped as, well, sockeye, they will whack a #6 Tom Thumb dry fly just above the lake as will cutthroat and rainbows. Good stuff! Try also bead-head nymphs, stoneflies, small fry patterns, Egg-sucking Leeches and, as noted, simple dry fly patterns.

The bottom end of Nimpkish Lake has poor access, but good rainbow and cutthroat trout fishing. Below the lake, the river is once again best taken with a guide. Just above saltwater, where the highway crosses over the river, the turnoff to the local hatchery is on your left, just before the highway crosses the Nimpkish River in its tidal reaches. There is good sockeye fishing—again, unusually bitey sockeye—in this brackish water a quarter mile from the sea, to the right of the highway on a small track. Take them on orange and red bugs and egg patterns or 3/8" and small orange spinners.

**Access:** There are multiple access points as there is a well-established system of logging roads in the area, and Highway 19 first touches the Nimpkish River in Woss about 15 miles (24 kms) north west from the Eve River. The road that takes you through Woss to Woss Lake, continues across Woss River and down the Nimpkish Main South that turns into Nimpkish Road. This system of logging roads shadows the west/south side of the Nimpkish River and has some better access points than Highway 19 that runs on the other side of the river. The Highway follows the Nimpkish River on a 15 mile (24 km) long journey until it enters Nimpkish Lake that is 16 miles (26 km) long.

Once you have turned off the Highway on the Zeballos turnoff, fifteen minutes north from Woss, and crossed the Nimpkish River, bear right onto the River Main that takes you down past the Anutz Lake turnoff (it has campsites) and becomes a less well used track across the flat to the end of the lake where it ends at what once was a large log sort. Though it would be nice if the logging company had removed all its sort pilings, these hundred or so provide cover for trout and before the wind rises in the afternoon, you can paddle among them in the morning casting for trout. You can also walk or paddle around the corner to the right for half a mile and find where the Nimpkish River empties into the lake, a good place to fish.

At the bottom of the large and very windy Nimpkish Lake—take caution on this lake—the Nimpkish River then flows through the Lower Nimpkish Provincial Park where drifting is not recommended. It is a real beauty of Vancouver Island for about five miles (eight kms) down to where the highway crosses the river just above tidewater and you look across to Alert Bay on Cormorant Island. From the river crossing, the highway rolls on another eight miles (13 km) to Port McNeill.

## Cluxewe River

The Cluxewe contains multiple species of fish: both winter and the odd summer steelhead, productive runs of pink and coho salmon, and has a solid reputation for Dolly Varden char. Try for the Dollies close to the beach with bugs, the California Neil and minnow patterns. Some days deliver double digit catch-and-release fishing for them.

You will find a busy, well-established campsite, with a boat launch for saltwater anglers (90% of the fishing effort) zipping across to Malcolm Island for salmon fishing.

The estuary gives way to a wide easy-access beach of three miles long and you can walk the entire beach fishing. Use #6 to 8 shrimp imitations in hot pink on silver hooks in the mouth of the river. This is a productive spot, larger than the popular Oyster River estuary south of Campbell River. Try your floating line or on windy days a slime line intermediate sink. This is where Port Hardy anglers come for beach fishing before the Quatse and Keogh turn on.

Keep your eyes open on the calm waters of late summer for the large schools of pink salmon that rove the beaches. Cast where you see fish. Small pink Buzz Bombs will serve the spin caster well. As the tide begins to rise, move on to the estuary, where schools of salmon will begin flowing past the tight choke point that separates the river from the ocean. There is a very flat beach here, and with neoprene waders on, because the ocean is very cold, you may walk out in pursuit of jumping salmon quite a distance. A slime line tip does a good job of reaching the fish zone in this region with its currents from either the river or tide. A bug-eyed pink streamer with pink Lazer Wrap will offer a little bit of sink and the pink will move forward and stop the fly. In September, the coho begin showing and you can use your Pearl Mickey fly or spoons like Kroks in silver that attract the attention of the coho that will hit with a decided smack.

**Access:** The Cluxewe River is five m (8 km) north of Port McNeill on Highway 19. The highway provides access to the river and the estuary at the Cluxewe Beach Resort. Turn right at the sign and follow the gravel road to the cottage, camping and RV Park. Ask at the office where to park. At the same time buy something from their stores as you are asking to use their property to access the fish.

## Keogh River

The Keogh is one of three Vancouver Island Living Gene Bank Rivers (the Quinsam and Little Qualicum rivers, being the others). They are the recipients of a world-recognized program for bringing back steelhead populations. There are three aspects to the program. First, in-stream fertilization is achieved through the planting of slow-release briquettes of the basic building blocks of

# Keogh & Marble Rivers

life—nitrogen and phosphorous—in the river; thus the base of the food chain is stimulated, that is, the algae, and this stimulates the insect life on which all fry and resident fish feed. Second, there is steel cabling of woody debris, as in logs, with boulders, in sections to provide cover for growing fry, over wintering "alcoves," spawning channels and the addition of headwater storage. Finally, there are the Living Gene Bank steelhead, planted in the river. To avoid the possible genetic damage of using hatchery fish, local, wild fry are raised in captivity and spawned, putting the fry back in the river in which their parents were raised.

Check out: http://www.bccf.com/steelhead/living-gene-bank.htm, for further details.

As for fishing, the Keogh River receives, along with steelhead, pink, chum and coho salmon. Fish for salmon at the estuary, with pink shrimp imitations, particularly for the pinks and, as in all other locations, garish is the right word to describe a chum pattern, including hot pink. The steelhead in this tea-coloured river will rise to a dry fly (check regs closely).

Access: Take Highway 19 another ten miles (16 kms) north of the Cluxewe River and take the right hand turn to the Fort Rupert airport. This gives access along the shore to the mouth of the Keogh River. This is a long beach walk of about a half hour. It is reputed that if you hunt long enough, you will find an access road to the right of the airport. Good luck, I've never been able to find one. But remember, that if you have to walk, there will be fewer people fishing.

The Keogh is also accessed from Highway 19 where the river flows beneath it.

## Marble River

The nearby Marble River flows into Rupert Inlet that joins up with Quatsino Sound, giving access to the west coast of Vancouver Island. The top end of Vancouver Island is nearly cut in half by the sound and thus, access is relatively short from the east side to the west side south of Port Hardy.

Marble River Provincial Park is a popular destination for anglers and skilled kayakers. The river, with its hatchery at the head of Alice Lake, offers diverse quarries, including, steelhead, cutthroat, rainbow and Dolly Varden char and chinook and coho salmon.

On summer days you can often look down from the bridge into the shallow water where the Marble River begins and see steelhead and rainbow trout, along with, as the season progresses, salmon, often surprisingly bright chinook.

*Coho salmon caught on a warm fall day while drifting downstream in the versatile Watermaster raft.*

From the boat launch you can begin fishing down to the pool under the bridge with small spinners like the Panther Martin series, in gold with orange and yellow-tail Courtney Buggers.

From below the bridge you can walk down the river and through the very good campground to access the pools that the river creates as it falls over rocks into sequential pools downstream. The Marble River Trail offers a number of access spots to specific pools. You go off the trail and down to fish the pool and then climb back up to the trail and carry on to the next trail down to a pool. The pretty Bear Falls is about half way down the trail to the ocean.

The Emerald Pool at the bottom end is the best spot on the river to fish—it can contain big cutthroat trout of three pounds (1.4 kgs) and larger. The springs can go very big here, too, to legitimate 50- to 60-pounders (22.7- to 27.3-kgs). They provide great sport on the standard river rod and baitcaster setup, fishing wool flies below a dink float and pencil lead. The coho are not that bitey in freshwater so they should be targeted in saltwater. Big Gibbs spoons in the Ironhead and Illusion line are good for big springs.

The saltwater in front of the river has excellent crabbing, and you can access the very big springs as they leap here and there and charge around in the estuarial reaches, giving you a thrill just to see them.

The Marble is a river and lake system to savour and you can easily spend a week camping here and sampling all that the area, about 15 minutes from the main highway, has to offer.

Access: Five miles (eight kms) west of the Cluxewe River on Highway 19, turn left onto the Port Alice Highway. Carry on another six miles (10 kms) and you will cross the Marble River near Alice Lake. The campsite is on your right and you walk down through it, picking up the river trail between the last Mens and Ladies facilities for the access to this four mile (7 km) section of river.

For saltwater access to Rupert Inlet where the Marble flows into saltwater, take the Rupert Main left turn from Highway 19 just the other side of Beaver Lake from the Port Alice Highway. In about five miles (eight kms) you will come to Rupert Inlet where there is a boat launch, camping and picnic area. From here it is a three mile (five kms) journey until you spot the one mile deep bay that receives the Marble River.

*Winter-run steelhead taken with a black Bunny Leech.*

its entrance. Note that the deeper water is near the entrance of Fairy Creek and this is a good spot to cast spinners and to drop a worm under a trusty red-and-white bobber under your boat (bait is legal in the summer months). Alternatively, gently troll a Wedding Band adorned with a worm.

Chironomid flies do the deed for the experts, but for families on holiday, the usual suspects, including Doc Spratleys in red, green or black, along with black Woolly Buggers topping the list of casting and trolling flies. Small Mepps Aglia spinners are your best bet for these pan-sized trout.

Fairy Lake has a number of campsites. And there are campsites nearer to Port Renfrew on both sides of the road after you have crossed the San Juan River, both supervised and unsupervised ones.

## San Juan River—Estuary

All of the estuarial water above the bridge over the San Juan near Port Renfrew is considered freshwater, the bridge being the arbitrary demarcation between fresh- and saltwater. Take your self-propelled water craft and row up with the tide, keeping your eyes open for the rises that spell sea-run cutthroat trout. It is common to catch and release several in a fish in this broad, winding river mouth. Try amphipods, and other shrimp patterns, along with minnow patterns.

Do remember that there is a convection wind most days, blowing up the river. This means that your row back down to the bridge area in the afternoon is against the wind and difficult, even more so when the tide is rising.

## San Juan River Proper

On the first torrential rain of the fall season in October—as in an inch or more— the coho salmon commit to freshwater. The first place they stop is the pool on the last big corner before the river sprawls into its estuary.

On this very wet day, you will be smiling because you will be at the corner pool with a goodly assortment of good quality spinners and spoons. Vibrax Blue Fox spinners in sizes three to five, with red, green and blue, along with silver blades will come in handy as will the heavier and thus easier to cast Bolo spinners in silver, gold and red. Gibbs Nortac makes high-quality spoons and the larger sizes of Ironhead, Kit-A-Mat, Illusion, Koho and Croc do the deed in silver, gold, blue and green. For extremely dirty water, as in less than knee-deep visibility, use big gold wobblers because gold transmits better than any other finish.

After your morning's fish, come back up to the long pool at the confluence of the Harris and San Juan rivers and get a second chance at the coho. Give a look at the pool under the Harris Creek Bridge as some days it can be chock-a-block with coho. Further up the San Juan at the junction with Lens Creek is another coho spot—this spot requires a decent hike. All three pools should be on your day's fish when you are after cutthroat trout.

## Fairy Lake

The freshwater fishing in the Port Renfrew area is diverse, with Fairy and Lizard (stocked annually with rainbow trout) lakes, in-river salmon fisheries and summer and winter steelhead in local watersheds.

## Fairy & Lizard Lakes

Both of these small lakes offer fishing for rainbow trout and cutthroat trout, with Fairy also having Dolly Varden char. These are good lakes for float tubes and small rowed or paddled water craft.

Fish the shallows in the morning and evenings. You will see trout dimpling the surface as they sup up the day's hatch of insects. At Fairy Lake, row out the narrow channel that grants access to the San Juan River and the pool at

## Harris Creek

Both summer and winter steelhead move up the San Juan, with most turning left and following Harris Creek. The summers are in from May through September and tend to get "pooled up" as late summer is usually pretty dry, making the pools the only decent water for the fish to rest in, waiting for the rains of fall.

The key to this fishery is not to be seen by the fish, and this requires a great deal of stealth. And, if you are lucky enough to spark a take, it will be the last in the pool. I have landed a fly, quite softly, I thought, but it made 50 steelhead shatter the pool.

You may want to try out some of the simple Spey patterns including the well known, Green Butt Skunk, Skykomish Sunrise and the Silver Hilton. Unless you hit the creek while it is up after rain, consider the Harris a non-starter for gear. One plop of a lure does the same, and more, than a fly.

Your best time for winter steelhead is January and February. There are a few regular pools, including the canyon and above it that hold the fish. Standard river gear includes dink floats, Lil' Corkies, Spin 'N Glos and smaller Gooey Bobs along with pencil lead.

This is a medium difficulty river with the canyon being a place that is not safe to go alone. Use a guide.

## Gordon River

The Gordon River holds summer steelhead higher in the river and has searun-cutthroat trout below the bridge in any likely looking pool toward the river mouth near the marina. There is easy access along the paved road just above the marina, but take care in the rain as this is one river that can flash flood in a hurry.

The Gordon is only fished by fly-fishing anglers, though the pool below the bridge on the bottom end is definitely big enough to plumb with gold wobblers in the summer, provided you can find a spot not filled by someone on an inner tube.

Very quickly above saltwater, the Gordon becomes a river in a huge canyon. Stand on the bridge at TR 11 and look down, look way down. It's got to be 600 feet. Consequently, you are strongly advised to take a guide if you wish to fish the upper reaches of the river. Do not go on your own.

**Access:** The drive from downtown Victoria is one and three quarter hours over, first, Highway 1 and then Highway 14; the latter, a twisty road, gives high vistas of Juan de Fuca Strait in the distance, but keep your eye on the road as logging trucks with their huge loads dominate the highway.

For all of the freshwater fishing, turn right just before Port Renfrew and go down to the bridge over the San Juan River, with its beach-front campsites on the estuary. Carry on and cross the bridge on the other side of the broad estuary (1.5 m—3km). Turn left and move on to the Gordon River on the River Main to the next bridge. Turn right from the San Juan estuary and you pass Fairy Lake, with its campsites on your right. The Harris Creek Bridge is about ten miles down the road.

Right before the Harris Creek bridge on the right is a four-wheel drive access gravel track—take care as it has some pretty deep wet spots. It takes you pretty much in a straight line west, giving access to the long pool at the junction of the Harris and San Juan Rivers, and then farther along to the corner pool on the San Juan River. Lots of mud on this one. You can put pontoon boats in beside the bridge and take them out at the corner pool—and carry them on your back back to your vehicle.

**Spot of Interest:** The West Coast Trail Botanical Beach is a great spot to take the kids for a good look at tide pools and their fascinating, highly- coloured inhabitants. Check the tide guide – you want low tide – and route in Port Renfrew.

**Guides:** Catchsalmonbc. com

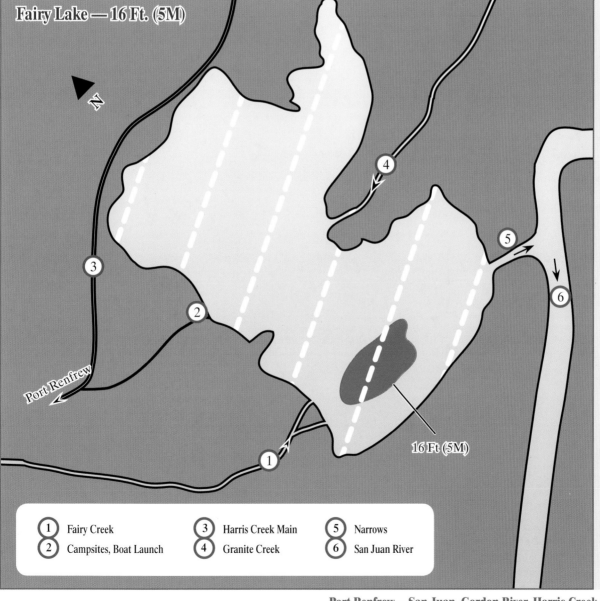

Fairy Lake — 16 Ft. (5M)

Port Renfrew

16 Ft (5M)

| | | | | | |
|---|---|---|---|---|---|
| ① | Fairy Creek | ③ | Harris Creek Main | ⑤ | Narrows |
| ② | Campsites, Boat Launch | ④ | Granite Creek | ⑥ | San Juan River |

## Little Qualicum River

At the outlet from Cameron Lake the Little Q is little more than a stream, but in the fall can fill with very big brown trout indeed and November is the time to hit them with big bushy flies like black Woolly Buggers—a good fly for browns wherever they are found.

In the section above the falls park, you can add cutthroat trout to the list of species in the river. Try a Tom Thumb or Elk Hair Caddis dry fly on a stream that gets very little traffic in the summer—this is partially because of its smaller size and over-hanging trees. Do check out the falls park a few miles below Cameron Lake as they are a spot of high drama.

On the lower end, you start below the hatchery and this can be a lovely fish for an angler on his own, but a bit much for kids. On a summer day you will see rainbow and cutthroat trout and the occasional Dolly Varden char, and at the railway trestle you can climb up to get a good view of the very productive nature of this stream, with small to large fish wavering in the noon sun. There are winter steelhead in the river, but do check the regulations if you fish in the cooler months.

In the fall months, chinook, pink and coho salmon come back, with the outlet down on the beach being a good spot for those casting spoons (often an area closure must be observed), and fly fishermen with Pearl Mickey's and small streamers with eyes. Minnow imitations along with Muddler Minnow flies can often be the ticket. Saltwater regulations usually apply a closure of near shore waters until October 15, so consult DFO regulations.

**Access:** The Little Qualicum may be accessed at the top end by taking the Highway 4 exit from the Island Highway 19 north of Nanaimo and Parksville. This is a 2.2 hour drive north from Victoria, or about 40 minutes north of Nanaimo. At the Cameron Lake resort, turn right or simply access the stream along the highway near the railway tracks.

The River is accessed on the bottom end from the town of Qualicum at Garrett Road that takes you up to the hatchery.

## Big Qualicum River

The Big Q is perhaps the best, well shaded little river on the island, in terms of its fishability. This is because it received a $1 million facelift some years ago, with cabling in of big logs and deposit of good big boulders, turning the river into a cascade of small waterfalls from pool to pool.

The fecund nature of the river is easily seen in its dark algae bottom that is the source of the food chain for this river that seldom blows out. It remains fishable year-round and is a good bet for its long walk to adult anglers and to short walks up from the hatchery to open spots in the vegetation for families having picnics.

The river has resident cutthroat (in the upper end), as well as sea-run cutthroat trout, winter steelhead, chinook, coho and chum salmon. Hence spinners and spoons that imitate fry are good on this river—when allowed. Flies include tarted up Woolly Buggers, featuring such colours as black Glo-brite chenille, red Schlappen, olive marabou, purple, yellow, black with gold bead heads in combination.

This delightful river can have good sea-run cutthroat fishing at its upper end as well, particularly in the spring and fall.

For salmon in the fall, lean to the simple rigs including yarn flies, in pink, and chartreuse, dink floats and pencil lead as this is a snaggy river that can rip off a lot of gear in a day. It's hard to get the big fish to stop before they get you into trouble, so think cheap gear, for example, home-assembled Colorado blades in silver and gold for coho rather than ready made and thus more expensive spinners.

## Horne Lake

This large deep lake receives roughly 15,000 cutthroat trout each year and similar numbers of rainbow trout from time to time.

**Access:** A 2.25-hour drive north from Victoria on the Island Highway 19, turning right into Qualicum Beach and then following the old Island Highway 19A north until you see the sign for the Big Qualicum hatchery on your left. You park in the asphalt parking lot and saunter over to the river where there is wheelchair access to the best pool below the hatchery for salmon fishing in the fall. You can walk upstream to the main highway and all the way up to the upper end, alternatively accessed from above, near Horne Lake, the source of the Big Q, on the circuitous Horne Lake Road, from the junction with the Island Highway 19.

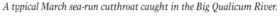

*A typical March sea-run cutthroat caught in the Big Qualicum River.*

# Saltspring Island—St. Mary Lake

*This rainbow wacked the fly so hard, I almost dropped the rod.*

Should you find yourself where the clock seems not to have moved since the hippy age of the 1960s, you will be on Saltspring Island. Put on your bell-bottomed trousers and take yourself down to St. Mary Lake. It has a fine—and well-deserved—reputation for smallmouth bass and for stocked rainbow and cutthroat trout, receiving more than 10,000 in the aggregate each year.

It is a relatively shallow lake with much shrubbery, shallow reed beds and tree cover, just the thing for bass. Make sure to creep up on the shallows where bass spend most of the summer in water as shallow as one foot. Fling your Texas rig and its rubbery scent exuding lure and if the bass don't whack on the plop, wait a few seconds and give a small tug and that should do it. Top water plugs are also attractive.

Bring along your float tube and slowly fin the lake trolling a fly for the ever present trout. Use a type 3 full-sink line, Muddler Minnows, Black Leeches and black Woolly Buggers, along with chironomids for the hatches.

Troll short gang trolls and worms for trout, fling spinners from shore including Mepps and the Panther Martin with small blades in orange.

**Access:** Drive a half hour north from Victoria to Swartz Bay Ferry terminal and take the half hour ferry to Saltspring Island. Then follow the main drag from Fulford Harbour toward Ganges. Pick up North End Road that goes from Central to the east side of St. Mary Lake. Tripp Road goes up the other side and both sides have several spots where you can stop and cast. Several boat launches dot the lake.

*The Salmon River produces some of Vancouver Island's largest steelhead. Many break the 20-pound (9.1 kgs) mark.*

On your drive north from Campbell River you will pass from time to time within view of a river on your left side. When you cross over it you are at the junction of the White and Salmon rivers. The Salmon brings jitters to the veins of Island fishermen because it has the largest wild winter steelhead on Vancouver Island. Legitimate 30-pound (13.6-kg) fish were the rule in the past. While logging damage has reduced the numbers of steelhead, fish that still go over 20 pounds (9.1 kgs), live here.

The Salmon is a medium-sized river that in its lower end provides good spots for wading. Along with steelhead, there are good-sized cutthroat trout that are the same opportunistic fish they are in other rivers. These fish will whack the same flies that will take winter steelhead, along with pink plastic worms, Jensen eggs, even spoons and spinners that are the easiest lures to fish. The simple but effective gold wobbler is still a lure that rules with steelhead.

The winter steelhead in the Salmon are willing to come to some unusual preparations. I have found that, contrary to the usual cannon of using pink and black, including marabou, that if I emphasize contrast—making the fly easy to see—that other combinations work as well or better. For example, using red, chartreuse and black bunny in that order on a size 1 salmon hook with bead eyes, this tri-colour fly, ugly by anyone's standard, makes for a fly that is extremely visible and thus gets followed and whacked.

Use whatever combinations of cross cut and length cut bunny that suits your taste, for example, I use magenta bunny with a bit of Flashabou and the fish come swimming. For an alternative silhouette, use a mallard feather on top of purple bunny, opposite to the way nature colours things, and it is as effective as putting the darker colour on top. Another variation is blue, yellow and red with Krystal flash. In other words, the flashier the better.

Also, in winter, there is a luminous quality to the water and in shade very dark, so using great wads of marabou, in black, orange, purple, red, pink along with bead chain eyes and a stack of hot-orange Glo-brite chenille before the bend of the hook adds a shrimpy look that sometimes triggers a bite. The more the glow, the better.

Cutthroat and Dolly Varden char may be caught in the lower river most commonly, but in most of its fishable 15 miles (25 kms) below Kay Creek, too. Summer steelhead also enter this river and may also be angled in the pools of the White River. You can add pink, chinook and coho salmon to the Salmon River from July on to early November. Do remember that the cutthroat enter during the pink fry emergence in April and hang around for the other species of fry that migrate later in the summer.

Despite it being beneath their dignity, chinook are pushovers for wool, in the same garish oranges and greens and blood reds that chum prefer, in fact, the two species of salmon have very similar likes and dislikes in lures and flies, preferring the primary colours, or combinations thereof—more garish for chum. Wool fished below a dink float is the standard method on the island.

The Salmon has been the subject of one of the longest in-stream fertilization (1989) programs and in-stream repair work and thus has the greatest long term potential for winter steelhead, other than the Stamp or Gold. The Nimpkish is the other river system that in the long run promises a great deal.

**Access:** Before you reach the Sayward region, you used to pass two white trash cans on the left side of the highway (look for the 53 km marker back to Campbell River). This is the first access to the Salmon River, but you should only venture down the path with a guide. It is not that difficult a trail physically—other than the first hill—but it is about a mile long and if you get off the trail you will be very quickly lost. This is known as the—you'll never guess—the

Garbage Cans, (even now, after they have been removed) and it gives access to the Memekay and Salmon Confluence, a classic steelhead run that is very fishy. This is one pool that if you take a steelhead, you should come back and explore it thoroughly, as it usually holds several fish every day.

The Dy-R trail, from the highway, also moves just by the Salmon which in its lower reaches is a wide washout style of river that meanders here and there, a victim of logging damage, but that property makes it easier to access at less than the highest water. As noted, the highway also crosses the confluence of the White and Salmon, with a good pool with a wicked back eddy under the bridge, and extending below it. You may venture above the bridge to gain access, too. Check the White River regulations as they may complicate things depending on the time of year that you intend to fish.

A little farther north, as in three quarters of an hour north from Campbell River on Highway 19, you turn right onto Sayward Road (it is another 15 minutes to Sayward and Kelsey Bay) that soon crosses the Salmon River in a broad slow run. The bridge is easy to spot as it is a one-way single lane crossing on which there is a traffic light. Access here is a left turn onto the first dead end road. There is an access to the tailout (that you saw from the bridge) through a clear cut, but if this is too difficult to find on a day by yourself, continue on down that road to the next left turn dead-end road and find your way down to the Salmon. You will come out just around the corner from the run and tailout you saw from the bridge above. Do walk back up as the run below the tailout and under the trees on the far side is a sleeper but a classic, as is the tailout above it.

Alternatively carry on down the road toward Sayward. It crosses the river once more, providing access to the river. There are also small tracks on both sides of the bridge that you can move down and along – look closely to find them. . The bridge is broad and flat in its lower reaches, and the issue is deciding what is the structure that fish will follow most frequently on their passage up-river.

## McCreight Lake

A number of local lakes are stocked each summer in the Sayward area. Two, the McCreight and Stella receive 5,000 and 10,000 cutthroat trout each year respectively. From mid-April to the third week in June is best, along with September when the water cools. But gang trolls and green and black Kwikfish will work all summer long, particularly when trolled in deeper water.

McCreight has well developed shoal water at the southern end and is a definite bet for morning and evening fishing. Although less extensive, the highly productive shallows at the north end are also fish attracting. Along Rock Bay Road, the lake drops quickly from shore and thus where you can easily access the lake, are spots to cast spinners and spoons particularly on the outside bends —outside bends almost invariably produce more fish than inside bends. In addition, there are four campsites on the lake and these provide lakeside waters and a boat launch at the far end of the lake.

Do bear in mind that as cutthroat trout grow larger they focus on fry for their meals. That is why trolling the deeper waters with larger lures is a worthwhile way to wile away the day. And that contour where shallow water deepens into dark water at the south end of the lake is a good tack to take.

**Access:** Access to McCreight Lake is a right turn from Highway 19 where it crosses Amor de Cosmos Creek (well before the Salmon River comes into view on the left) onto Rock Bay FSR gravel road and is two miles (3 kms) from the highway. Stella Lake is on the same road, but a good 15 miles (24 kms) from the highway. Both lakes have several campsites.

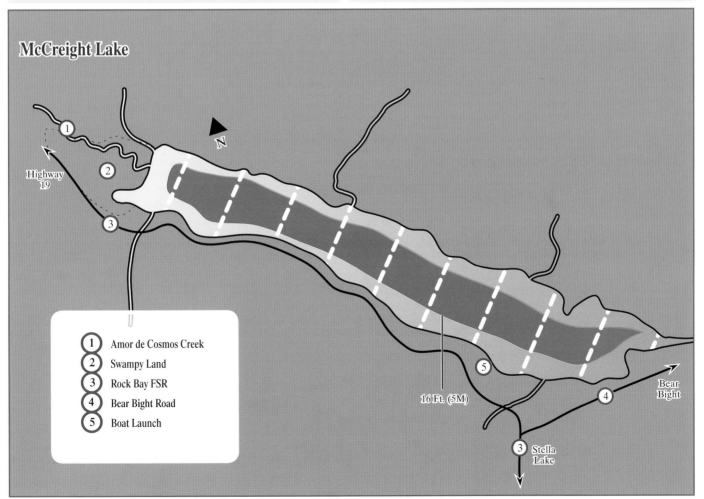

**McCreight Lake**

Highway 19

N

1. Amor de Cosmos Creek
2. Swampy Land
3. Rock Bay FSR
4. Bear Bight Road
5. Boat Launch

16 Ft. (5M)

Bear Bight

Stella Lake

# Sooke—Sooke River, Highway 14 Streams

*A bright hen chum salmon caught with a Spey rod in the Sooke River.*

West of Victoria on a good quality road, Sooke is a picturesque town set on the five mile (eight km) long Sooke Basin. Surrounded on the north, east and south by rolling rock hills several hundred feet high, the Basin is well sheltered from winter blasts.

While Sooke is better known for its saltwater fishery for salmon, there are a number of freshwater, on-foot fisheries within the basin. There are also some of the stocked CRD lakes mentioned in the freshwater Victoria write-up in this area, including, Matheson Lake toward Pedder Bay, Kemp Lake and Glinz Lake (that is stocked occasionally).

A local volunteer hatchery raises coho and chinook on the Sooke River.

## Sooke River

In the fall, a good quality fly fishery for chum, coho and chinook, in that order, takes place on the upstream side of the silver bridge in town—you can't miss it. Below the bridge is deemed saltwater and salt rules apply, and that includes retention of salmon, with shore anglers below the pub or on the spit on either side casting out for entering salmon with drift jigging lures like the Buzz Bomb, Stingsilda or Perkins, among many others.

But above the bridge it is fly fishing only, and the All Sooke Day's Park—take the first right turn after the silver bridge and park on the right, but not in front of the gate, before the small bridge over De Mamiel Creek—kindly allows fisher dudes to enter the park and fish in the open expanse.

One very good aspect of this fishery is that the area is a great big lawn; all the trees have been cleared and this affords prime territory with back casting room for as many as two dozen anglers. Another good aspect is that it has to be considered a very good bet for chum salmon and is a great area for learners to cut their teeth on the sport without their errant casts being dangerous to their neighbours.

As you stand on the lawn and look out into the estuarial Sooke River, there are a number of spots that are higher percentage areas. These include right in front of De Mamiel Creek on a high tide as most of the coho are trying to enter it. It tends to hold chum, too, presumably tasting the water and deciding whether to keep moving up the river or enter the creek.

Down where the bank takes a cut in to the right is a good spot too, and a sleeper. The reason is that there is a small reef that creates a "pool" on either side. The chum move over in schools up to 100 fish and as the water is knee deep, the fish zone is much more easily reached than in deeper water. Resist the temptation to move into the water here as you are pushing the fish into deeper water and thus making the fish zone larger and harder to pin point. Consider this a general rule of thumb: try to fish salmon where the fish zone, as in right in front of their nose, is easily reached. Estuaries are the most difficult place to catch salmon, because their habits are changing and the bite periods can be frustratingly short and sporadic, anything that you can do to tip the scales in your favour become more important.

Across the river on the far side under the evergreen trees is a trench that the springs lie in before heading up stream. This is best fished on a low tide, first thing in the morning as you can get closer to it and the fish have not been flayed over night. A Spey rod with an intermediate sink tip finds good use here, as the distance can be great, and the current can prevent penetration by the line and fly..

Farther down the bank, the chum tend to come to rest against the right hand shore and as they stay put there for some time, it represents a high quality spot. This is only reached on a low tide as the property below mean high tide is legally public. At high tide, the only access is by pontoon boat, as the land route is trespassing over private property.

Many flies will do the deed. As this is an estuary, the fish want one colour and one pattern on any particular day and another on another. But if you hit it right you and all the other fly guys will catch and release several salmon. A very social and agreeable fishery.

Colours that I have seen work include white, pink, grey, purple, green, gold and combinations. Try white Woolly Buggers with hot pink thread, sparse blue streamers with 1.5 ml eyes, other coho streamers in the one inch length, including pearl Mickeys, blue and gold with pearlescent Krystal flash. Or make up Zonkers with grey and white chinchilla fur, or try hot pink and furry flies, even ones made with rabbit. I have even caught fish on 3-inch open-ocean bucktails in cream, but the fish must have been crazy. Also try sparse orange streamers with glow in the dark chartreuse or orange materials for fishing before dawn or into dark. On some days, though, the chum will prefer something as simple as a hot pink Woolly Bugger.

There is also some river access afforded up stream. Take the bridge over De Mamiel Creek and go a half mile up to the small housing development and bear right. Park your car and walk down to the river. There is a big rock downstream that sits in a good pool on a medium tide. Alternatively, move upstream where the river bears to the left (as you look upstream) and there is a narrow

pool between the high trees on the left and the cliff on the right. By this point the fish have changed from breathing salt-water to being able to breath freshwater and the bite is much more reliable. Depending on the flow you can wade up the river and cross, the next pool and its white-water head, being in view as you wade; this can be a hot spot, indeed, for coho and chum. Above is Martin's Pool.

## Sooke Basin Sea-run Cutthroat Trout

For the nomadic angler, the Sooke Basin and surrounding waters can offer up a nice day's fish for the lovely silver and brown-spotted sea-run cutthroat trout. These fish are also on the move, prospecting for food in shallow waters that are seldom more than three feet deep. Everywhere there is an entrance stream, is a good spot to look for trout touching the surface or leaving the water.

The spots include the beach off Esquimalt Lagoon, Whitty's Lagoon, and the unnamed stream that flows into the ocean near Pedder Bay. In Sooke Basin proper, try Roche Cove, the old mill site and Ayum Creek, the entrance to the Sooke River, under the docks to the right of the oyster and seafood operation and along Whiffen Spit at the head of the basin.

Use fly fishing methods with an intermediate slime-line tip and small sparse streamers. Mickey Finn varieties, Muddler Minnows and one-inch green or blue epoxy flies will take these more than willing fish. The key is to find them and then release them once they have been located. Who knows, you may want to catch them again on your next trip to Sooke.

## Streams from Sooke to Port Renfrew

Continuing west from Sooke on the rolling, twisting Highway 14 to Port Renfrew, you will cross over many streams. A number of these support chum and/or coho salmon, sea-run cutthroat trout, and, in one or two streams, small populations of winter steelhead.

During the fall salmon migrations, add Tugwell and Muir creeks to your day if the saltwater gear and fly-fishery below or freshwater fly-fishery above Sooke's silver bridge is not producing. Simply park nearby and explore on foot, keeping your eye open for salmon.

King, Kirby, Jordan, Loss and Parkinson (that can be accessed via the steep, gravel Pazant Main) are also worth a look. Use the same flies as noted above, while adding reliable steelhead flies such as the egg-sucking Leech in pink and purple, and colourful marabou creations with bead chain eyes.

Where ocean access is easy, particularly Muir Creek and Jordan River, try your silver Krocodile spoons in the ocean out front.

**Access:** Sooke is 20 m (32 km) west from Victoria on Highway 1 that exits to Highway 14 for the remainder of the journey. Sooke to Port Renfrew is another 45 m (72 km) on Highway 14. All the creeks mentioned flow under the highway and are evident by signs on the road. Be sure to add fuel to your vehicle in Sooke as there is no real gas station in Port Renfrew. In a pinch, you can buy gas in the summer at the marina or—so they say—year-round in Beach Camp.

**Accommodation:** The Sooke Harbour House is an excellent couples' weekend get-away spot. Check the Chamber for an extensive list of other accommodation.

**Information:** Sooke Harbour Chamber of Commerce, PO Box 18, Sooke, V0S 1N0; Phone: 1-250-642-6112; Website: sookeharbourchamber.com; Email: info@sookeharbourchamber.com.

**Guides:** Catchsalmonbc.com. I can fix you up with someone. Toll Free: 1-877-610-1011

# Tofino

Most people go to Tofino for its saltwater fishing on the banks—gear fishing on the open ocean, or to Weigh West Resort for its "skiff" fly fishing, for coho in more protected, inside saltwater. But there is also some beach fishing in the marshy edges of the ocean along Grice Bay and Tofino Mudflats.

Those who come may also bring along a spinning rod and the venerable Krok silver lures, and ones, from Gibbs Nortac that feature half orange, for sockeye salmon. The Tequila Sunrise, Popsicle, and fluffy orange marabou flies do the deed for sockeye salmon.

In addition, reached only by boat or helicopter are the rivers of Clayoquot Sound including the Megin, Moyeha and Bedwell. The Cypre, Megin and Tranquil rivers are legendary with the very high end resort up the sound believing they have more wild steelhead than any other place in the world. Indeed! In other words it is the old maxim: the more difficult the access, the better the fishing. They also do fly outs to Megin and Pretty Girl Lake for cutthroat trout, on float tubes and pontoon boats.

**Access:** Take Grice Bay Road on your right about ten miles after you turn right at the T-junction, (turning left at the T-junction takes you to Ucluelet) and continuing on Highway 4 that takes you farther, to Tofino. There is also a small boat launch best accessed and egressed at higher tides. Check the saltwater write up for the boat launches in town.

It you want to go to the rivers of Clayoquot Sound, you will be traveling on inside, often glassy water—a good thing for the seasick-challenged among us. Do be advised that later in the summer that fog is an every day reality and thus a GPS Chartplotter is vital. In addition, the crossing from Tofino to Meares Island and into Maurus Channel is extremely shallow. Follow the track on the local chart exactly, or you will head off and become high centred, or worse, on a bank. Perhaps the trickiest passage on Vancouver Island—even in sunshine.

**Accommodations:** Clayoquot Wilderness Resort drops freshwater anglers off by boat and then it's walk or drive up. For the discriminating moneyed class, this resort is associated with Nimmo Bay Resort, also posh beyond the pockets of the average traveler. Inter-resort helicopter rides are very expensive but also very cool.

*An angler fly-fishing a beautiful pool and a remote stream.*

# Ucluelet—Kennedy River & Lake, Toquart River

Continuing on Highway 4 over the summit beyond Taylor River (west of Port Alberni), you come to the ultra-clear Kennedy River that follows the highway down to the flattish land near the west coast where the waves roll in seemingly from infinity. Along the way, the Kennedy flows or tumbles really from pool to pool on the right hand side of the highway and on summer days people stop to swim at the natural potholes formed over the ages in the rocks. Very beautiful, but this is not a river to drift in its upper end—it is too rough.

**Access:** On Highway 4, there is a left turn onto Maggie Lake Road, a gravel surface, that passes Maggie Lake and on to fishable sections of the Toquart River. Access to the Toquart is difficult to find, but there is the bridge. Beyond this, take a guide to do this gem.

## Kennedy River and Lake

Near the river's entry into Kennedy Lake it flattens and has some nice ultra-clear slots that can take an afternoon's fishing. The lake is a very large and broad one that has daily winds that should be avoided. This is a pity as with its sockeye run their fry spend up to two years in the lake and thus, along with native stickleback fry, form the basis of the food chain for other fish—making them larger than in lakes that do not have large populations of fry.

The lake's cutthroat trout and sea-run cutthroat trout thus take minnow imitation flies and any spinner in size 3 along with Kroks and small silver spoons. It has the distinction of having sockeye that will attack an orange spinner or fly, a Comet for instance—not common for sockeye.

**Access:** Take Highway 4 west from Port Alberni about 40 m (64 km) and one hour traveling on the sometimes twisty highway, particularly near Kennedy Lake. For lake access, there are boat launches at Cedar Creek, Kennedy Lake Provincial Park and just beyond the Kennedy River Bog Provincial Park where the river flows from the bottom of Kennedy Lake into the ocean, reached by boat in less than half an hour from Tofino.

## Toquart River

The Toquart is home to summer and winter steelhead runs as well as coho in the fall. The lake of the same name is home to resident wild rainbows. Maggie Lake, on the road to the Toquart, has wild rainbows and cutthroat trout. Troll past the creek mouths. The Toquart is unusual in that it has one of the Island's very few summer-run coho runs that comes in with the summer steelhead in late spring and early summer.

Larry Lake near Ucluelet receives stockings of rainbow trout in most years.

*A spectacular rainbow hooked in the Toquart River located near Ucluelet.*

*Jay Hitch took this smallmouth bass from the weeds with a Texas-rigged bait in Elk Lake.*

The Capital Regional District (CRD) of Victoria stretches from the Swartz Bay Ferry terminal some 25 miles (40 km) south to Victoria, and the other four municipalities that comprise Greater Victoria, to the Malahat Drive west of town and to Sooke on Juan de Fuca Strait, as well as including some of the Gulf Islands, most importantly Salt Spring.

There are 35 lakes in the area, virtually all of which are stocked by the Freshwater Fisheries Society of B.C. These people stock more than 10,000,000 fish across the province each year, about 1,000,000 of which are released into Vancouver Island waters. These include rainbow trout, cutthroat trout, sea-run cutthroat trout, kokanee, eastern brook trout and steelhead.

Local lakes are stocked from April into late October, some receiving as many as six stockings in a season. Hence, they must be considered prime and easy waters for you on your holiday.

In the Victoria area, the more important lakes include Elk and Beaver lakes beside Highway 17 (aka the Pat Bay highway), into town from Swartz Bay ferry terminal and Victoria Airport, and receive an average of 25,000 trout per year. Other well stocked lakes include, Prospect, Thetis, Langford, Durrance, Florence, Shawnigan (on the Malahat Drive and Highway 1) and Glen Lake.

Prior to fishing the Victoria area, visit the gofishbc.com website for stocking information. That will give you the best advice on the most recently stocked lakes.

## Elk and Beaver Lakes

These joined lakes have good access, as they lie along the Pat Bay Highway some seven miles (11.2 km) from downtown Victoria. Along with stocked trout, the lakes also hold introduced small and largemouth bass, pumpkin seeds and perch. Shore fishing occurs anywhere along side the highway that has access for casting. The fishing pier on the opposite side of Elk Lake is also a good spot for shore casting. Access by turning left, when coming from Victoria onto Sayward Road that leads to Hamsterly Road. You will see people fishing along the shoreline and so, find your spot and toss in your offering.

Still fishing is king for kids and shore fishers. To the mainline attach a one ounce weight two feet from the tag end. Attach a size 6 to 10 freshwater hook to the tag end. Round a small ball of pink, orange or chartreuse Berkley Powerbait around the hook to bury it. Because this kind of artificial bait floats, the baited hook will float up from the weight on the bottom and hang suspended waiting for the fish, usually a trout, to come along. Other good bait includes worms below a old reliable red and white bobber, or a rig with a one-ounce egg weight on the bottom end and a snelled hook and its leader off a loop, three to six feet from the bottom.

Boating anglers troll the highway side of Elk Lake as well as past the public beach nearby, and in the deep water to the north of the rowing course. Do not enter the course, as rowers, facing backwards, cannot see you and their sculls are moving very quickly.

Trout trollers use Willow Leafs and worms, small Flatfish in rainbow and frog patterns, Wee Tads, Mepps Aglia spinners and Len Thompson spoons in red and white or yellow with red spots. Fly fishermen use a Type 3, full-sinking line and troll Black Leeches, Woolly Buggers, Doc Spratleys and damselfly nymphs. Try also chironomids, for example, Pheasant Tail, Halfback and Gold Ribbed Hare's Ear nymphs. Hatches occur from March right through into November, with some hardy little bugs coming off in nearly all of the cooler months in the middle hours of warm days.

Casting into shore cover results in success for both fly fishermen and bass fishermen. Bass may be taken with straight forward Texas and Carolina rigs, as well as crankbaits. Cast into cover and get ready for a smash. Do note that in the early summer months when water temperature sends trout to the deeper

# St. Mary, Shawnigan

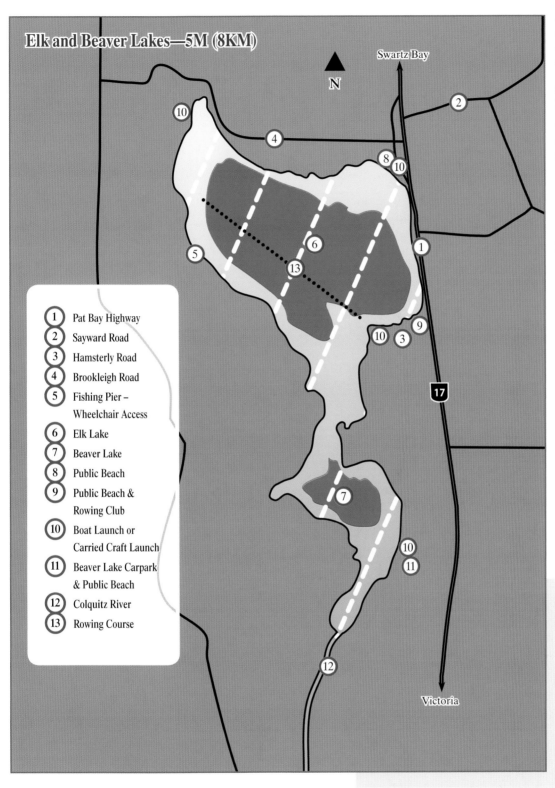

## Elk and Beaver Lakes—5M (8KM)

Swartz Bay

N

1. Pat Bay Highway
2. Sayward Road
3. Hamsterly Road
4. Brookleigh Road
5. Fishing Pier – Wheelchair Access
6. Elk Lake
7. Beaver Lake
8. Public Beach
9. Public Beach & Rowing Club
10. Boat Launch or Carried Craft Launch
11. Beaver Lake Carpark & Public Beach
12. Colquitz River
13. Rowing Course

Victoria

that stimulate eating, or garlic or salt, because fish tend to hold on to the lure longer, making it easier for you to strike the rod.

The Texas rig is niftily rigged to hide the barb. First the point of the hook is inserted into, say, a tube jig, directly down on the head. Then it is turned out of the jig one third of the length from the head. From there the shank of the hook, as the right-angle bend on top is pulled snug to the jig's head, is pulled down to the fronds (tube jigs look like saltwater hootchies) and inserts through the body of the jig. The hook point that protrudes from the far side is then embedded into the side of the jig so that there is nothing for the lure to get snagged on. Black and the much higher contrast, char-treuse, are good places to start. The lures are tossed close to structure, allowed to sink and retrieved with little jerks to give them action.

Check out the great amount of shallow water in Beaver Lake and consider the shorelines in among the lily pads and logs to be your prime territory – this means pretty much the whole lake. The public beach and the opposite side with the rock face against the lake are good places to spin cast to rising trout. From time to time the cutthroats ap-pear on the public beach, in the spring and fall, in a low-pressure system.

**Access:** Elk and Beaver Lakes are easily accessed from the Pat Bay Highway 17, to the Beaver Lake, Rowing Club or Sayward Road access points.

Anglers with boats launch beside the rowing club on the south end of the lake and from Brookleigh Drive on the north end. Those with craft they can carry, usually launch at the public beach on Brookleigh. For shore anglers there is a chip trail around the entire circumference of these joined lakes—six miles (ten kms) that is well used by

central waters that bass fishing in the weedier, stumpier sections of the lakes is usually hot. Try 4-inch tube jigs, with pork rind, lizards and other soft baits that have been weed-rigged to slip right on over. Even algae-stained shallows harbour bass, right into two feet of water.

In the Texas Rig put a lead cone on the ten-pound (4.5-kg) mainline and tie on a bass hook. The point of the hook is embedded in a soft, squishy, plastic bait that usually has some type of scent in it, such as the specific amino acids

runners, dog walkers and horseback riders—you can reach any shoreline spot that looks fishy to you.

## Durrance Lake

Little more than a few acre pothole set in large fir trees, Durrance Lake war-rants a look for a few reasons. It is a good family location on a calm body of water, close to Victoria that is suitable for a picnic and a fish from shore or from

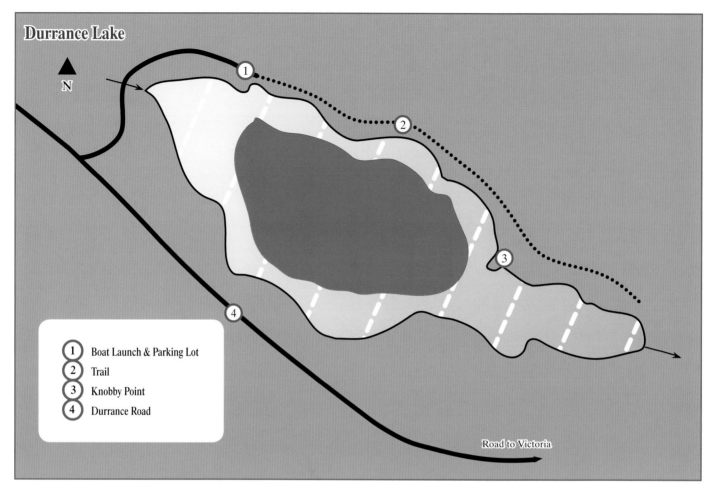

**Durrance Lake**

N

1. Boat Launch & Parking Lot
2. Trail
3. Knobby Point
4. Durrance Road

Road to Victoria

a boat—electric motors only. It also receives annual stockings of enough fish that it is a very good bet for landing one or two. In some years several thousand cut-throat are stocked and in recent years several thousand catchable-sized rainbow trout have been released each season.

The north side where there is a good trail offers a few spots to toss out a bobber and worm or small spinning lures. Many trout hide in the underbrush to the left of the boat launch, and the short walk down to Knobby Point offers a few, through the trees, views. The point itself has enough room to sit down and toss in your offering—straight out or to the right hand side.

If you stand on the boat launch and look across the lake, you will be sighting along the 16-foot (five m) contour which is a good little trolling line. You may also cast from this contour into the lily pads where the stream flows into the lake, but do not venture among them as your line will soon be caught on vegetation.

Carry on trolling to the other side—a Wedding Band and a worm are your best bet on this small lake—then, on the other side, troll as close to the fallen timbers as you can get without catching your lines on them. This is also a good spot for fly fishermen to work and even in the winter there are a few small insects hatching in the warm, middle part of the day. Pursue them with a floating line and nymph, chronomid or even a dry, such as a Parachute Adams and Vancouver Island's favourite dry fly, the Tom Thumb.

Bear left toward Knobby Point and then continue your troll close to the brush, as it is deep here, all the way back to the boat launch. Do not go past the Point as the lake shallows rapidly, and, few fish seem to lurk in this end of the lake toward the outlet stream.

Access the lake by exiting Highway 17 at Royal Oak and then pick up West Saanich Road for a gentle, rolling, turny ride through the country to Wallace Road on your left. Another left puts you on Durrance Road and the lake is marked on your right. This is a 12 m (19.2 km) jaunt from the centre of town and takes about half an hour's driving.

## St. Mary Lake

Located on Salt Spring Island (via ferry from Swartz Bay), St. Mary has a well-deserved reputation for bass fishing with the same gear as for Elk Lake. It is also well stocked with trout. Fish the brushier, more struc-ture filled water for bass, for example, docks, lily pads and over-hanging branches.

## Shawnigan Lake

Shawnigan is renowned for its bass fishing—and has been the host of the B.C. bass championship—anglers regularly release double digit numbers of bass in a day's fish. Because few people retain bass the numbers are truly outstanding. And of course the lake is stocked with trout, often in excess of 30,000 cutthroat and rainbow trout. So consider this easy access lake a good bet. Use the same tackle as noted under Elk and Beaver lakes above

About 15 miles (24 kms) north west from Victoria on the No. 1 Island Highway, take the well-marked left turn or stay on the Highway until Mill Bay, 28 miles (44.8 kms) from Victoria, and take the well-marked left turn at the second light.

On the north end of the lake you will find access points and boat launches: Dougan Park and the government wharf. This is a complex lake with multiple drop off points, islands and shoals. A real winner.

If you come along in the cooler time of year, bass will be in their winter pattern suspended 20- to 35-feet (12.3- to 21.4-m) deep. Give purple or black a try on a weighted rig. Let it sink to the bottom and bounce it very slowly across the bottom as you reel in. A good spot would be right off the round point on the way into the long arm. The inside turn is a softer bottom with some rocks and vegetation. Look for these kinds of spots and fish deep around them, or drag across the bottom with weedless rigs as described above.

# Other Local Waters

## Gorge Waterway

While sea-run cutthroat trout are a saltwater species, Victoria's Inner Harbour leads to the Gorge waterway that runs through the centre of Victoria, Esquimalt and View Royal. Sea-run cutthroats are stocked from time to time and form the basis of a fishery that both adult and child can enjoy.

You can actually walk from your hotel in the morning, catch a fish or two and then be back for breakfast. The best spots are under the Johnson St. Bridge, by the Laurel Point Inn, under the Bay St. Bridge, and along the west shore to the Galloping Goose Trestle by the rowing club and up near the Gorge itself where the tidal flow makes the water surge through like a river.

The rule for sea-run cutthroat trout is: fish for half an hour and if you do not catch any or see any, move on. These fish are relentlessly on the move and you must follow them. Fortunately they love to jump, seemingly for the sheer joy of life and when you see them you have an 80% chance of catching them; when you don't, you have an 80% of being skunked.

Fly-anglers take along minnow patterns such as Muddler Minnows

### Victoria: Shawnigan Lake — 6M (10 KM)

1. Shawnigan Lake Road
2. Renfrew Road
3. West Shawnigan Lake Road

*This truly beautiful wild coastal cutthroat trout couldn't resist a summer steelhead fly.*

and small, 1-inch saltwater streamers on silver hooks. These are sparse patterns that include green or blue epoxy minnows, Mickey Finns and knock offs using colours other than red and yellow and green and blue saltwater streamers with eyes epoxied on. Various amphipod and shrimp patterns will take these fish, too.

Sea-run cutthroat trout can be non-selective, and the simple one inch silver Krok is perhaps your best choice for a small lure. Try also Mepps Aglia spinners with some green in them. Do remember to rinse them in freshwater or they will rust.

**Access:** Many Victoria Lakes have good asphalt road access. Ask at local tackle shops for directions or visit Tourism Victoria as it has online road maps.

# Index

# Index

To Receive a FREE sample copy of
*Flyfishing & Tying Journal* magazine

call 1-800-541-9498 or email
customerservice@amatobooks.com
and make a request

(This offer applies only to non-subscribers)